WARPLANES
OF THE FUTURE

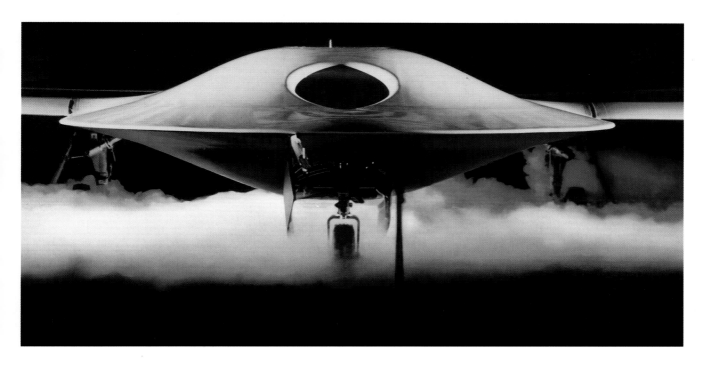

WARPLANES OF THE FUTURE

David Oliver & Mike Ryan

PUBLISHED BY

SALAMANDER BOOKS LIMITED

LONDON

A Salamander Book
Published by Salamander Books Limited
8 Blenheim Court
Brewery Road
London N7 9NT
United Kingdom

©Salamander Books Ltd. 2000   A member of the Chrysalis Group plc

ISBN 184065 0850

1 2 3 4 5 6 7 8 9 10

All correspondence concerning the content of this volume should be addressed to Salamander Books Ltd.

CREDITS
Project managed by Ray Bonds
Designed by Mitchell Strange/Mel Raymond

Color separation by Studio Tec

Printed in Spain

THE AUTHORS

DAVID OLIVER is an aviation writer and photographer who began his career as a photo-journalist working for Duckhams Oil Company's in-house motor sport publications. He learnt to fly and was appointed Editor of *AirForces Monthly* magazine and Co-ordinating Editor of *Air International.* He subsequently formed his own consultancy company working with specialist defense publications, television production companies, and the aerospace industry. He has written 14 books on various aviation and defense subjects ranging from flying boats to unmanned aerial vehicles (UAVs).

MIKE RYAN is Managing Director of AVPRO UK Ltd, a conceptual design and research company committed to the design of advanced aerospace and defense technology. Close working relationships with the UK aerospace and defense industry and the Defence Evaluation Research Agency (DERA) enable the company to offer a custom design service for air, land, and sea platforms. He also serves in the UK Reserve forces as an Army officer, and frequently acts as a technical consultant to the film, television, and publishing industries.

PICTURE CREDITS

With the exception of those indicated below, the photographs and color scenarios have been drawn from David Oliver's collection, and he and the publishers wish to thank the manufacturers, services, and private individuals who have provided illustrations for this book. Special thanks are accorded to Eric Hehs, Editor of *Code* One magazine, Lockheed Martin Tactical Aircraft Systems, for permission to use the F-22 development material.

Illustrations on the following pages were supplied by AVPRO UK Ltd: endpapers; pages 2-3; 4-5; 80-86; 106-107; 109 (bottom); 111 (bottom); 112-113; 114; 118-119 (top); 120-121 (top); 122-123; 126-127; 130 (bottom); 139-141; 156-157; 159; 163 (bottom); 164-165; 168 (top).

Illustrations on pages 8, 9 (top and bottom), 10 (top), 11 (center and bottom), and 12-14 were provided by Salamander Picture Library. Photographs on pages 153 (bottom) and 154 (top) are by Patrick Allen (via David Oliver).

ADDITIONAL CAPTIONS

Jacket front: Boeing's CV version of Joint Strike Fighter. Jacket back: the F-22A Raptor, AVPRO UK's Marauder concept, and Lockheed Martin's proposals for CTOL and STOL unmanned strike aircraft operating from advanced assault ships.

Endpapers: Operational concept of manned and unmanned strike aircraft package.

Page 1: Lockheed Martin/Boeing DarkStar UAV design.

Pages 2-3: UCAVs used for suppression of enemy air defenses (SEAD), clearing the way for manned strike aircraft.

Pages 4-5: Concept for closely integrated packages of UCAVs led by manned "mother ships."

Pages 6-7: Boeing's Airborne Laser system, based on a 747 and designed to shoot down theater ballistic missiles while they were still

CONTENTS

INTRODUCTION

I n the time since man first battled with his fellow man, aerial warfare takes up a milli-second. Heavier-than-air flight is less than a century old and it was not until 1910 that a military firearm was fired or a dummy bomb dropped from an aeroplane in flight. In the following decade, World War I accelerated aviation technology out of all recognition and airplanes had become an important weapon.

I n five short years, they had photographed the front line from the air, sunk submarines, bombed capital cities, and pursued and shot down other aircraft. Over the next two decades, military aviation marked time, with developments of World War I biplanes being used by most air forces until war clouds again loomed over Europe in the late 1930s.

From the first day of World War II, it was clear that aerial warfare would play a crucial role in the outcome of the conflict. The German Blitzkreig unleashed over Poland, Norway, the Low Countries, and France swept all before it. RAF fighter aircraft saved the British Isles from a German invasion during the Battle of Britain in the summer of 1940, while the Japanese aerial attack on Pearl Harbor just over a year later at first caught the world's most powerful nation totally unprepared, but unleashed aerial retribution such as the world had never witnessed before.

For the next five years, the race for superiority saw unprecedented advances in aviation technology ranging from the development of the jet engine, radar, aircraft carriers, airborne assaults, helicopters, pressurized cockpits, and hydraulically operated folding wings for naval aircraft. Weapon technology saw the introduction of 30mm cannons, flying bombs, guided missiles, "Grand Slam" bombs, ballistic rockets, and the atomic bomb.

By the end of the war, air power could now reduce the world to a wasteland and an even longer struggle for air superiority was about to begin. The dying months of the conflict had seen the so-called Allies involved in a deadly race to capture German aviation designers, technicians, and the experimental aircraft that they had been developing. The results of the captured German research, which were divided between the victorious nations, mainly the United States and the Soviet Union, were integrated with that carried out by their own designers, paving the way for a quantum leap in technology over the next decade.

The impetus for these advances was yet another war, one of a different kind—the Cold War that "broke out" following the Soviet blockade of Berlin in June 1948. This blockade was defeated by an unprecedented US and British airlift to sustain the city that lasted for more than a year. US and Soviet defense bugets mushroomed as the two "Superpowers" raced to replace outdated World War II combat aircraft with state-of-the-art jet warplanes. Some idea of the pace of change can be measured by the world absolute air speed record which stood at 486mph (777kmh) at the end of the war and would more than double in the next decade.

When communist North Korea invaded South Korea in June 1950, the conflict was about to test Soviet and US aviation technology as the Cold War threatened to escalate into World War III. The latest combat aircraft from both "Superpowers" faced each other in a deperate battle for air superiority in the remote Southeast Asian skies. The most successful fighters involved in the Korean War were very similar in

Strategic Air Command's first jet-powered nuclear bomber was the futuristic B-47 Stratojet, more than 2,000 of which were built in the 1960s.

The Soviet Union's first swept-wing fighter, and the Sabre's main rival in Korea, was the MiG-15, also created with German research, and British jet engines.

design, size and performance. Both the North American F-86 Sabre, which first flew in October 1947, and the Soviet MiG-15 which flew a month later, benefited from German swept-wing research while the Soviet fighter also utilized British jet-engine technology by reverse engineering the Rolls Royce Nene. However, the US fighter had a 10-to-1 kill ratio over the MiGs by the time the conflict ended in July 1953, the Sabre's ability to absorb battle damage, and the quality of its pilots, being the deciding factors.

The Korean War further escalated the Cold War arms race. The largest slice of the US defense budget at the time went to the US Air Force's Strategic Air Command (SAC) which ordered more than 2,000 B-47 Stratojet global mission bombers. The futuristic three-man nuclear bomber, powered by six turbojets fitted in pods under a thin swept wing that again was based on German research, had an unrefueled range of nearly 3,000 miles (4,800km). Vast amonts of money was also being poured into the development of supersonic "second generation" fighters which culminated in the American Century Fighter series in the mid-1950s. The first of these was the F-100 Super Sabre which was quickly followed by the F-101 Voodoo and F-102 Delta Dagger and F-106 Delta Dart.

Many of these aircraft had been developed in great secrecy, but one US facility was to remain under wraps not only from the prying eyes of the Soviets, but also from the American public and most of its government. This was Lockheed's ultra-secret "Skunk Works" which was responsible for some of the most successful and innovative Cold War warplanes. Established at the end of World War II under its legendary designer Kelly Johnson (who was responsible for America's first jet fighter, the P-80 Shooting Star), it was here that the supersonic F-104 Starfighter—dubbed "the missile with a man in it"— was created in the late 1950s. Although used by the USAF in only small numbers, more than 2,000 Starfighters were operated by 11 overseas air forces over three decades.

One of Kelly's best known and enduring products, built at the Skunk Works for the CIA in extreme secrecy, was the subsonic U-2 high altitude "spyplane." Little was known about Lockheed's remarkable surveillance aircraft until one was shot down by a surface-to-air missile (SAM) over Sverdlovsk in the Soviet Union in May 1960 while making an overflight from Pakistan. This incident created added tension between East and West. The Soviets also recognized that they were falling behind in the development of

The first of USAF's Century Fighter series designed during the Korean War was the supersonic North American F-100 Super Sabre.

USAF's first swept-wing fighter, the F-86 Sabre, inspired by German wartime research, was the mount for most Korean War "aces."

The sleek Convair F-106A Delta Dart interceptor, which set a world absolute speed record of 1,525mph (2,440kmh) in December 1959, was the last of the Century Fighters.

The agile MiG-17 flown by North Vietnamese pilots managed to shoot down many more modern US fighters using its cannon armament.

The Soviet MiG-21F "Fishbed" point interceptor, here seen in North Vietnamese markings, was limited by its restricted combat radius.

high performance air defense fighters, since its response to the US Century fighters had been the development of the MiG-19 "Farmer," a supersonic, single-seat, twin-engined day-fighter, which was unable to reach the U-2 when tasked with its interception in May 1960.

Mikoyan's successor to the MiG-19 made its first flight in 1956 and was destined to be built in greater numbers than any other jet fighter to date. Designed as a result of lessons learned during the Korean War, the compact, supersonic, delta-wing MiG-21 "Fishbed" became the Warsaw Pact's standard air defense fighter for almost 30 years. More than 10,000 MiG-21s were built. It has served with no fewer than 46 nations and it remains in production in China, giving it the longest operational and production life of any combat aircraft in history.

While the Cold War settled to a NATO/WarPac stalemate in the early 1960s, with SAC B-52 Stratofortresses armed with nuclear weapons maintaining round-the-clock airborne alerts and Soviet Tu-95 "Bears" probing Western air defenses from Norway to Florida, America became involved in yet another conflict in Southeast Asia—Vietnam.

Warfare broke out in 1963 between US forces supporting the South Vietnamese government and the communist Viet Cong guerrillas supported by North Vietnam. In 12 years of conflict, nearly every type of USAF and US Navy combat aircraft was committed to air operations in the region. They were pitched against Soviet-built North Vietnamese air defense fighters. In the early years of the war, US Century

Fighters escorted Korean War veteran piston-engined attack aircraft such as the A-1 Skyraider and B-26 Invader, although these were quickly replaced by the F-105 Thunderchief in the close air support role. However, when Operation *Rolling Thunder*, the sustained bombing campaign against North Vietnam, began in 1965, US losses began to mount not only from anti-aircraft fire, but also from North Vietnamese fighters. Initially, USAF fighter bombers proved to be particularly vulnerable to the highly maneuverable MiG-17 and had to be escorted over enemy territory by one of the most successful western warplanes of all time—the F-4 Phantom II.

Conceived originally as a ship-borne multi-role fighter, the supersonic two-seat F-4B first went into action in Vietnam with the US Marines in 1964 . That was followed a year later by the first F-4C Phantoms, which had been adopted by the USAF as its standard tactical fighter. Flying MIGCAPs over North Vietnam, the Phantom soon began to gain the upper hand in air-to-air combat, although it would never emulate the Sabre's success in Korea.

By the end of the conflict, the success rate for American fighters was little better than two-to-one despite the relatively small numbers of operational North Vietnamese MiGs they encountered. Many other US aircraft were downed by SA-2 surface-to-air missiles (SAMs) which were first deployed by the North Vietnamese in July 1965, as well as by "old fashioned" AA batteries.

Other US aircraft that won their battle spurs during the Vietnam conflict included SAC B-52s which dropped thousands of tons of conventional bombs over North Vietnam and Cambodia. But 16 of these huge, long-range bombers were shot down over an 11-day period of Operation "Linebacker II" in December 1972. The USAF rushed its new variable-geometry F-111A fighter-bomber into operations in 1968 but, after several losses on their first missions, they were soon withdrawn. The US Navy introduced

▼

Having made its operational debut during the Vietnam conflict, the McDonnell Douglas F-4 Phantom II became one of the classic jet fighters of its era.

◄

Vietnam was the birthplace of the attack helicopter in the form of a two-seat development of the famous Huey, the AH-1 Cobra.

▼

The heavy-lift CH-47 Chinook helicopter entered service at the beginning of the Vietnam conflict and has remained in production ever since.

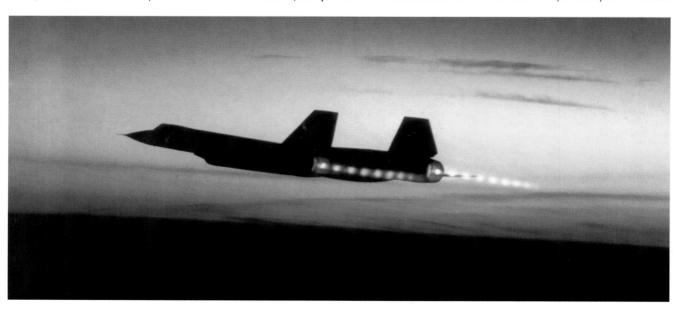

INTRODUCTION

▶

The Mach 3 SR-71 Blackbird strategic reconnaissance aircraft remained USAF's highest performance combat aircraft for more than three decades.

▼

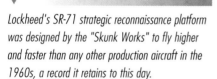

Lockheed's SR-71 strategic reconnaissance platform was designed by the "Skunk Works" to fly higher and faster than any other production aircraft in the 1960s, a record it retains to this day.

a large number of new combat aircraft into the conflict. Apart from the Phantom II, the F-8 Crusader, A-3 Skywarrior, A-4 Skyhawk, A-5 Vigilante, A-6 Intruder, and A-7 Corsair II all saw action there. The A-7 made its combat debut in 1967 only two years after its first flight and the compact single-seat attack aircraft, designed to replace the Skyhawk, was rapidly adopted by the USAF as a medium attack aircraft and subsequently deployed to Southeast Asia.

Vietnam also saw the baptism of fire of the battlefield helicopter, and the two-seat dedicated gunship development of the ubiquitous Huey, the AH-1 Cobra, was one of the most successful products of the Vietnam conflict. Another star of the helicopter war was the twin-rotor heavy-lift Boeing CH-47 Chinook which could carry as many troops and cargo as its illustrious fixed-wing predecessor, the C-47.

The Vietnam War left more questions than answers for a US Air Force and Navy that had been developed to confront the Soviet Union in Europe. Some 1,800 US aircraft were lost in combat, and the conflict had shown up serious shortcomings in aircraft design, performance, and armament, as well as pilot training and tactics.

On the positive side, strategic reconnaissance carried out by detachments of SAC U-2s and its Skunk Works stablemate, the incredible SR-71 Blackbird, were extremely effective. Developed in great secrecy from the highly classifed A-12—the world's first Mach 3-capable single-seat strategic reconnaissance aircraft—the twin-engined, two-seat Lockheed SR-71 first flew in December 1964. A detachment of Blackbirds flew unchallenged high-altitude (over 80,000ft/26,000m) missions over China, North Korea, and North Vietnam from Kadena Air Base in Japan from March 1968 under an operation codenamed *Senior Crown*.

The conflict also saw the first deployment of small, pilotless surveillance aircraft based on the Ryan Q-2 target drone. Launched from DC-130 Hercules aircraft, Firebee remotely piloted vehicles (RPVs) flew more than 34,000 operational surveillance missions over Southeast Asia—and, of course, without the loss

of a single pilot.

Great advances in the development of electronic warfare (EW), electronic countermeasures (ECM), airborne early warning (AEW), and command, control and communications (C$_3$) were generated by the huge defense contracts placed with the US aerospace industry during the Vietnam period, while a profusion of "smart" weapons also began to appear in the forces' inventories. One of the most important of these was the AGM-45 Shrike, a specialized anti-radar missile used by "Wild Weasel" units flying with F-105F and later F-4G defense-supression aircraft equipped with Radar Homing and Warning (RHAW) systems.

Again, the lessons learned from combat led to the development of another generation of fighter aircraft in the 1970s. The first of these was the twin-engined, two-seat, variable-geometry F-14 Tomcat, a Mach 2 carrier-borne fleet defense fighter. Designed to replace the US Navy's Phantom II, the Tomcat (which first flew in December 1970 as a private venture competitor to the US Navy's F-111B which was later canceled) became one of the most potent long-range interceptors. The USAF selected the twin-engined, two-seat McDonnell Douglas F-15 Eagle air superiority fighter to replace its Phantom fleet in 1969, and in the early 1970s two aircraft—the General Dynamics YF-16 and Northrop YF-17—were in

▲

One of USAF's many F-4G Phantom units was the 37th "Wild Weasel" Tactical Fighter Wing (TFW) which was dedicated to the suppression of enemy air defenses (SEAD) mission.

▼

The F-15 Eagle, which first flew in July 1972, quickly built up a formidable reputation as a "MiG killer" in air combat over Israel, in the Gulf, and in the Balkans.

competition for the USAF's lightweight fighter program. In February 1974, the single-engined F-16 Fighting Falcon emerged as the victor over Northrop's twin-engined fighter. So began the service life of one of the world's most important and versatile combat aircraft, which a year later was selected to replace NATO's F-104G.

The YF-17 was not a total failure since the design was developed in collaboration with McDonnell Douglas as a ship-borne fighter and attack aircraft to replace the Corsair II. After a protracted development, the result—the multi-role F/A-18 Hornet—achieved operational status with the US Marine Corps and Navy in 1983.

Other post-Vietnam combat aircraft of note that were developed in the 1970s were the Rockwell B-1 bomber and the more successful AH-64 Apache attack helicopter. Designed as a supersonic strategic bomber capable of penetrating Soviet defenses and launch stand-off nuclear weapons, the variable-geometry B-1A first took to the air in December 1974. In 1977, President Carter canceled the bomber on grounds of cost, although it was resurrected by President Reagan four years later, albeit in a revised form. The B-1B incorporated much recently developed "stealth" technology which reduced its radar cross-section to significantly less than that of the B-52 it was designed to replace. It was also given an additional low-level, high-subsonic penetration role when the first of 100 production B-1B Lancers entered service with SAC on July 1985.

As well as proving a formidable strike aircraft, the multi-role F-16 Fighting Falcons have shot down more than 70 aircraft in air combat over Israel, Pakistan, Iraq, and the Balkans — with no losses.

▼

Although it was designed to replace the B-52, the variable-geometry B-1B bomber was not used in combat until the end of 1998 when it took part in Operation Desert Fox in the Gulf, alongside veteran B-52s.

Designed to meet the US Army's requirement for an Advanced Attack Helicopter (AAH), the two-seat Hughes, later McDonnell Douglas, AH-64A was flown for the first time in September 1975 and was built to attack Soviet tanks on the plains of northern Europe. Armed with a 30mm chain gun, Hellfire laser-guided anti-tank missiles, 70mm FFAR rockets, and Sidewinder or Stinger air-to-air missiles, the Apache was equipped with the advanced Target Aquisition and Designation Sight/Pilot's Night Vision Sensor (TADS/PNVS) with the gunner using the novel Integrated Helmet And Display Sighting System (IHADSS) which had a monocular sight slaved to the chain gun.

During this period, the Soviets developed a family of supersonic variable-geometry fighter and attack aircraft, the MiG-23 and -37 "Floggers" as successors to the many MiG-21 air defense and ground attack variants. They proved to be fast (Mach 2.3), strong, and reliable warplanes that were built in large

◄
The latest variant of the world's most popular fighter, the MiG-21bis, and its stablemate, the MiG-23 "Flogger," here in Indian Air Force markings, were both deployed to Afghanistan in the 1970s.

numbers—more than 5,500 MiG-23s— but were better suited to Third World operations rather than facing American third generation US F-15s and -16s.

The Soviet Union was about to become embroiled in its own "Vietnam" when it invaded Afghanistan in December 1979. It was its chance to test the effectiveness of its air forces and combat aircraft in a war environment, and they were found wanting. During the 10-year conflict more than 110,000 troops, supported by 300 fighters, 100 long-range bombers, and 250 combat helicopters, battled with 40,000 Mujaheddin guerillas. Several types received their baptism of fire during the conflict, including the "Flogger," the ground attack Su-25 "Frogfoot," which proved vulnerable to the Mujaheddin's shoulder-mounted SAMs, and the capable Su-24 "Fencer" that carried out bombing missions over Afghanistan alongside Tu-16 heavy bombers operated from within the Soviet Union.

The aircraft that became a symbol of Soviet air power in the conflict was the Mi-24 "Hind," at the time the world's most formidable helicopter gunship, christened the "Devil's Chariot" by the Mujaheddin. With a speed of over 200mph (320kmh), the "Hind" was heavily armed with cannon, rockets, and "Spiral" laser-guided anti-tank missiles, and could transport nine assault troops. Many Mi-24s were shot down when flying at low level by US-built Stinger SAMs and small arms fire.

The war in Afghanistan had been a severe strain on the Soviet Union's defense budgets and the war-weary withdrawal in 1989 heralded the Union's collapse two years later, and with it the end of the 40-year Cold War.

In the following chapters we shall see how Cold War technology adapted to a new period of global uncertainty as "local" conflicts broke out in the Middle East and the Balkans, and civil war threatened to engulf Africa and former Soviet regions. At the same time the United States and Europe became involved in a new race to produce post-Cold War fourth and fifth generation combat aircraft that would push technology, and defense budgets, to the limit.

Russia's once powerful aerospace industry has been defeated by economics. The undoubted skill and resourcefulness of its designers has been stifled by a complete withdrawal of defense funding in the 1990s, although the innovative fourth generation MiG 1.44 and Sukhoi S-37, which were designed during the Cold War, eventually took to the air. They have little chance of ever becoming operational, however.

Along with new aircraft, new missions have evolved in the "New World Era," many of them covert and highly specialized. We shall examine the growing importance of special forces (SF) operations, combat search and rescue (CSAR) missions, the development of the unmanned combat air vehicle (UCAV), which is being designed to undertake many of the "dirty and dangerous" missions now flown by manned aircraft, and how new and exotic propulsions will take strategic strike and reconnaissance airplanes into space within the next decade.

▲
The Soviets' tank-busting Su-25 "Frogfoot" was used against Mujaheddin guerrillas in Afghanistan, and several were shot down by shoulder-mounted Stinger surface-to-air missiles.

▼
Christened the "Devil's Chariot" by the Mujaheddin in Afghanistan, the heavily armed Mi-24 was vulnerable to Stingers and ground fire.

OUT OF THE COLD INTO THE STORM

T he delicate nuclear balance between the East and West was maintained for nearly four decades of the Cold War, with each side of the Iron Curtain maintaining vast stocks of air-launched, submarine-launched, and land-based missile-launched thermonuclear weapons. Each side also had to develop ever more complex and expensive defenses against a multi-layer attack by the other.

The potential World War III battlefield was a divided Germany which was the front line between opposing WarPac and NATO forces. Dozens of giant air bases supported by thousands of military personnel were built by the United States and Great Britain in West Germany, and by the Soviet Union in East Germany. Here the most sophisticated air defense and attack combat aircraft from all three countries were deployed, along with the latest ground-based air defense missiles and tactical nuclear weapons.

In a gamble to break the nuclear stalemate, US President Reagan implemented the Strategic Defense Initiative (SDI) that came to be known as the "Star Wars" program in the mid-1980s. This was intended to create a defensive shield over the USA autonomously operated by intellingent computers which would detect and prioritize all threats and destroy them with a variety of advanced weapons. Most of these weapons were only in the concept stage of development and would have required unprecendented investment over a long period.

However, whether the "Star Wars" program was bluff or reality, it was an important step in the United States' ultimate victory in the Cold War. SDI would force the Soviet Union into competing in the development of a comparable system, but its ecomomy was already doomed to self-destruct and it fell to General Secretary Gorbachev to deliver the unthinkable truth to the Soviet Union's millions. With *glasnost* ("openness," Gorbachev's policy of liberalizing various aspects of Soviet life) came the break-up of the Warsaw Pact and, to the West, the most significant sign of the collapse of the Eastern bloc, the fall of the Berlin Wall.

At the same time that Mikhail Gorbachev was receiving the Nobel Peace Prize his successsor as public enemy number one, Iraq's President Saddam Hussein, launched a land, sea, and air invasion of neighboring Kuwait on August 2, 1990. As with the Soviet invasion of Afghanistan a decade earlier, the US and Europe were taken completely by surprise. Despite all the sophisticated satellite and aircraft reconnaissance assets available to the west's superpower, Kuwait was occupied and Saudi Arabia under threat by Iraqi forces before the international community could react. Responding to a United Nations resolution condemning the unprovoked

A symbol of the Cold War, this East German Sukhoi Su-22 seen low over the Baltic was destined for the scrap yard when Germany reunited in 1990.

This "Vietnam Vet" US Navy A-7E Corsair II carried out its last operational missions attacking Iraqi ground positions during the Gulf War in 1991.

aggression, the United States and Great Britain were the first to deploy combat aircraft to the Middle East in an operation codenamed *Desert Shield.*

The UN ultimatum gave Iraq until January 15 1991 to withdraw from Kuwait, giving Coalition forces five months in which to assemble the largest deployment of military hardware since World War II. During that period more than 700,000 troops and their equipment from 32 countries were transported, largely by air, to Saudi Arabia and the Gulf States. Also moved to the Gulf area were more than 1,000 combat aircraft from the USA, Great Britain, France, Italy, Canada, Saudi Arabia, Qatar, and the UAE, and almost as many support aircraft—transports, tankers, heavy-lift helicopters, and maritime, electronic and photographic aircraft—joining the remnants of the Kuwait Air Force which managed to avoid capture or destructon by Iraqi forces. It was the largest deployment of UN air power seen since the Korean War.

Facing it were some 800 Iraqi Air Force aircraft, only half of which were combat capable, mostly of Soviet and French origin. Fewer than 100 Mirage F1s and 50 MiG-29 "Fulcrums" made up Iraq's air defense element, while many of its ground attack aircraft (including MiG-23s, Su-25s, and Mi-24s) were battle-weary from a decade of conflict with another of its neighbors, Iran.

Among the most powerful assets of the Coalition Force were the US carrier battle fleets deployed to the Persian Gulf and Red Sea during *Desert Shield.* Each had air groups comprising F-14 Tomcats, F/A-18 Hornets, A-6 Intruders, and A-7 Corsair IIs. They were supported by Hawkeyes, Prowlers, Vikings, and Sea King helos.

As the deadline for Iraq's withdrawal drew closer, Coalition commanders prepared plans to liberate Kuwait utilizing aircraft, tactics, and weaponry designed to defend western Europe from the Soviet Union and its WarPac allies. US, British, and Italian combat aircraft had regularly taken part in "Red Flag" exercises over the deserts of Nevada, and these had given these air forces valuable experience in combined operations in a Gulf-like environment. Though it would turn out to be a short, sharp air campaign, the upcoming Gulf War would prove to serve as a valuable lesson for the future of air warfare just as the much longer Vietnam War had two decades earlier.

The January 15 deadline came and went without Coaltition forces being unleashed. It was to be more than 24 hours later that *Desert Shield* became *Desert Storm.* The air assault began with 950-mile (1,530km) round trip mission by AH-64H Apache helicopters which successfully attacked Baghdad air defense radar stations during the night of January 16/17. Within minutes, the initial offensive on Baghdad itself began with Tomahawk cruise missiles armed with conventional warheads and fired from US warships in the Persian Gulf.

These were closely followed by salvos of BQM-74C target drones which resembled the cruise missiles in size, speed, and flight profiles. It was some of these that were shot down by Iraqi air defenses, leading them to claim they had destroyed waves of cruise missiles and attack aircraft. The first manned US fixed-wing attack aircraft committed to the Operation *Desert Storm* was the F-117A Night Hawk.

Developed under the deep "black" project *Senior Trend* by the Lockheed "Skunk Works" in the early 1980s, the world's first "stealth fighter" was designed to carry out covert strike missions against terrorist targets or rogue nations without exposing their identity of origin. The unique arrow shape and faceted construction, which deflects most radar energy in multiple directions, and its skin of composite radar absorbant material (RAM) give the F-117A a radar cross-section (RCS) of about one-hundreth of a square

Having first dropped bombs in anger over North Vietnam in 1965, the veteran B-52 took part in Operation Desert Storm *and was air-launching cruise missiles at Yugoslavia in 1999.*

yard, making the Night Hawk the equivalent of a bird of prey. Despite rumors and sightings over the Nevada deserts, a wing of 59 F-117As, which were built at a cost of nearly $100 million each, remained under cover at a remote and closely guarded base at Tonopah in the Nellis AFB range complex, its precise shape and official existence not being revealed until the end of 1988.

The subsonic Night Hawk can carry GBU-10 or GBU-27 Paveway laser-guided-bombs (LGB) in its internal weapons bay, being dropped from medium altitude. The "stealth fighter" acquires a target with its forward looking infra-red (FLIR) turret mounted in front of the cockpit. Close to its target, control is passed to the downward looking infra-red (DLIR) turret positioned next to the nose-wheel door which is equipped with a laser designator. As the *Desert Shield* build-up gained pace in late 1990, it was decided to deploy F-117As of the 37th Fighter Wing to Khamis Mushayt in Saudi Arabia to exert additional pressure on Saddam Hussein.

By way of a dress rehearsal for a possible future conflict, two Night Hawks had been deployed to Panama to support American special forces troops tasked with capturing its errant leader, General Noriega, in Operation *Just Cause* almost exactly a year earlier. Their attack on a military barracks during the night of December 19/20 1989 with 2,000lb (1,000kg) LGBs was the F-117A's first taste of action, but their lack of accuracy was blamed on the poor performance of sensors due the high humidity.

However, there was fortunately little humidity over Baghdad on the night of January 16/17 1991 when two waves of F-117As carried out very successful missions, targeting command and control centers, barracks, and Presidential palaces without loss or damage. More AGM-86C conventional air-launched cruise missiles (CALM) were launched by seven B-52Gs flying direct from the US mainland, a record distance which broke the one previously held by RAF Vulcans that had flown non-stop bombing missions from Ascencion to the Falkland Islands in June 1982.

At first light on the morning of Janaury 17, airfield strikes were carried out by USAF F-111 Aardvarks

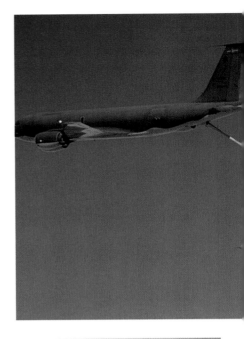

US Navy F-14A Tomcats operating from US carriers in the Persian Gulf and Red Sea seen refueling from a USAF KC-135 during Operation Desert Storm.

Although it made a less than successful operational debut in Vietnam, the F-111 Aardvark flew over 4,000 successful Gulf War missions without loss.

USAF's "secret" weapon during the Cold War, the futuristic Lockheed F-117A Night Hawk "stealth fighter" made a high profile appearance during the Gulf War.

and F-15E Strike Eagles, while RAF Tornados made low-level attacks unleashing their JP233 runway denial weapons. One of the British all-weather attack aircraft was the first Coalition casualty when it was shot down over Ar Rumaylah Air Base. Supporting the low- and medium-level strike packages were F-4F and F-16 Wild Weasel teams and US Navy EA-6B Prowlers, taking out SAM sites with high-speed anti-radiation missiles (HARM), while EF-111A Ravens jammed Iraqi communications.

On the first full day of the air battle, Iraq Air Force fighters, including three MiG-29s, two MiG-21s, and two Mirage F1s, were shot out of the sky by F-15C Eagles and F/A-18 Hornets. One Hornet and a Kuwaiti Skyhawk were lost to ground fire. Night raids on Iraqi airfields by F-111s, F-15Es, and Tornados continued, while during daylight hours it was soon obvious that the much-vaunted Iraq Air Force was not going to be a threat to Coalition fighters which slowly built up a growing tally of air-to-air victories. The F-15C Eagle, which had won its battle spurs over southern Lebanon with the Israeli Air Force almost a decade earlier, proved to be the top scoring type during *Desert Storm,* accounting for 33 Iraqi aircraft in air combat.

Although air superiority was virtually achieved by Coalition air forces within the first week of the war, their aircraft were still being shot down by Iraqi ground fire, both "triple-A" guns and surface-to-air missiles (SAM).

Some 16 different types of Coalition combat aircraft took part in *Desert Storm* operations against Iraqi forces in Kuwait and Iraq. These ranged from the A-6 Intruder, A-7 Corsair II, F-4 Phantom, F-111 Aardvark and B-52 Buff—all veterans of the conflict in Southeast Asia— to the F-117A Night Hawk. The most numerous fixed-wing type was the F-16, some 250 of which were deployed to the Gulf, a total that was matched only AH-64 Apache helicopters. Both these types had seen action with the Israelis in the 1980s but several US types made their operational debut in the Gulf War, including the A-10A Warthog, Strike Eagle, and the AV-8B Harrier II.

Typical of the state-of-the-art electronic warfare (EW) assets employed to great effect during Operation Desert Storm *for monitoring electrical signals and emissions was the RC-135U Rivet Joint.*

Of the carrier-borne aircraft in action (all of which were American since the British mini-carriers were held in reserve), the F/A-18 Hornets and F-14 Tomcats had been "blooded" in the Gulf of Sirte, off Libya. In August 1981 US Navy Tomcats shot down two Libyan Su-22s that were approaching the US Sixth Fleet; and in January 1989 two Libyan MiG-23s fell to Tomcat AAMs. Both the Tomcat and Hornet also took part in Operation *Eldorado Canyon* in April 1986, a USAF/USN air strike on Libyan targets in response to General Gadhaffi's involvement and support of international terrorism.

In contrast, none of the three British combat types deployed to the Gulf had seen action before. The two-seat, variable-geometry, multi-role Tornado GR.1 flew one of its primary Cold War missions from day one of *Desert Storm,* that of airfield denial using JP233 weapons dispensers. Designed for low-level high-speed delivery, the JP233 contained 30 bomblets and 215 mines capable of destroying a runway. However, it was during low-level airfield strikes that six Tornados were shot down by SAMs. In view of mounting losses and the realization that the only hostile threat was from ground fire, Tornado operations switched to medium level using "smart" weapons for the first time in its career.

British weapons and equipment rushed into service for *Desert Storm* included the BAe air-launched anti-radar missile (ALARM) and the thermal imaging and laser designation (TIALD) pod, both of which were used by RAF Tornados from the second week of the war. A force of 65 RAF Tornados based in Saudi Arabia and Bahrain flew more than 1,600 strike and reconnaissance missions, while the type was also flown by the Italian and Saudi Arabian Air Forces, each of which lost one aircraft.

The second RAF strike aircraft deployed to Bahrain was the 20-year-old Anglo-French Jaguar strike reconnaissance fighter, which at the time was under threat of imminent retirement. Twelve of the twin-engined, single-seat, tactical attack aircraft flew over 600 daylight missions from the first to the last days of the war without loss. Although a relatively unsophisticated aircraft which

Low over the deserts of Saudi Arabia carrying out stand-off jamming of Iraqi air defense radars and command and control systems in the Gulf War is an EC-130E Compass Call "electric" Hercules.

lacked radar but possessed an excellent nav/attack system and a laser rangefinder, the Jaguar GR.1 proved extremely effective in attacking Iraqi artillery positions and barracks in Kuwait and enemy shipping with 1,000lb (500kg) "iron" bombs, cluster bomb units (CBU), and CVR-7 rockets. France also deployed a similar force of Jaguars with equal success.

One of the oldest combat aircraft to see action in the Gulf was the RAF's Buccaneer, or "Flying Banana." Designed 30 years earlier as a Royal Navy carrier-borne, low-level strike aircraft, the twin-engined, two-seat Buccaneer was adopted by the RAF in 1970. After a long career in the maritime strike and reconnaissance, and—in Germany—the nuclear strike roles, the Buccaneer S.2 was slated to be replaced by the Tornado GR.1 when it was called up to make its operational debut in the Gulf. Ironically its *Desert Storm* mission was to support RAF Tornados not fitted with TIALD pods with its Pave Spike laser designator. Twelve Buccaneers flew a total of 216 missions over a four week period, assisting in the destruction of 24 bridges and several hardened aircraft shelters (HAS).

One other British type saw service in the Gulf, the two-seat, long-range fighter development of the Tornado. Having entered RAF service three years earlier, the Tornado F.3 was held back from the front line and made no contact with enemy fighters during its 700 air defense missions.

By the second week of the air war, much of the Iraqi Air Force had disappeared—quite literaly. After sporadic, one-sided air-to-air encounters with Coalition fighters, the Iraqis decided to run away to fight another day, seeking refuge in Iran, Chad, and even as far away as Tunisia. Almost 150 of its most effective combat aircraft—including MiG-29s, Su-24s, and indigenous Adnan AEW aircraft designed around the Il-76—fled to its erstwhile enemy Iran, while a similar number were estimated to have been destroyed on the ground. This fact did not slow the Coalition's aerial destruction of Iraq's war machine prior to the ground war, especially the "carpet" bombing by B-52s.

Extensive use was made of every aerial intelligence asset in the US inventory, including Israeli-built tactical unmanned aerial vehicles (UAV) which were used by the US Marine Corps for the first time. Signal Intelligence (SIGINT), the generic term for both Communications Intelligence (COMINT) and Electronic Intelligence (ELINT), was gathered by USAF U-2R/TR-1As, RC-135 Rivet Joints, EC-130H Compass Calls, as well as EF-111A Electric Foxes, and US Navy EA-6B Prowlers and Lockheed EP-3E Aries which made up the overall theater electronic order of battle (EOB).

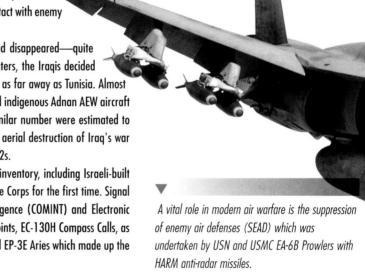

▼ *A vital role in modern air warfare is the suppression of enemy air defenses (SEAD) which was undertaken by USN and USMC EA-6B Prowlers with HARM anti-radar missiles.*

◄

Seen in its desert camouflage is one of more than 50 Marine Corps AH-1T SeaCobras that took part in the ground war phase of Operation Desert Storm.

▶

The first US Air Force fighters to arrive in-theater during Operation Desert Shield were F-15C Eagles of the 1st Tactical Fighter Wing (TFW) at Dharan in Saudi Arabia.

▼

US Navy, Marine, and Canadian forces F/A-18 Hornets were heavily engaged in Desert Storm air strikes. They shot down at least two Iraqi MiG-21s.

Electronic warfare (EW) technology had made considerable advances since the Vietnam War and, in addition to protection afforded to most strike packages by dedicated jamming aircraft, all Coalition tactical and many support aircraft were fitted with comprehensive self-protection electronic countermeasures (ECM) suites. These took the form of jamming pods, chaff/flare dispensers, infra-red (IR) countermeasures, decoys, and radar warning receivers (RWR). Although in the event there was little call for ECM assets against air-to-air threats, Coalition air forces had to face sophisticated ground-based threats of Russian- and French-built SAMs as well as lethal barrages of radar-ranged "triple-A." All of the 30 Coalition aircraft lost to enemy action, including an AC-130H Spectre gunship and its 14-man crew, were bought down by ground-based air defense systems.

Watching over the unfolding air war were numerous reconnaissance/surveillance assets which, apart from a pair of KH-12 photo reconnaissance satellites, consisted of six USAF U-2Rs and a similar number of TR-1As deployed to Taif in Saudi Arabia, plus six veteran RF-4C Phantoms at Incirlik Air Base in southern Turkey performing pre-strike target development and battle damage assessment (BDA) missions. Missing from the USAF's reconnaissance inventory was the Mach 3 SR-71 Blackbird which had been inexplicably retired from USAF service in March 1990, five months before Saddam Hussein's invasion of Kuwait. The US aircraft were backed up by six recce versions of the RAF Tornado, while the Jaguar force flew a number

of daylight tactical photo-reconnaissance missions over Kuwait.

One of the most important *Desert Storm* debutants was the E-8 Joint-Surveillance Target Attack Radar System (J-STARS). Two development E-8A aircraft, using the Boeing 707 airframe, designed to be jointly operated by USAF's Air Combat Command (ACC) and the US Army, were rapidly deployed to the Gulf theater a few days prior the start of the ground war. The long-range battlefield reconnaissance aircraft uses a synthetic aperture radar (SAR) to detect ground vehicle movements within a theater of operations, and this proved invaluable during the fast moving ground war when the two E-8s flew a total of 49 operational missions.

This bewildering array of Coalition aircraft was controlled by a fleet of another Boeing 707-based aircraft, the E-3 AWACS. Together with US Navy E-2 Hawkeyes, USAF E-3s flew round-the-clock to monitor Iraqi Air Force movements, and provide an air traffic control service for the numerous attack packages ingressing and egressing the battle area and guiding them to the waiting tankers.

Air refueling was vital to the success of Operations *Desert Shield/Storm*. With Coalition tactical aircraft based in Saudi Arabia, the Gulf States and Turkey, and B-52s operating from the UK, Spain, and Diego Garcia in the Indian Ocean, tankers were at a premium. A total of 256 USAF KC-135s and 40 KC-10As, plus 15 RAF Victor, VC.10, and TriStar tankers flew an amazing 5,500 refueling missions, offloading some 70 million gallons of fuel during the six-week Gulf War.

Having gained complete air superiority, Coalition aircraft continued intensive air bombardments of Iraqi positions in Kuwait, as well as bridges, roads, and rail communications to Iraq. The ground war began on February 24 when 2,000 troops of the US 101st Airborne Division were airlifted by 100-plus Chinook and Black Hawk helicopters to what was called Cobra Base inside Iraq. The operation was supported by Apache, Cobra, and SeaCobra attack helicopters, while special operations forces were moved around the covert battlefield by MH-53J Pave Low, MH-60G Pave Hawk, and Puma helicopters, which also flew several successful combat search and rescue (CSAR) missions during the war.

Two days later, Iraqi troops began blowing up Kuwaiti oil installations, trashing Kuwait City, and making a run for Baghdad. The highway from Kuwait to Basra became a "turkey shoot" for US Army AH-64s and USAF A-10As as Iraqi resistance crumbled, but it was another two days before Iraq finally agreed to implement all the UN Security Council resolutions and a ceasefire came into force, during which time an F-16 and an AO-10A were shot down. The first war claimed to be won by air power was over—or was it?

The statistics of the Gulf War were awesome. F-16s flew more than 13,500 missions; B-52Gs dropped 25,500 tons of bombs, one third of the Coalition's total; but it was the massive logistic effort required to sustain *Deserts Shield* and *Storm* that produced some staggering numbers. Military transport aircraft from a dozen nations supported by commercial aircraft from more than 100 civilian airlines airlifted more than half a million troops to the region, plus 650,000 tons of equipment—four times the total tonnage carried throughout the year-long Berlin Airlift. Almost half this total were flown by one type only, the ubiquitous C-130 Hercules, 250 of which flew nearly 50,000 missions between August 1990 and March 1991.

Lessons learned from the Gulf War were even more deep-rooted than those from Vietnam nearly two decades earlier. From the TV pictures beamed to the world during the early stages of the air war showing "smart" bombs entering windows, doors, and roofs of target buildings with pinpoint accuracy, the assumption was that they were the majority of the weapons used. This was not the case. Fewer than 10 percent of bombs dropped were "smart," and of those nearly 20 percent missed their targets. Also, several million-dollar air-launched ACM-86C CALMs malfunctioned before or immediately after launching.

▶

Four RAF warplanes that took part in the Gulf War—the Tornado GR.1 leading, the Jaguar GR.1 in the background, and the Buccaneer S.2B, all in Desert "Pink" camouflage, with a Tornado F.3 in trail.

▼

Carrying a centerline ALQ-131 jamming pod and Rockeye CBUs under the wing, this 363rd TFW F-16C with 35 mission symbols under the cockpit was one of 250 Fighting Falcons that took part in the Gulf War.

Armed with Super 530D and 550 Magic air-to-air missiles, French Air Force Mirage 2000Cs have taken part in Operations Desert Storm, Deliberate Force, and Allied Force.

Much was made of the F-117A "stealth fighter" which was an excellent propaganda weapon, although rather less effective as a strike aircraft. It must be remembered that it was designed in the 1970s, entered service in 1982, and had limited payload and range. The subsonic Night Hawk could carry only one third of the F/A-18 Hornet's weapons load of 15,50lb (7,000kg) despite using the same twin GEF404 turbofans and its landing gear, and one fifth of the Strike Eagle's weapons load. Although some 40 F-117As flew more than 1,200 *Desert Storm* missions, they proved difficult to maintain and their IR-weapons system was affected by bad weather, smoke from targets, and dust storms. Its distinctive faceted, low-observable design has never been copied.

Aircraft that performed particularly well in difficult out of area (OOA) operations included the multi-role F-16, especialy those fitted with low altitude navigation and targeting infra-red night (LANTIRN) pods, the veteran F-111, and the "simple" Jaguar. "Top gun" was the F-15C Eagle, but there was little chance to prove its superiority after the first few days of the air war. Coalition fighters shot down fewer than 50 Iraqi aircraft, some of which were helicopters. Some 70 Coalition aircraft were lost during *Deserts Shield* and *Storm*, more than half that number due to non-combat causes. Nevertheless, 28 modern Coalition combat aircraft were shot down by relatively unsophisticated SAMs and "triple-A" and some Cold War tactics, particularly those involving low-level attacks against heavily defended airfields, had to be rapidly re-assessed. RAF Tornados and Jaguars were quickly fitted with TIALD pods, and the Buccaneers were "retired," as were US Navy Corsair IIs and Intruders, along with USAF Phantoms and the F-111.

The Gulf War had also shown up a requirement for a swifter, heavier airlift capability to be used to transport rapid reaction forces to known, or even potential, troublespots. Many of Coalition's transport assets, both fixed and rotary wing, were "worn out" by the high rate of utilization and operating in harsh climatic conditions. The Gulf War hastened many types' retirement or, at the very least, major rebuilds. What was clear, however, was that the oil-rich Gulf States were patently incapable of defending themselves against a ruthless aggressor such as Saddam Hussein, despite their state-of-the-art military equipment.

What also soon became obvious was that Iraq, having been forced out of Kuwait, was not defeated. Within weeks of the ceasefire, Coalition forces had to establish Operations *Northern* and *Southern Watch*—"no-fly" zones over North and South Iraq to prevent Hussein from annihilating factions within his own country that he saw as internal threats. He also blatantly disregarded some of the UN resolutions

he had agreed to honor in order to bring *Desert Storm* to an end. These involved the UN monitoring of Iraq's weapons of mass destruction (WMD) capability and, ten years after the end of the Gulf War, Saddam continues to taunt the "western invaders."

After repeated Iraqi violations of the "no-fly" zones, and numerous expulsions of UN WMD monitors, the US and Britain, and initially France, carried out a series of air strikes against Iraq's air defense sites and control centers. The first major operation took place in January 1993 when more than 100 aircraft, including F-117As, F-15s, F-16s, RAF Tornados, and French Mirage 2000s, joined by naval aircraft from the carrier USS *Kitty Hawk* and Tomahawk cruise missiles fired from other US warships in the Gulf, hit targets around Baghdad. Two Iraqi MiG-23s were also shot down by F-16s.

However, it was a full six years later that another expulsion of UN monitors led to the largest air operations against Iraq following the Gulf War. Operation *Desert Fox* was a concentrated, 70-hour campaign that commenced on December 19 1998 with the launching of Tomahawk cruise missiles from US warships in the Gulf, followed by strike by US Navy and Marine Corps Hornets and LANTIRN-equipped Tomcats from the carriers USS *Enterprise* and *Carl Vinson*. Land-based aircraft taking part included F-16s and F-15Es on suppression of enemy air defenses (SEAD) missions, RAF TIALD Tornados attacking air defense sites with Paveway III LGBs, and B-52Hs from Diego Garcia launching more than 50 CALMS.

In action for the first time was the B-IB Lancer, held back during *Desert Storm* due to the fact that the supersonic high-altitude bomber was converting to a new role, that of delivering conventional munitions at low-level. During *Desert Fox*, two B-1Bs based in Oman dropped Mk 83 "dumb" bombs on Republic Guards barracks from high altitude. It was rumored, but not confirmed, that F-117A Night Hawks, some of which had been continually based in the Gulf region since 1990, also took part in the action.

A total of 348 US and British aircraft took part in *Desert Fox*, flying some 650 strike missions against 93 designated targets. Nearly 350 Tomahawk cruise missiles were launched at Iraq, more than all those fired in the six-week Gulf War. However, within weeks of the strikes, the southern "no-fly" zone was violated by a suprising number and variety of Iraqi fighters, including MiG-21s, Mirage F1s, MiG-29s, and even MiG-25s. The Gulf War continues!

War in the Balkans

Even as the desert dust was being washed off Coalition aircraft involved in the Gulf War, a new and potentially more serious conflict was breaking out in eastern Europe. On June 26 1991 the Yugoslav republic of Slovenia declared independence from the Federal Republic of Yugoslavia. The Balkans War was about to begin.

To prevent cessession, Federal troops surrounded Slovenia while Yugoslav Air Force Super Galebs (Super Gulls), Jastrebs (Hawks), and MiG-21s bombed and strafed Ljubljana Airport and TV and radio transmitters. After a short, sharp battle, during which Slovenian militia shot down two Gazelles and a Mi-8

RAF Tornado GR.1 "Foxy Mama" shows off its Desert Storm mission markings and one of its two 27mm IWKA-Mauser cannon at Dharan Air Base in Saudi Arabia.

Armed with Skyflash and Sidewinder air-to-air missiles and carrying long-range fuel tanks, this RAF "Desert Eagle" Tornado F.3 flies a combat air patrol (CAP) along the Saudi/Iraq border.

An upgraded RAF Jaguar GR.1A strike aircraft carrying overwing AIM-9L Sidewinders for self protection seen over Bosnia during an Operation Deny Flight mission.

"Hip" helicopters, the Yugoslav presidency decided to withdraw from Slovenian territory on July 18. Unfortunately, this was only a prelude to a more savage conflict in Yugoslavia when Croatia also decided to claim independence. There followed five months of intense fighting on the ground between Croatian militia and Federal Army defectors on the one hand, and the Federal government forces on the other, supported by air strikes by Yugoslav ground attack aircraft, which included the J.22 Orao (Eagle) using AGM-65 Maverick air-to-surface missiles.

Over this period more than 20 Yugoslav Air Force fighter bombers and helicopters were shot down by ground fire and SA-2/6 SAMs. They included three MiG-21s, two Oraos, and a Super Galeb. Three more MiG-21s were flown to Zagreb by defecting Croatian pilots. In August a Yugoslav air brigade of 50 MiG-21s and Super Galebs was withdrawn from Pula Air Base on the west coast of Croatia to Bihac in Bosnia-Herzigovina which had underground shelters. By the end of October, the European Community (EC) had brokered a ceasefire. To oversee the ceasefire, a United Nations Protection Force (UNPROFOR) was sent to Croatia in February 1992 but again, like a house of collapsing cards, the conflict had moved on.

The republic of Bosnia-Herzigovina, the largest in Yugoslavia, was where Serbs, Croatians, and Bosnians had lived together in peace for generations. When Bosnia voted for independence, it provoked a three way battle for control of the province. Civilians caught in the crossfire were slaughtered if they were in the wrong place at the wrong time, despite UNPROFOR's good intentions. Without military support for UN designated "safehavens" the savage civil war continued to tear the former Yugoslavia apart.

In response to Bosnian Serb aircraft bombing these Muslim "safehavens," the UN ordered air space

over Bosnia to be closed to military aircraft in October 1992. Serbia ignored this until NATO was asked to enforce the "no-fly" zone in June 1993. Over the next year, fighter, tanker, and AWACS aircraft from eight NATO nations, including France, flew 2,000 missions a month in support of combat air patrols (CAP) over Bosnia as part of Operation *Deny Flight*. With very limited powers of engagement, the NATO aircraft could only monitor violations which were mainly by low-flying helicopters. However, 1994 was the first year in its history that NATO "fired in anger." An air strike against Serbian ground forces attacking the Muslim "safe haven" at Goradze was mounted in April, and in November a package of 42 NATO aircraft attacked the Krajina Serb airfield at Udbina during Operation *Volcano*. The following year saw the first downing of *Deny Flight* aircraft, a British Sea Harrier and a USAF F-16. Although both pilots were rescued, international patience with the Serbs was running out.

On August 30 1995 NATO launched Operation *Deliberate Force*, at the time the largest military air operation in Europe since World War II. Over a three week period, US, British, French, and Netherlands aircraft flew 3,500 missions from bases in Italy and carriers in the Adriatic, hitting Bosnian Serb positions with "smart" weapons, while 13 cruise missiles were launched from US warships. Within weeks of the operation, the warring factions in Bosnia had signed the Dayton Accord agreeing a ceasefire overseen by a 50,000 NATO-led Implementation Force (IFOR).

This in turn led to the largest airlift since the Gulf War. The USAF C-17A Globemaster III won its battle spurs as it joined Air Mobility Command C-5s, C-141s, and the ubiquitous C-130s in flying more than 20,000 US troops to IFOR and later Stabilization Force (SFOR) bridgeheads. Years later, NATO forces on the ground and in the air continue to police the uneasy ceasefire in Bosnia, while in 1999 yet another part of remaining territory of Yugoslavia erupted into violence.

In the decade during which the former Yugoslavia imploded, East and West Germany re-unified, and former East German MiG-29s and Mi-24s became the first Russian-built aircraft to join NATO with the new *Luftwaffe*. although the last Russian Air force units were not withdrawn from the former GDR until 1994.

That same year saw the Russian republic of Chechenia in the Caucasus, led by General Dzhokar Dudayev, a former commander of a Soviet Long-Range Aviation Unit in Estonia, declare independence. After initial skirmishes, Russian aircraft bombed Chechenian airfields, destroying most of its embryo air force, and some 40,000 Russian troops backed by helicopters, tanks and armored personnel carriers (APC) invaded the country. After nearly two years of bitter fighting, Russian forces retreated from a devastated Chechenia, having lost some 20,000 personnel killed or wounded. A dozen strike aircraft, mainly Su-24s and Su-25s, and more than 25 helicopters had been shot down by Stinger SAMs and ground fire while flying more than 15,000 missions over the battlefield. One of these missions killed rebel General Dudayev in April 1996. The war destroyed the reputation of Russia's armed forces, particularly that of its air force, which clearly were not equipped or organized for guerrilla warfare and had learned nothing from their operations in Afghanistan a decade earlier.

As if inspired by events in neighboring Yugoslavia, civil war broke out in Albania in 1996, which led to the establishment of yet another NATO peacekeeping force. More than 7,000

RAF Tornado GR.1Bs taking part in Operation Desert Fox *operated from Ali al-Selem in Kuwait whose hardened aircraft shelters (HAS) had been targets for* Desert Storm *strikes when occupied by Iraqi fighters eight years earlier.*

Born in the Cold War, American F-16 Fighting Falcons and Russian MiG-29 "Fulcrums" were locked in air combat in the skies over Iraq and Yugoslavia in the 1990s.

AGM-86 convential air-launched cruise missiles (CALMs) were first carried to war by the veteran B-52H "Buff" during the Gulf War and eight years later were being launched against Belgrade.

troops supported by helicopters were deployed with Operation *Alba* in April 1997 to protect the delivery of humanitarian aid and provide security during elections. The knock-on effect of the chaos in Albania was that the Albanian minority population of the Yugoslav province of Kosovo formed an underground army to fight for its independence in late 1998. This in turn provoked decisive and violent reaction from Yugoslav security forces which caused heavy civilian casualties and their mass exodus from the rebel strongholds.

Determined not to see the situation deteriorate into another Bosnia, NATO warned the Yugoslav government that, if it did not withdraw it troops from the province and allow NATO troops to monitor a ceasefire, air strikes on military targets would follow. Yugoslavia's President Slobodan Milosevic, who became a rival to Saddam Hussein as the world's number one villain, refused to accept NATO's ultimatum and during the night of March 24 1999 cruise missiles were again targeted on the Balkans.

Operation *Allied Force* saw NATO at war with a sovereign nation for the first time in its 50 year history. Following a pattern of operations similar to those against Iraq, an attack on Yugoslav air defense assets around the capital Belgrade and the Kosovo provincial capital Pristina were carried out by Tomahawk cruise missiles launched from US warships in the Adriatic and CALMs from B-52s flying from RAF Fairford in the UK. These were followed by packages of 250 aircraft from 13 NATO air forces, including the *Luftwaffe* which fired in anger for the first time since the end of World War II.

Among this first wave of NATO aircraft were two B-2A Spirit "billion-dollar" stealth bombers making their operational debut. Designed as low observable strategic nuclear penetration bombers in the dying years of the Cold War, the blended flying-wing aircraft flew non-stop from their base at Whiteman AFB in Missouri, USA, to drop up to 80 Mk82 "dumb" bombs on priority targets.

The air attacks, designed to "degrade and if neccessary destroy" Milosevic's ability to wage war on the ethnic-Albanian majority in Kosovo, continued unabated in the following weeks during which time five Yugoslav MiG-29s were shot down—including one by a Dutch F-16 using AMRAAMs, two by USAF F-15Cs over Bosnia—and a USAF F-117A Night Hawk was shot down by a Yugoslav SAM near Belgrade. The downing of the much-vaunted "stealth fighter," whose type had flown almost 1,800 combat missions over Panama and Iraq without loss, was a psychological boost for the Yugoslavs and an embarrassment for NATO, which nevertheless continued to deploy the F-117A in the operation.

As the air strikes continued for days and then weeks, serious doubts about their effectiveness began to surface. Bad weather prevented the use of many air-launched precision weapons and although main fighter bases and fixed air defense positions were severely "degraded" it was clear that the large numbers of tanks, armored personnel carriers, and troops of the Yugoslav security forces were able to continue to harass the Albanian population in Kosovo with impunity. On the eve of its 50th anniversary NATO had to rethink its strategy if Milosevic was to be forced to the negotiating table.

In April, NATO widened its target base by destroying Yugoslavia's civilian infrastructure such as power stations, oil refineries, and bridges in major cities. In Operation *Allied Force*, the preferred weapon was the cruise missile, more than 150 of which were launched on Yugoslavian targets in the first two weeks of the war, and although some 350 NATO aircraft, most operating from bases in Italy, were involved in initial air strikes, the results were disappointing. Bad weather and smoke over targets caused missions to be aborted or laser-guided munitions to miss their targets, and with Yugoslav air defense radars shutting down prior to the air raids, NATO's anti-radar missiles were rendered ineffective.

Although the air strikes damaged Yugoslavia's air defense assets, they did not prevent its security forces from effectively evicting the entire ethnic-Albanian population from Kosovo, which sought revuge in neighboring Macedoniac and Albania, in the process destabilizing both those countries. Russia, which had supported Milosevic with arms and equipment during the Bosnian conflict, sent warships to the Adriatic as a warning of a much larger conflict if NATO were to invade Yugoslavia.

Another electronic platform that made an impressive debut in the Gulf War was the E-8 Joint-Surveillance Target Attack Radar System (J-STARS), subsequently used over the former Yugoslavia.

However, after 78 days of NATO air strikes, Milosevic agreed to withdraw his forces from Kosovo and Operation Allied Force ended on June 10 1999. In the months that followed , it was found that NATO seriously overestimated its success in destroying Yugoslavia's military assets as more than 75 percent of the Serbian tanks, APCs, and mobile SAM units left Kosovo in pristine condition, while several MiG-21s flew back to Belgrade. Clearly NATO's overwhelming superiority had failed to achieve its main objectives.

So by the end of the 20th Century, former WarPac members Poland, Hungary, and the Czech Republic joined NATO on the eve of its 50th anniversary, while unresolved conflicts in the Middle East and Eastern Europe continued and Africa was being torn apart by brutal civil wars in nine different countries ranging from Ethiopia in the north to Angola in the south. As we will see in the following chapters, the future of air warfare will have to address the difficult balance between the escalating costs of developing sophisticated and specialized air defense fighters, and the acquisition of multi-role attack aircraft, helicopters, and support aircraft for deployment in ever increasing numbers of out of area (OOA) or so-called peacekeeping operations.

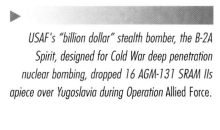

Veteran of Operations Just Cause, Desert Storm, Deliberate Force, *and* Desert Fox, *the "unsinkable" F-117A Night Hawk eventually fell prey to a Yugoslav SAM near Belgrade in Operation* Allied Force.

USAF's "billion dollar" stealth bomber, the B-2A Spirit, designed for Cold War deep penetration nuclear bombing, dropped 16 AGM-131 SRAM IIs apiece over Yugoslavia during Operation Allied Force.

THE FOURTH GENERATION

I n the early 1970s the Soviets had been working on the development of a new generation of advanced air superiority fighters, including the MiG-29 "Fulcrum" which first flew in October 1977, and the Su-27 "Flanker" that took to the air three years later. The Soviets were also rapidly advancing their surface-to-air and air-to-air missile technology, and the West's military planners were becoming increasingly concerned that the projected exchange rates between Western and Soviet-built fighters were looking unacceptably even.

These aircraft were a quantum advance from the rather "agricultural" MiG-23s and Su-22s developed only a few years earlier. At the same time, the supersonic swing-wing Tu-160 "Blackjack" strategic bomber, the heaviest and most powerful combat aircraft ever built, was making its first flight. Suddenly the West seemed to be coming from behind in the race to counter these extremely capable Soviet aircraft, but their response would be fragmented by differing political and operational requirements.

EUROFIGHTER

T he British have had a checkered history of producing state-of-the-art interceptors, which stems from the protracted development of the Hawker Hunter which first flew in 1951. Deliveries to the RAF were delayed by teething problems with the four 30mm Aden cannon pack and Canadair Sabres had to fill the gap until the Hunter became available in 1956. Although built in large numbers, almost 2,000, the short-range Hunter had more success in the ground attack role. The RAF's first all-weather radar-equipped interceptor fighter was the two-seat, twin-engined, subsonic Gloster Javelin which when it entered service 1957 was also the first to be armed with air-to-air missles.

That same year the the British government issued a disastrous White Paper that declared the end of manned fighter development,

Soviet-era's most formidable fighter is the Sukhoi Su-27, which proved to be superior to many Western fighters in the 1980s. Seen here is the naval "Flanker-D" with canard foreplanes.

projecting the supplementing of the aircraft by the missile. As a consequence, innovative supersonic fighter projects such as the mixed-power, rocket/jet-engine SR.177 and a supersonic development of the Hunter, the Hawker P.1121, were abandonned. The only survivor of this carnage was the English Electric Lightning which was to become the first, and only, all-British supersonic interceptor. Powered by two afterburning Rolls-Royce Avon turbojets, the Lightning had a maximum speed of Mach 2.25 and was capable of climbing to 50,000ft (15,150m) in one minute. However, it gulped fuel at a prodigious rate and had a maximum endurance of little more than one hour. Its dated monopulse radar was soon outdated but that did not prevent the Lightning from remaining the RAF's main air defense fighter for almost three decades, later lining up alongside a fleet of Phantoms powered by Rolls-Royce Spey turbojets.

The advanced MiG-29 "Fulcrum," a Ukrainian example of which is seen here with USAF F-16s, shook the West when it was first revealed in the late 1970s.

Their replacement was a compromise designed as a high-altitude, long-range bomber "destroyer," the Panavia Tornado ADV. This was a dedicated fighter derivative of the successful multi-national variable-geometry interdictor strike Tornado. After a seven-year development, the Tornado F.2 entered service in 1986 but early problems with its Foxhunter radar meant that it was not fully operational for another three years, by which time the Cold War was over and the role it was designed for had virtually disappeared. The RAF was left without an agile air superiority asset throughout the 1990s.

This shortcoming had been recognized 20 years earlier when British Aerospace (BAe) was attempting to initiate a "European" research and development program for a new Agile Combat Aircraft (ACA). This project attracted no government interest but in 1982 the UK Ministry of Defence supported BAe in the design and production of Britain's first-ever fighter technology demonstrator, the Experimental Aircraft

▼

The RAF's first and only all-British-built supersonic fighter was the English Electric Lightning which served as the backbone of its interceptor fleet for more than three decades.

▶

British Aerospace's Experimental Aircraft Programme (EAP) technology demonstrator for the European Fighter Aircraft (EFA) program that became Eurofighter.

Programme (EAP). This served as a technology prototype for the multi-national European Fighter Aircraft (EFA), later Eurofighter, that was launched in August 1985, and first flew exactly one year later.

The highly agile, single-seat, short-take-off and landing (STOL), air superiority Eurofighter is being produced by a four nation consortium comprising the UK, Germany, Italy, and Spain—France having withdrawn from the project in 1985 to develop its own aircraft in the same class. Having to contend with the integration of cutting edge technology—carbon-fiber composites, stealth materials, variable-camber wings with canards, quadruplex fly-by-wire (FBW) flight control systems, hands-on-throttle and stick (HOTAS), multi-function displays (MFD), and direct voice input (DVI) – the aircraft also had to be produced in four different countries. Inevitably there have been setbacks and delays, not helped by the fact that Germany threatened to pull out of the project in 1992 because of escalating costs. However, after reconsidering the alternatives, Germany stayed on board and it was the German development Eurofighter which made the first flight in March 1994, almost 10 years after the program's launch.

Seven development Eurofighters (now named the Typhoon), including three two-seaters, had flown by the end of 1999 and there are 232 aircraft on order for the RAF, 180 for the Luftwaffe, 121 for Italy, and 87 for Spain. Greece has a requirement for 60+ Typhoons and Norway and Australia are being targeted as potential customers in 2000. In the meantime a Continuous Technology Insertion (CTI) program will incorporate BAe's Terprom Terrain-Referenced Navigation (TRN) system which will allow the Typhoon to fly "hands-off" at night and low level. Uprated EJ230 turbofans with thrust-vectoring (TV) nozzles, an active array radar, and the integration of more advanced infra-red (IR) homing missiles are also being considered before the first production aircraft enter service with RAF's Evaluation Squadron in 2005.

▲

The first of seven development aircraft of the four-nation twin-engined Eurofighter, optimized for beyond-visual-range (BVR) and close air combat, first flew in 1994.

▲

Italy's Eurofighter Typhoon DA3 on finals showing its canard foreplanes, large chin-mounted inlets, variable-camber delta-wing, and excellent visibility from the cockpit.

▼

DASA's Eurofighter DA5, the second German aircraft to join the development program, seen carrying two underwing AIM-120 AMRAAMs and four semi-recessed under the fuselage.

RAFALE

When France pulled out of the EFA project in 1985 it was because its Dassault ACX, originally promoted as the basis for a European fighter, failed to meet either the technical or political requirements of other countries.

Dassault had produced a long line of battle-proven combat aircraft which had been involved in numerous Middle East conflicts. The very capable Israeli Air Force started with the Ouragan (Hurricane) which fought in the Suez campaign with both the French and Israeli Air Forces. Dassault's swept-wing development, the Super Mystere, was followed by the first of the very successful family of supersonic, delta-winged, multi-role Mirages, some 2,000 of which had been produced since 1961. The latest variant, the Mirage 2000, will continue to leave the Dassault production lines well into the 21st Century.

The design of France's proposed EFA contender, the Rafale (Squall), placed more emphasis on the ground attack role with air defense as a secondary mission, and it was also to be the common airframe for a carrier-borne version to replace the Aeronavale's aging F-8 Crusaders and Etendards.

Dassault had already developed the Mirage 4000 multi-role fighter as a private venture during the late 1970s and, although it attracted no contracts from the French government, it was later re-engined and participated in the Rafale program. The twin-engined Rafale A technology demonstrator was first flown in July 1986 and shared many of the Eurofighter's design characteristics—compound sweep delta wing with foreplanes (canards), composite construction, digital fly-by-wire system, side-stick, and advanced multi-function displays. Although its dimensions and performance are almost indentical to those of Eurofighter, the Rafale's radar cross-section (RCS) is less, due mainly to the design of the flank-mounted engine inlets.

Some 300 Rafales were ordered in three basic versions: the single-seat, carrier-capable Rafale M fleet defense fighter, 60 of which will operate from France's new supercarrier, *Charles de Gaulle*, from 2001;

▲ This head-on view of the Dassault Rafale emphasizes the small radar cross-section which is compromised by the three auxiliary fuel tanks and Apache dispensers on the inner pylons.

▶ The French Air Force's two-seat Rafale B seen here in low-level ground attack mode carrying a full 9-ton load of underwing stores.

▼ Dassault's unsuccessful Mirage 4000 was later converted into an engine test-bed for France's fourth

the single-seat, multi-role combat Rafale C for the French Air Force which can carry 17,640lb (8,000kg) of ordnance, including the ASMP nuclear stand-off missile, on 14 external hardpoints; and the two-seat Rafale B originally designed as an operational trainer, but which is now the French Air Force's primary combat version.

The multi-mode functions of Rafale's RBE2 electronic scanning radar include long-range detection and tracking of multiple targets in lookdown or look-up mode, the generation of 3D maps for terrain following, and real-time multi-function secure data links. Rafale offers several advanced operational capabilities such as the Front Sector Optics (OSF) system which operates in visible and infra-red (IR) wavelengths to provide discrete long-range detection, multi-target angular tracking, and range-finding for air, sea and ground targets in adverse weather or under radar jamming. The latest generation of French air-to-air, air-to-surface, anti-ship, and stand-off missiles are integrated with the Rafale's upgradable weapons system. Rafales B and C will replace French Air Force Mirage F1s, Jaguars, and eventually Mirage 2000s with the first production two-seater finally entering service with a test unit at Istres in 1999.

▲
With strengthened under-carriage, the carrier-capable, single-seat Rafale M, designed to replace the Aeronavale's F-8 Crusaders and Super Etendards, is seen about to grab a cable on the flight deck of the carrier Foch.

▼
Rafale's state-of-the-art cockpit, showing the wide-angle head-ip display (HUD), head-level tactical multi-image display (HLD), two lateral system management displays, and hands-on throttle and stick (HOTAS).

JAS 39 GRIPEN

Perhaps one of the most unlikely fourth generation combat aircraft to attain production, and in fact the first to enter service, was the Saab JAS 39 Gripen. Produced by a country that had successfully protected its neutrality through two world wars and the Cold War, the Gripen is the latest in a long line of innovative fighter designs that have made the Swedish Air Force one of Europe's best equipped forces since the end of World War II. Designed specifically to its customer's requirements, Saab's aircraft were not compromised by constraints imposed on designs that have to consider potential exports, since these have been strictly limited to other neutral countries by successive Swedish governments.

The Saab 29 was Europe's first swept-wing jet fighter to attain service in 1951, the Saab 32 Lansen (Lance) was one of Europe's first all-weather attack aircraft, while the unique double-delta Saab 35 Draken (Dragon) multi-role fighter was the first European Mach 2 fighter, entering service in 1960, and the first to be armed with license-built Sidewinder AAMs. Its successor was the mighty Saab 37 Viggen (Thunderbolt) which was a complete weapons system, including support facilities integrated into Sweden's air defense network. It entered service in 1971. Once again its design broke new ground by being the first operational combat aircraft to feature a close-coupled canard delta configuration which two decades later was adopted by most fourth generation fighters. Viggen was a multi-role fighter with a maximum speed of Mach 2.1 but capable of operating from temporary roadway airstrips thanks to its suberb low-speed handling and reverse thrust of its 28,100lb (12,745kg) thrust Volvo turbofan.

The Viggen was a hard act to follow but Saab managed to pull off another first with its JAS 39 Gripen (Griffin). JAS stands for Jagt-Attack-Spaning (Fighter-Attack-Reconnaissance), the Gripen's roles, which three different variants of the Viggen previously fullfilled. Also designed as a single-engined cropped delta with close-coupled all-moving foreplanes, the JAS 39 differs from the Saab 37 by being two thirds its size, less than half its weight, but with the same performance. Incredibly, it can carry the same weapons load of 14,332lb (6,500kg). Thirty percent of the airframe structure, which has an extremely small radar cross-section is constructed of composites and the 18,101lb (8,210kg) thrust GE/Volvo afterburning turbofan gives the the JAS 39 an excellent power-to-weight ratio.

▲

Saab's lightweight JAS 39 Gripen multi-role fighter, seen here carrying AIM-120 AMRAAMs, entered service with the Royal Swedish Air Force in 1993.

Mission profiles can be changed after take-off using on-board programmable software and its integrated weapons systems. Information is presented to the pilot on three head-down CRT multi-function displays and a wide-angle head-up-display (HUD), while the Ericsson radar has a look-down shoot-down capability. A comprehensive variety of Swedish, US, French, and British smart weapons have been integrated with the Gripen's weapon system, a fact that will help future export sales which, since the end of the Cold War, the Swedish government has encouraged.

The JAS 39 first entered service with the Royal Swedish Air Force in June 1993 and in January 1999 the first export customer for the Gripen International, which is being jointly marketed by Saab and BAe, was announced. South Africa selected 28 Gripens to fullfill its light fighter requirement for the South African Air Force (SAAF). While not in the same class as the twin-engined Eurofighter, Rafale, and Raptor, the Gripen utilizes similar advanced technologies designed into a practical and cost-effective package which is proving to be serious competition to the US aerospace giants.

▼

A formation of two Saab Gripens flying at low-level armed with Sidewinders and AMRAAMs, the world's first fourth generation fighter to enter service.

◄

The JAS 39 Gripen's Ericsson EP 17 computer-controlled cockpit display system featuring a wide-angle head-up display (HUD), and three head-down high resolution CRT displays (HDD).

BIRTH OF THE F-22 RAPTOR

To give an insight into the complex and protracted development process involved in the creation of a fourth, or fifth generation fighter aircraft, as the Americans consider the latest of their breed, it is worth looking in some detail at the 20-year gestation period of the Lockheed Martin F-22A Raptor

Integrating stealth, speed, and maneuverability became the fundamental challenge of the USAF Advanced Tactical Fighter (ATF) program. No one had ever attempted such a complex combination before. As the F-117 had shown, stealth affects every aspect of a design. Internal weapon carriage, a must for a stealthy design, increases the cross-section of an aircraft. Larger cross-sections increase supersonic drag and work against supercruise. "A stealthy aircraft requires a big weapon bay," explains Dick Hardy, Boeing's F-22 program manager. "And the landing gear and the inlet duct want to be in the same place as the weapon bay. You wind up with a guppy that will not be supersonic unless you make it very long with huge engines. Such an approach is a non-starter because the aircraft would be way too expensive."

Maneuverability requirements tend to increase the size of the wings and tails and make the engines bigger than necessary for supercruise alone. Those few pilots who were briefed on the F-117 knew about compromises in speed, maneuverability, payload, and other capabilities that went along with an all-out approach to stealth. Fighter pilots who would be flying the ATF would not willingly sacrifice these capabilities for stealth.

Nine airframe companies and three engine manufacturers responded to the challenge when the USAF Aeronautical Systems Division (ASD) re-entered the game and issued its request for information (RFI) for an ATF in 1981. At this early stage of the program, the USAF had not decided whether the new aircraft would emphasize air-to-air or air-to-ground missions and invited industry to share ideas for the new fighter.

The companies submitted a wide range of configurations in their responses. Lockheed favored a derivitive of the YF-12A, the forerunner of the two-seat SR-71 Blackbird. The YF-12A, designed for air-

The experimental Lockheed Y-12A interceptor successfully fired several AIM-47 air-to-air missiles in the mid-to-late 1960s.

One of Lockheed's first proposals for the USAF Advanced Tactical Fighter (ATF) program was the Mach 3 YF-12A that first flew in 1963.

to-ground missions, carried several kinetic-energy penetrator weapons in a central weapon bay which would be released at supersonic speeds at high altitudes and guided to the target by a laser. The approach, which was worked through in early 1982, built up technical data gathered from a series of air-to-air missile launches from the YF-12A conducted in the mid-to-late 1960s. The YF-12A had fired seven Hughes AIM-47 missiles at altitudes of up to 80,000 feet (24,250m) at speeds of over Mach 3. The shots, at aerial targets at ranges of over 30 miles (48km), were highly successful. This high-altitude, high-speed approach was also one of Lockheed's candidates for the F-X program which became the F-15.

Like Lockheed, Boeing submitted a supersonic air-to-ground design. "After studying a broad spectrum of airplanes including flying wings, canards, four-tails, two-tails, side inlets and nose inlets, Boeing homed in on a design fairly quickly," recalls Hardy. "We thought the aircraft should be designed for higher speed so we concentrated on designs with a higher fineness ratio. It was also obvious that we needed a good maneuverability aircraft. When the prime mission of the airplane later shifted to air-to-air, we quickly got rid of those things that did not have good control authority."

Boeing also stressed stealth with clever internal arrangement and weapon bay designs that carried munitions semi-submerged.

The General Dynamics response favored two of the four concepts originally developed in its 1976-78 studies for the Flight Dynamics Laboratory. One was Model 21 which looked like a traditional member of the modern fighter family, but it was not totally conventional. It had frontal shaping and treatment to reduce its radar cross section, strut-braced wings, and a rotating nose that combined a radar with an infra-red search and tracking (IRST) system. Composite materials comprised 40 percent of the aircraft structure. Its air-to-ground weapons included glide bombs with square cross-sections.

General Dynamics' other candidate could not be shown to USAF officials because of its classification and the company substituted surrogate drawings of a notional fighter that was soon dubbed the "Marshmallow." The real design was the starting point for all-wing studies explored in the next phase of the program.

After a year long study and report by industry, ASD performed mission analyses on four generic fighter designs that spanned the variety of aircraft investigated by the companies. They were labeled N,

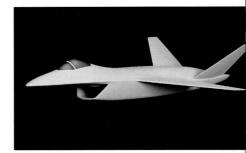

a small, cheap concept that could be puchased in quantity; SDM, a supersonic dash and maneuver; SLO, subsonic low observables; and HI, high-Mach/high-altitude. The results, which were presented to all participants, favored the the SLO flying wing, and the more conventional SDM placed second in effectiveness.

As the RFI results were announced, the ATF program gained momentum and funding. A mission element need statement was issued in late 1981 with Tactical Air Command, later Air Combat Command (ACC), creating a corresponding statement of need that addressed threats, theaters of operation, and capabilities required to accomplish the mission described.

The requirements formally made the ATF a replacement for the F-15 in the air-superiority role and an ATF System Program Office was formed at Wright-Patterson AFB in1983.

A request for proposals (RFP) for the ATF engine was issued and General Electric and Pratt & Whitney were awarded contracts to build and test competing engine designs, the F120 and F119, respectively. At the same time, USAF requested proposals for a concept definition investigation for ATF. Boeing, General Dynamics, Grumman, Lockheed, McDonnell Douglas, Northrop, and Rockwell responded and prepared proposals for submission by mid-1983. Just before the deadline, ASD announced a delay during which time the companies were asked to add highly classified stealth-related information to their proposals — in no more than five pages!

"Originally the ATF program did not contain stealth," explains Al Piccirillo, the then ATF program director. "People on the program were aware of what was going on in the F-117 and B-2 programs and we would have been really stupid to develop an advanced fighter without using this new technology. Without stealth, I am not sure USAF could have justified ATF."

Including stealth set an unusual security precedent. The security level of the original RFPs at this stage of the program precluded any details on stealth, a topic that was highly classified in the early 1980s. Companies that could claim low-observable (LO) technologies would be considered in a design but they could not reference any actual experience or techniques in their proposals. Stealth technologies were considered "black" and as such did not exist to anyone not cleared on them. The last minute change in the RFPs placed the program in both the "black" and "white" worlds.

The next phase in the program was the demonstration/validation (dem/val) phase in which companies would have to prove their technologies and refine their designs. Lockheed, however, took a radical departure from its high-speed, high-altitude design. "Clearly, ATF was going to be superstealth and not a cousin of the YF-12 or SR-71," explained Bart Osborne, Lockheed's chief engineer during this phase of the ATF program. "I stopped the YF-12 derivative effort and we started working on an F-117 derivative for ATF. The design submitted looked like a larger and elongated F-117 with some significant differences. It had a high wing rather than a low wing and four tails instead of two. The inlets were placed below and behind the leading edge of the wing. The highly faceted aicraft weighed around 80,000 pounds (36,290kg) and was far from aerodynamic. We knew we would have serious problems with the supersonic requirements but it was a real dog of an airplane. With enough power you can make a brick fly! We did not know how to analyze a curved stealthy shape in those days; the software was not sophisticated enough and we did not have the computational capacity we needed. We had our hands tied by the analytical problems. Lockheed had become convinced that if we could not analyze a design as a stealthy shape, then it could not be stealthy. We would not break through that barrier until 1984."

Lockheed's submission for the concept exploration phase was not received well by USAF, and the company was placed last in the field of seven which all received a contract for about $1 million for this phase. In the demonstration/validation phase, four winning companies would be given some $100 million each to demonstrate technologies needed to build their ATF.

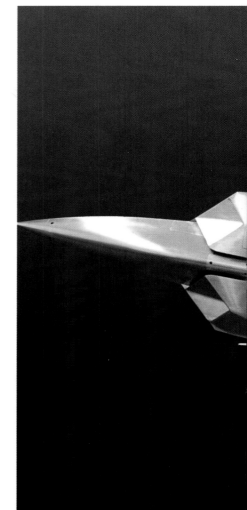

▲

The final Lockeed Boeing F-22 Raptor design traces its roots to the three ATF demonstartion/validation concepts submitted by Boeing (top left), General Dynamics (top right), and Lockheed (center).

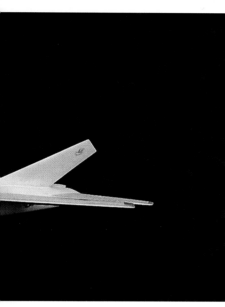

LOCKHEED ATF

After its poor showing, Lockheed had to turn around its ATF program before the next proposal was due in December 1985. The company had just lost what was to become the B-2 bomber with its faceted design compared to the more aerodynamic flying wing design from Northrop. Lockheed had also been cut out of the US Navy's Advanced Tactical Aircraft (ATA) program after entering the competition with another highly faceted design.

USAF's response to its latest ATF concept forced the company to rethink its commitment to faceting for stealth. "We simply started drawing curved shapes," recalled Osborne. "Even though we could not run the designs through our analytical software models, when we went to curved airplanes we began to get more acceptable supersonic and maneuver performance. Instead of relying on software models, we built curved models and tested them on the company's radar range which performed quite well."

The Lockheed configuration which just preceded the company's final dem/val design, called Configuration 084, was smooth except for a faceted nose. "We knew how to make a stealthy flat radome," recalled Osborne, "but we did not know until early 1985 how to make a stealthy curved radome. We started drawing them in 1984 before we knew how to analyze them."

The final configuration, called 090P, had a streamlined nose, trapezoidal wing planform with positive sweep on both leading and trailing edges, and four tail surfaces—two horizontal and two vertical. The large vertical tails were canted outwards while the leading and trailing edge sweep angle on all surfaces were aligned to common angles. The design had a wide strake that ran in a straight line from the leading edge outboard of the inlets to the point of the nose.

One requirement that drove all of the ATF designs was a wide field of regard for sensors. The requirement called for a 120-degree radar field of regard on each side of the nose. A forward-looking infra-red search and tracking (IRST) capability was also desired. The Lockheed design included three radar arrays placed in the nose of the aircraft, one facing forward and two facing sideways. Each wing root carried an IRST system that operated through faceted windows.

The aircraft carried six air-to-air missiles in a rotary missile launcher which was loaded away from the aircraft. When closed, the bottom of the launcher became the lower skin of the aircraft.

"The real question USAF had was whether Lockheed could design a curved stealthy airplane," Osborne explained. "We showed them with the range model that we could do curves." Lockheed's biggest advantages going into the next phase were its revamped approach and vast stealth experience. It had also earned a good reputation for rapid-prototyping in a variety of programs, most recently the F-117's predecessor, the "Have Blue."

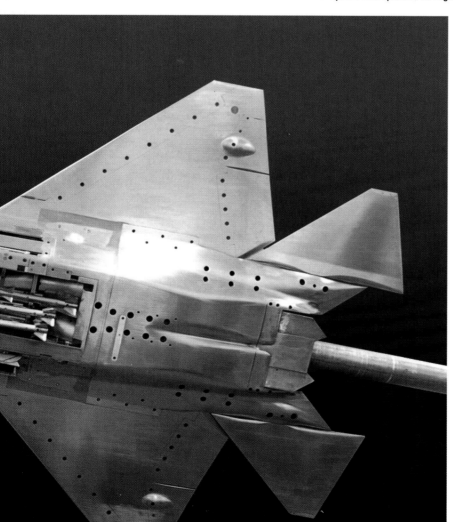

◄

The final F-22 design is the result of many thousands of hours in the wind tunnel. This model was used to measure various forces associated with the internal weapons bay.

BOEING ATF

The Boeing concept was a larger aircraft than the designs submitted by Lockheed or General Dynamics. The company retained the higher operating speeds assumed in its previous work. The most notable features of the design were twin vertical tails located well aft on the fuselage behind a trapezoid planform wing. The vertical tails were sized to provide the same vertical and horizontal control power as four tails.

"Our designers argued most over two tails or four," recalled Hardy. "The whole Boeing Company got involved in the argument. We had special teams set up to study the problem. Two tails won out. Our higher operating speeds led to a longer airplane which produced a longer moment arm for the tails so we did not need as many surfaces. We thought we could meet all the requirements with two tails which gave our design a lower signature and a lighter weight."

Boeing designers focused on the weapon bay and essentially designed the aircraft around it. Wind tunnel results, especially those related to flight at high angles of attack, affected the arrangement, size, and cant angles, and the placement of the tails. The design used a single chin inlet with an internal splitter to feed the two engines. The inlet had an internal variable ramp to reach its higher design speeds. Boeing designers moved the nose landing gear aft of the inlet in one of their later design changes.

The company had been working with advanced composite materials for USAF labs and in some classified programs in the 1970s and 1980s. As a result the design used a unique thermoplastic manufacturing process and material for the wing.

Air-to-air weapons were carried internally, although larger air-to-ground weapons were carried partially submerged while heat-seeking missiles were carried in separate bays placed forward in the fuselage. The weapon bay concept relied on quick-change pallets to position the munitions so they could be loaded speedily to meet the rapid turnaround requirements. The Boeing design also had three radars in the nose, one large forward-facing array and two smaller side-facing arrays to meet the 120-degree field of view requirement. Two IRST sensors were placed near the nose.

Boeing had done well in the previous phase of the program and its design was well developed and wind tunnel tested. Further, the company had extensive experience in integrating avionics which dated back to to the AWACS program, and more recently the B-2 bomber program.

GENERAL DYNAMICS ATF

The General Dynamics design evolved from a variety of inputs. During the previous phase, the company had focused on three separate families of aircraft: "C" - conventional, "W" - all-wing, and "T" - semi tailless. After a series of internal design competitions and trades, the company went with the "T" ser tailless approach.

The wing planform and airfoil design were chosen to minimize weight while providing the maximu turn capability and supersonic cruise. The single vertical tail, however, presented problems in achievin totally stealthy design. GD ran many wind tunnel tests to find a location and shape for twin canted vertic tails on the "T" configuration. The vortex-flow off the forebody and delta-wing produced unstable pitchin moments when it interacted with twin tails. A single vertical tail with no horizontal tails was final identified as the best overall approach despite the degradation of radar cross-section in the side sect The proposal configuration was designated T-330.

General Dynamics took a unique approach to the sensor requirements, using two radar arrays and a IRST sensor. The IRST sensor was placed in the nose and the two radar arrays were located aft of the cockpit. The radar beam from each array could be steered 60 degrees from the face of the array, allowing each radar to cover the area from straight ahead to 120 degrees aft. The arrays were located just above the engine inlets.

The GD configuration achieved a high state of detailed design. The company had built a full-scale

▶

Major sections of the YF-22 were built at three different locations and were assembled at the "Skunk Works" at Palmdale, California.

mock-up and was finalizing a half-scale model for testing the design's radar cross-section. Preliminary structural designs were developed along with locations for manufacturing breaks to allow the aircraft to be divided among potential partners. GD had done well in the concept phase. Among its strengths were its extensive experience in fighter design and manufacturing gained in the F-16 program. The company also had experience with rapid prototyping with the YF-16.

A few months before the final proposals were to be submitted, USAF amended its proposal request, significantly increasing the importance of stealth in the design. Lockheed, with a stealthy configuration derived from the F-117, made no modifications while Boeing made some slight modifications to the design of the inlets. The upgraded requirements forced General Dynamics' engineers to again reconsider twin tails in a variety of locations including out on pods on the wing. The trailing edge of the wing and control surfaces were cut into chevrons aligned with the leading edge, giving the wing a bat-like look. In the end, no acceptable location for twin tails was found and the design was submitted with a single centerline tail and a serrated trailing edge. The new final configuration was labeled T-333.

As it had done with the proposal for the previous phase, the USAF delayed the submission date of the dem/val proposals; this time the deadline for the prototyping was put off. The amendment required contractors to build two prototypes, one with the F119 engine and the other with the F120. The last-minute change resulted from a reaction to a report released in the early 1980s by a Congressional commission which had been asked to look at reforms in Pentagon acquisition practices. The report, influenced by the recent success of the F-16 program, favored prototyping for new military aircraft.

"Initially, the proposal request did not contain prototypes," Piccirillo explained. "ATF was patterned on the F-15 program which did not have prototypes. The Air Force has gone back and forth over fifty years

The first flight of the YF-22 PAV1 took place at Palmdale on September 29, 1990. Supercruise flight was first demonstrated on October 25.

in the value of prototyping. In the 1960s through the F-15 program, we did not prototype. We performed studies, ground and wind tunnel tested and went straight into full-scale development work. We built test airlpanes but they were very close to the production configuration. After amendment, the dem/val phase of the program called for best-effort concept demonstrators. We left it up to the contractor to decide how they would demonstrate the critical technologies behind their concepts for an ATF. One of the most critical was shaping for supersonic flight and low observables."

General Dynamics program manager Moran later recalled, "We had actually finished the proposal and were within a few days of turning it in when we got Modification Request MR-006 to the RFP. Instead of approximately $100 million contracts for four winners, USAF awarded only two contracts of about $700 million each. We were directed to write one more proposal volume describing how we would design, build and test two flying prototypes—one with each of the designated engines. We were also required to build a ground-based avionics test lab and we could offer a flying avionics test-bed if we thought that was desirable."

The companies were given 60 extra days to modify their proposals. At the same time, USAF sent out a letter to the competing companies to encourage teaming. Moran commented that, "The Air Force encouraged teaming because it wanted the best resources from industry to be brought to bear on the program which was going to be expensive and big. The more commitment we had from industry, the more likely the program was to succeed."

A complicated dance among the contractors began immediately to see who wanted to partner with whom. Representatives from Boeing, GD, and Lockheed signed a teaming agreement in June 1986, while Northrop and McDonnell Douglas announced their team two months later. Rockwell and Grumman did not

team up. The teaming deal was done "blind" with none of the participants getting to see each other's design or program plans before the contract was awarded.

On October 31 1986 it was annouced that Lockheed and Northrop had each won $691 million contracts to proceed to the dem/val phase of the ATF program. The following day was the first time the respective team members were able to look at each of their team member's designs and the process of integrating their best aspects began in earnest. The Lockheed team had three designs to mesh into one YF-22 while Northrop had only two for their YF-23. Nevertheless they both had less than four years to virtually redesign a viable ATF contender within an ever-decreasing budget.

Although the Lockheed team's final F-22 variant would trace its roots to some of the original ATF concepts submitted, including Lockheed's four-tail design, and General Dynamics' inlet configuration, none of these included the eventual diamond wing planform. This evolved over the next two years with the aid of ACAD, a three-dimentional software package developed by GD linked with CATIA, high-fidelity 3D software ironically developed by Dassault.

The final design freeze for the Prototype Air Vehicles (PAV) occurred in May 1988 and construction of PAV1 with GE YF120 engines and PAV2 with Pratt & Whitney YF119s, both of which featured thrust-vectoring, began at Fort Worth the following month. The YF-22 was unveiled to the public at the "Skunk Works" on September 29 1990, a month after its rival, the YF-23.

The McDonnell Northrop contender, the YF-23, was a slightly longer aircraft with a cropped-diamond planform, vee-tail and flat-bottomed fuselage. The widely spaced shallow inlets were set well back under the wing while the exhaust outlets, without thrust-vectoring, were positioned above the flattened rear fuselage which increased its stealth characteristics which Northrop had been developing for its low observable (LO) B-2 strategic bomber program. In an effort to cut costs and time, the YF-23 used a number of stock McDonnell Douglas components such as an F-15 cockpit and F/A-18 landing gear. Unveiled at Edwards AFB in June 1990, the YF-23 was the first ATF prototype to fly when it took off on August 27.

Lockheed's YF-22 PAV1 first flew on September 29 and after flying 92 hours in 74 test flights, compared with the YF-23's 65 hours in 50 flights, Lockheed and Pratt & Whitney were declared the winners of the ATF program on April 23 1991 by Secretary of the Air Force Donald Rice for "offering better

Although its basic shape is now well established, the F-22A Raptor continues to evolve in the flight test program at Edwards AFB, California, and at various other facilities across the United States.

The planform of the YF-22 (top) compared with the longer Engineering and Manufacting Development (EMD) F-22.

The first live-firing of an AIM-9 Sidewinder air-to-air missile from a YF-22 took place on November 28, 1990, while a live AIM-120 AMRAAM was launched a few weeks later.

capability at lower cost, thereby providing the Air Force with a true best value."

Although Northrop had lost their second major fighter contract in 15 years, it has long been rumored that the YF-23 optimized for stealthy supercruise was the prototype for the Advanced Stealth Technology Reconnaissance Aircraft (ASTRA) to replace the SR-71 Blackbird.

The subsequent $9.55 billion Engineering and Manufacturing Development (EMD) contract covered the manufacture of 11 single-seat F-22As, the first of which was scheduled for 1996, with the work shared equally between the three team members. In 1993 Lockheed purchased General Dynamics and took over its share of the F-22 production.

Since that time, the F-22's weight was reduced to little more than the F-15, its LO characteristics were improved, the IRST requirement dropped, a ground attack capability introduced, and the production program reduced. This phase originally included the production of 750 fighters with first deliveries in 2005. This was later reduced to 648 aircraft while subsequent post-Cold War funding and threat analyses have now reduced the planned buy to 339 F-22s, now christened Raptor. However, the potential for an air-to-ground version of the fighter to eventually replace the F-15E Strike Eagle is favored by the USAF.

DETERRENT FIGHTERS

Although undoubtedly ultra-capable combat aircraft, the West's fourth/fifth generation fighters were conceived in the Cold War to fight an enemy that no longer exists. Russia's long-range bomber fleets are being scrapped and its only fourth generation designs, the MiG 1.44 and Sukhoi S-37, remain technology demonstrators. With difficult and costly developments spanning more than twenty years, the 1999 prices of the West's new fighters — $68 million each for the Gripen, $98 million for Eurofighter, $115 million for the Rafale, and some $193 for the Raptor - make them, with the exception of the Gripen, prohibitively expensive for many countries.

However, they have stimulated the aerospace industries involved in each of these programs and have set the benchmarks for fighter aircraft standards for the next half century. They may never be used to defend the countries that developed them, but they are sure to deter any potential aggressor from provoking them into action.

JOINT STRIKE FIGHTER

Although the F-22, Eurofighter, and Rafale were conceived during the Cold War, the Joint Strike Fighter (JSF) was born out of several post-Cold War projects to replace the multi-role USAF F-16 and USN F/A-18 when they reach the end of their operational lives after 2010. The program had its roots in the USAF's Multi-Role Fighter (MRF), the US Navy's A/F-X project, and the Joint Attack Fighter (JAF) and Joint Stealth Strike Fighter (JSSF) which were both incorporated into the Joint Advanced Strike Technology (JAST) concept in 1993.

The JSF, claimed to be potentially the largest manned fighter program of the 21st Century, is being developed as a common advanced and affordable single-seat combat aircraft to fulfill three dedicated mission slots for four services. The USAF has a requirement for 2,000 primarily strike/attack aircraft with an acceptable air-to-air capability, to replace the A-10, F-16, and some variants of the F-15 with a projected in-service date of 2015. The USN wants early F/A-18s to be replaced by 300 stealthy, long-range strike, carrier-borne convential take-off and landing (CTOL) aircraft, while the US Marine Corps (USMC) requires 600 of the advanced short take-off and vertical landing (ASTOVL) close-air support (CAS) version to replace its AV-8B Harriers and fighter/attack Hornets. The fourth service is the Royal Navy, which needs 60 multi-role ASTOVL aircraft to replace its fleet of Sea Harrier F/A.2s.

Once the USN was persuaded to accept a single-engined, single-seat design, the program's timescale was set with the first demonstration aircraft scheduled to fly in 2000, the down-select to a single contractor in 2001, and the Engineering Manufacturing Development (EMD) commencing the following year. With a projected in-service date of 2010, the first production JSF should fly by 2005, but as with many multi-role aircraft programs in the past this may slip.

Another program rolled into JSF was the Common Affordable Lightweight

▼

An RAF Harrier GR.3 armed with Paveway laser-guided bombs (LGB) on the flight deck of the carrier HMS Hermes in the South Atlantic during the Falklands conflict in 1982.

▲

More than 300 AV-8B Harrier IIs were ordered by the USMC, some of which took part in Operation Desert Storm from air bases in Saudi Arabia.

Fighter (CALF) with "common" and "affordable" being the moving criteria behind the project. The JSF specification originally called for a stealthy Mach 1.5 strike aircraft with a combat radius for the CTOL version of 800 miles (1,300km) and 500-625 miles (800-1,000km) for the ASTOVL version. Its internal weapons bay has to be able to carry two 2,000lb (900kg) GBU-29 Joint Direct Attack Munition (JDAM) and two cropped AIM-120C AMRAAMs, with the heavier STOVL version carrying only two 1,000lb (450kg) "smart" bombs, while other ordnance can be carried on four underwing hardpoints. The common powerplant selected was a Pratt & Whitney F119 derivative developing at least 35,000lb (15,875kg) of thrust.

Commonality was initially a major stumbling block. The USAF and USN use different fuels, ejection seats, refueling systems, and even AIM-9 Sidewinder short-range air-to-air missiles. The Navy's primary attack aircraft was the two-seat, twin-engined A-6 Intruder that was retired during the mid-1990s and the role of its replacement, the twin-engined F/A-18E/F Super Hornet, which will not be operational until 2005, overlaps that of the CTOL JSF in certain aspects. Following the Department of Defense's 1997 Quadrennial Defense Review (QDR), a minimum of 548 Super Hornets were on order, and this could rise to 748 if the JSF is not available by 2008.

The STOVL version is the most complex and potentially most expensive of the JSF family. The US Marine Corps' and Royal Navy's requirement can be traced back over 40 years to when the British Hawker company developed the first STOVL P1127 as a private venture. A tri-national evaluation squadron was formed with Britain, Germany, and the United States in 1964 with nine Hawker Kestrel F(GA).1s, a militarized derivative of the P1127. US interest in the innovative STOVL ground attack aircraft began early in the program with America largely funding the Bristol Siddeley, later Rolls-Royce Pegasus, vectored-thrust turbofan, and six Kestrels were subsequently transferred to the USA in 1965 for evaluation by the USMC.

The Kestrel was largely a subsonic technology demonstrator for a supersonic derivative, the P1154, which was cancelled by the British Labour government in its 1964 defense economy drive. However, the

RAF was able to order more than 10? ?sonic, single-seat, close support and reconnaissance developments of the Kestrel which entere? ???ice in 1970, known as the Harrier. The USMC acquired a similar number of aircraft powered by ?? ???lb (8,710kg) thrust Pegasus 101, designated the AV-8A, with the Spanish Navy receiving a fur?? ?With the successful deployment of AV-8As on small Marine Corps assault carriers and the the an? ???ent in 1977 that t? ???Navy's large carriers were to be replaced with small anti-submarine ??? ? (ASW) STOVL carri? ?ne RN Fleet Air Arm ordered a mutli-role version of the Harrier.

The Sea Harrier (SHAR) FRS ?came operational in 1980 and an initial order for 34 aircraft was in the process of delivery when ?? ? broke out in the South Atlantic two years later. Operation *Corporate*, mounted to retake the Falkland islands from Argentine forces in the spring of 1982, saw the operational debut of both the RAF Harrier and the Royal Navy SHAR. In the subsequent three-month campaign, 28 SHARs flew 1,450 missions, downing more than 20 Argentine aircraft, mainly with AIM-9 Sidewinders, for the loss of five aircraft, none in air combat. Fourteen RAF Harriers flew 12? ground attack missions using "smart" bombs for the first time, losing three ?? ??und fire. Without t? ?perationally flexible, rugged Harrier and Sea Harrier with their unique ?????? ? operate from ?iort ???s, ??ads, heli-pads, and ships, the Falkland Islands, 8,000 miles (12,875km) away from the UK, could not have been ??ken.

Despite its operational success, the Harrier design was already more than 20 ? ?ars old and required a radical redesign to enable it to maintain its advantage over some conventional attack aircraft. However, the British government showed no further interest in advancing the design, and America's McDonnell Douglas acquired the production and development rights to the Harrier.

An improved Harrier II with a completely new composite wing and 21,500lb (9,750kg) thrust Rolls-Royce Pegasus vectored-thrust turbofan was already flying when Argentine forces invaded the Falklands. Ordered by the USMC, under the designation AV-8B, the Harrier II could carry twice the weapon load of the RAF's Harrier GR.1/3, had an advanced internal ECM system, and the Hughes Angle/Rate bombing system. The first of 336 AV-98Bs were delivered to USMC units in 1984 while the aircraft's second customer

was, ironically, the RAF which ordered 62 Harrier GR.5s in 1986. Over the past decade, USMC Harrier IIs have been upgraded to the AV-8B Plus specification with the fitting of the multi-mode Hughes APG-65 radar, giving AIM-120 AMRAAM, AIM-7 Sparrow, and AGM-84 Harpoon capability, while the RAF's GR.7 upgrade made it night attack-capable.

Royal Navy Sea Harriers have been fitted with a more capable Blue Vixen radar to ___ the type AMRAAM-capable, while AV-8B Harrier II Plus multi-role aircraft are operated from STOVL carriers by the navies of Italy and Spain. The Indian Navy also operates Sea Harriers.

However, it was during Operation *Desert Storm* in the Gulf in 1990/91 that the effectiveness of the STOVL Harriers was called into question. Some 35 USMC AV-8Bs operating from King Abdul Aziz air base in Saudi Arabia provided ground support for Coalition ground forces during the 100-hour land battle, attacking Iraqi armored vehicles and troop concentrations for the loss of only two aircraft, but RAF Harrier GR.5s were not considered combat ready, and the RN carriers and their Sea Harriers were held in reserve.

Since the Gulf War ended, USMC AV-8Bs have not taken part in any other li__ __eration ,although small numbers of RAF Harriers flying from large fixed air bases in Italy and Turkey ___ carrier-borne RN SHARs have been in subsequent actions over the former Yugoslavia. Some defense pl__rs h__e argued that the Harrier's original mission—that of close support from __akes __ forward operating bases (FOB) for ground forces as they made rapid advances on the setpiece battlefield —is now redundant in the present and projected limited war scenarios.

Nevertheless, more than 25 percent of the JSF program will be devoted to a STOVL version which will inevitably be a compromise between providing additional power for vertical lift and a reduced combat radius and weapon load. However, three teams—Boeing, Lockheed-Martin, and McDonnll Douglas with Northrop-Grumman and British Aerospace (BAe)— entered the JSF race in 1992, only two of which would be awarded contracts to build a CTOL and a STOVL prototype.

Boeing, which had not built a fighter aircraft since the XF8B-1—a prototype single-seat, shipboard, long-range, multi-role fighter that flew in 1944—was at first sight an unlikely JSF contender. Although it

___ the RAF's latest Harrier variant, the night-___ __.7 armed with 25mm Aden cannon pods, 6__ __t pods, and Sidewinder air-to-air missiles, took ___ __eration Allied Force *in Kosovo*.

had never produced a fast jet combat aircraft, the company had long experience of producing state-of-the-art long-range heavy bombers from the B-17 to the B-52, and military variants of its successful commercial airliners, such as the KC-135 and E-3 AWACS. As we have seen in Chapter Two, Boeing was also closely involved in the Advanced Tactical Fighter (ATF) program, having produced its own Dem/Val design before teaming with Lockheed-Martin to develop the F-22 Raptor.

Boeing's original JSF concept shared a number of design features with its ATF—a deep chin intake, shoulder-mounted wing, and twin canted "vee" tails. It differs by having a compact, thick, one-piece thermoplastic delta wing, a squat, blended wing/fuselage which contained the engine and weapons bays, and a deep forebody accommodating the pilot and small pointed nose with the electronics. It is the smallest, with a 36ft (11m) wingspan and length of 46ft (14m), and least complex of the JSF designs by virtue of the fact that the ASTOVL version is the only one of the three concepts powered by a single engine with no additional lift fan.

The system adopted for the Boeing ASTOVL is a three-segment powered lift arrangement with engine exhaust ducted forwards to two rotating direct lift nozzles via vortex flaps under the centerpoint of the fuselage. A front nozzle is fed by bleed air via a jet screen duct with an anti-recirculation shield which is extended aft of the nose wheel bay. Additional control in the vertical landing mode is provided by bleed air fed to wingtip roll-control nozzles via ducting along the wing trailing edges, and yaw nozzles located each side of the two-dimentional, pitch-vectoring propulsion nozzle.

To improve air flow to the engine at low speed to zero, a translating chin inlet cowl moves forward when the aircraft transitions from forward flight to the hover. Although it will not have to power a separate direct lift fan, the engine used by Boeing's ASTOVL JSF will have to be at a higher power rating than that of its competitors due to it providing all the lift through the three nozzles, and it will therefore use more fuel in the hover. However, in convential flight mode it will never have to use full power, thus saving engine life and improving fuel consumption.

Stealth features and advanced technology construction techniques learned from the F-22 program have been integrated into Boeing's JSF concept which, due to its lift system, could be considered as a third-generation Harrier.

Lockheed-Martin's original design concept for the USAF conventional take-off and landing (CTOL) version of the Joint Strike Fighter.

The carrier version (CV) of Lockheed-Martin's CTOL JSF for the US Navy, which features extended folding wings, beefed-up rear fuselage and landing gear, and tail hook.

The tailless JSF design submitted by McDonnell Douglas, teamed with Northrop-Grumman and British Aerospace, was eliminated from the multi-billion dollar contest in 1996.

Whereas Boeing had no experience of the designing and production of jet fighters, it must be remembered that the last fighter that Lockheed mass-produced was the F-104 in the 1960s, although 60 F-117A Night Hawks were virtually hand-built at its "Skunk Works" in the 1980s. In 1993, Lockheed-Martin purchased its erstwhile ATF partner, General Dynamics, and acquired its fighter division at Fort Worth, Texas, which had produced one of the world's most important and versatile warplanes, the F-16 Fighting Falcon, which was one of the aircraft that JSF was designed to replace.

Lockheed-Martin's JSF concept resembled a scaled down F-22 airframe featuring a trapezoidal wing, two horizontal and two canted vertical tailfins—the angles of both the wing and tail leading and trailing edges being identical—cheek-mounted inlets, and the F119 engine. It will even use a lightweight development of the F-22's APG-77 phased array radar. The three Lockheed Martin JSF versions will share wing sweep, tail designs, cockpit canopy, ejection systems, sub-systems, and most avionics. The USAF and USN versions will have a low observable asymmetrical nozzle (LOAN) and fixed-geometry main inlets with no boundary layer diverter channel—the space between the duct and the fuselage—to reflect radar energy.

The Navy version has larger wing and tail control surfaces for additional control authority during approach to a carrier landing, a strengthened internal structure and landing gear, and tailhook and refueling probe. These features will also be common on the USMC/RN ASTOVL version, which again is the most radical of the three versions and differs significantly from the Boeing proposal in its direct lift system.

Developed in the "Skunk Works," the Allison-built direct-lift fan, located behind the cockpit, is powered by a shaft drive from the main F119 afterburning turbofan derivative. Additional lift is provided by a stealthy, three-piece, rotating, asymmetric exhaust duct segment designed by Rolls-Royce and inspired by the innovative Russian Yak-141 "Freestyle."

The Soviet Union was the only other country to produce a successful STOVL attack aircraft to rival the

The advanced short take-off and vertical landing (ASTOVL) version of Lockheed-Martin's JSF, designed to replace the US Marine Corps AV-8B.

Similar to the USMC ASTOVL design, JSF is also aimed at the Royal Navy as a strike replacement for its fleet of Sea Harrier F/A.2 VSTOL aircraft currently operated on Invincible-class carriers.

Seen in the hover with its rotating afterburner nozzle at 95 degrees, exhaust deflector doors and lift engines inlet door extended, the Yak-141 inspired the ASTOLV version of JSF.

British Harrier. Designed by the Yakovlev Design Bureau, which had already built a series of STOVL prototypes in the 1960s, the multi-role Yak-38 made its operational debut with the Soviet Naval Aviation in the mid 1970s. Although similar in size to the Sea Harrier, it had a completely different direct lift system comprising two 7,200lb (3,265kg) thrust vertical-lift RD-38 turbojets mounted in tandem behind the cockpit, and a 15,300lb (6,940k) thrust main engine with thrust-vectoring nozzles. Due to the extremely high fuel consumption during STOVL operations, this arrangment severely limited its range and stores payload. The subsonic Yak-38's combat radius was less than 250 miles (400km) and, although this could be increased by carrying 158-gallon (600-liter) external fuel tanks on two of its four underwing hardpoints, its armament was restricted to only two AA-2 "Atoll" IR AAMs

Despite its shortcomings, the Yak-38 "Forger" gave the Soviet Navy valuable experience of operating a jet STOVL type. Some 200 were built and operated for over a decade in air groups aboard four Kiev-class cruiser carriers with the Northern and Pacific Fleets. It carried a number of advanced on-board systems such as full weapons system and a take-off control system which during a short roll automatically transitioned the aircraft into vertical take-off. Approach and vertical landing on a flight deck was automatitically guided by laser as soon as the "Forger" captured the carrier's ILS.

All Yak-38s were fitted with the extremely efficient K-36LV seat which automatically triggered the ejection sequence once the combination of vertical speed, height, and speed became out of limits. Of more than 30 pilots that ejected using this system, only one suffered fatal injuries.

Valuable lessons learned from the Yak-38 program were fed into its successor, the Yak-141 "Freestyle"—the world's first supersonic STOVL fighter which was optimized for the air defense role with a secondary attack capability. Adopting a similar layout to its predecessor of twin lift engines plus a main engine, the Yak-141 differed by having a single, rotating, afterburning nozzle slightly behind its center of gravity. A slab tailplane and twin canted fins were therefore mounted on deep booms, the inner walls of which were made of titanium while the airframe was constructed mainly of aluminum-lithium alloy although 26 percent was of composite materials. The underside of the fuselage, which had to withstand tremendous heat from the exhaust gases of the 34,000lb (15,422kg) thrust R-79 turbofan and twin 9,400lb (4,264kg) thrust RD-41 lift engines during vertical take-off and landing, was coated with heat-resistant resin putty.

Two protoype "Freestyles" were constructed in the late 1980s. They were fitted with Yak-38M Phase II avionics and digital fly-by-wire (FBW) flight/engine controls linked to its flight control computer to give all-weather manual or automatic take-offs and landings. The projected Yak-141M was designed to carry a 9,000lb (4,000kg) weapon load and operate on a combat radius of 550 miles (900km).

After more than 150 hours of successful flight trials, the program was terminated by two unrelated events. Firstly, following the disintegration of the Soviet Union, the new Russian Navy terminated further funding in September 1991, and a month later one of the prototypes was badly damaged during carrier landing trials when it caught fire following a heavy landing caused by partial engine failure.

For another year the Yakolev Bureau managed to continue flight testing the Yak-141, which was only a technology step toward the more advanced Yak-209, but the development program was cancelled at the end of 1992. However, the following year, Lockheed-Martin awarded the Yakovlev Design Bureau a $500,000 contract for assisting with the design of the rotating main jet nozzle for its ASTOVL JSF version, and Pratt & Whitney had a similar agreement with the Russian Soyuz Aero-Engine company.

Third JSF contender was McDonnell Douglas, the United States' most experienced jet fighter manufacturer with a 50-year history of successful designs for both the USAF and USN, including the F-4 Phantom, F-15 Eagle, and F/A-18 Hornet. Added to this, for the JSF it had teamed with Northrop-Grumman and British Aerospace (with which it had developed the Harrier II). It seemed to be a winning formula.

McDonnell Douglas's JSF design was the most unconventional of the three. It featured a low observable, low-drag, F-22-like fuselage with a shallow canted "vee" tail with split ailerons that acted as both rudders and airbrakes, and no vertical fin. The shoulder-mounted, blended wing planform closely

The mock-up of Lockheed-Martin's USAF version of JSF, the X-35A Concept Demonstrator Aircraft (CDA) which is scheduled to fly in the first half of 2000.

▲

Front view of the Lockheed-Martin X-35A which is being built at the "Skunk Works," showing the low observable (LO) inlets and canted tail fins.

▼

Lockheed-Martin's latest concept of the USAF CTOL X-35A version of JSF, seen dropping a "smart" stand-off weapon, shows a revised cockpit canopy and its air refueling receptacle.

resembled that of the B-2 stealth bomber built by team-partner Northrop. The CTOL version was powered by a standard 35,000lb (15,875kg) thrust F119, and had a thrust-vectoring nozzle for improved maneuverability.

For its ASTOVL concept, McDonnell Douglas followed the Yak-141 route by having an entirely separate and additional lift engine, a 16,000lb (7,255kg) thrust GE-Allison/Rolls-Royce GEA-FXL turbo fan. The ASTOVL's main engine was moved forward some 6ft (2m) and a diverter valve inserted between the F119 and its afterburner that was capable of diverting power to two Pegasus-style nozzles located one on each side of the rear fuselage. To avoid hot air ingestion and ground erosion during vertical take-off/landing, which had been experienced by the Yak-38/-141, an additional dorsal inlet was fitted to provide a screen of relatively cool air beneath the aircraft.

Although this arrangement meant that the ASTOVL version's main engine would have all its power available for transition acceleration and during cruise, it had to carry the extra dead weight of the lift engine, although McDonnell Douglas claimed it was capable of enabling the JSF to make a conventional landing if the main engine failed. The development of an additional lift engine, which had to be shut down after take-off and instantly spooled up on approach, increased costs, while the service's maintenance time and spares inventory would also be more than those required for the Boeing and Lockheed-Martin designs.

Despite these misgivings it was nevertheless a bolt from the blue when it was announced in December

▶

British Aerospace has now joined Lockheed-Martin in the development of the ASTOVL version of JSF proposed for the Royal Navy. The design differs from the USMC version by having folding wings.

▲

The US Navy's CV version of Lockheed-Martin's JSF, designed to replace F/A-18 Hornets and F-14A Tomcats, will operate from Nimitz-class carriers and the proposed CV(X).

▶

Boeing's CDA X-32A will retain the original delta-wing/two-tail layout with forward-raked, chin-mounted inlet, although its Preferred Weapon System Concept (PWSC) will differ considerably.

1996 that the McDonnell Douglas team had failed to make the pre-selection cut to produce the Joint Strike Fighter. The decision was a devastating blow to the company headquartered at St Louis, Missouri, known as "Fighter City." It had now lost out on a succession of major fighter programs, including USAF's ATF and the Navy's A-12 Avenger II Advanced Tactical Aircraft (ATA) which was cancelled before it flew in 1991. Its former JSF partners, Northrop-Grumman and BAe, both decided to join Lockheed-Martin and within a year of its elimination from the JSF competition McDonnell Douglas joined its other rival, Boeing, which bought the company in August 1997. Then there were two.

Both the two remaining companies now each received a $1.2 billion contract to build two JSF Concept Demonstrator Aircraft (CDA) by the end of 2000. The first CDAs—the CTOL version of JSF—Boeing's X-32A and Lockheed Martin's X-35A, are scheduled to fly in the first half of the year, and the ASTOVL X-32B and X-35B a few months later. The "A" versions will then be "re-manufactured" by the end of 2000 as the US Navy carrier version (CV) with wing extension/folding, strengthened rear fuselage with arrester hook, and beefed-up nosewheel gear. The program includes not only the manufacture and flight test of the CDAs but also the design trade studies for the Preferred Weapons System Concept (PWSC). Down-select is scheduled for mid-2001 and the winner will proceed to the Engineering and Manufacturing Development (EMD) phase, followed by production.

By early 1999, Lockheed-Martin was confident that it had refined the detailed configuration of its planned PWSC, which fundamentally differed little from its original concepts submitted in 1996. All three versions share a 51ft (15.5m) long fuselage while the USAF, USMC, and Royal Navy JSF will have a

▼

The CV version of the Boeing JSF proposed for the US Navy differs from Lockheed-Martin's by not having a folding wing system although the wing span will be more than the USAF CTOL version.

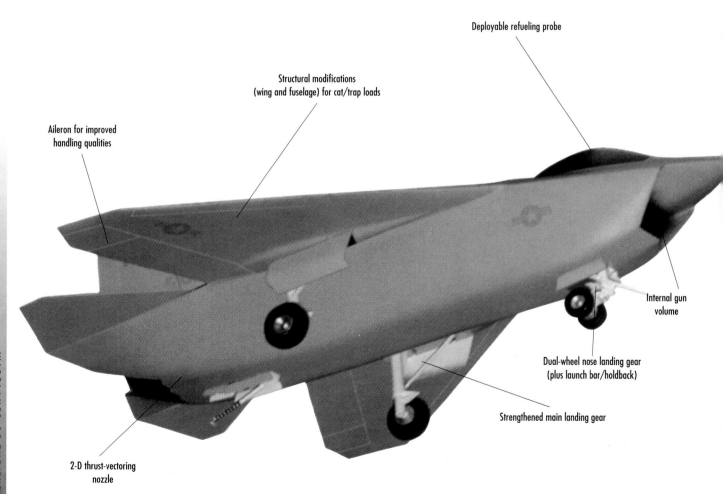

Deployable refueling probe

Structural modifications
(wing and fuselage) for cat/trap loads

Aileron for improved
handling qualities

Internal gun
volume

Dual-wheel nose landing gear
(plus launch bar/holdback)

Strengthened main landing gear

2-D thrust-vectoring
nozzle

common 33ft (10m) span wing. The US Navy JSF's larger folding wings will have ailerons in addition to the flaperons and enlarged vertical and horizontal tail surfaces for additional low approach speed control authority. The USAF version will have a refueling receptacle, while the Navy/Marine JSF will incorporate a retractable air refueling probe. Their stealthy, twin curved inlets were tested on an F-16 in a "black" program some years ago.

Boeing, however, announced at the same time that it had decided to substantially revise its PWSC design although it was too late change its CDA's configuration. Reasons given for the changes were to save weight, decrease low observability, and increase low-speed control authority of the CV version. This was achieved by replacing the original delta wing—which due the the fact that most of its area was behind the center of gravity made carriage of external stores difficult—with a smaller swept wing, as well as adding a separate horizontal tail. A smaller, raked, chin-mounted inlet replaced the former translating cowl and the cockpit canopy was reduced in size to save weight. The propulsion systems, including the powered lift fan of the ASTOVL version, remained unchanged.

However, by this time it was obvious that the JSF program was running into a funding crisis. The original $1.2 billion contract awarded to both Boeing and Lockheed-Martin was divided two thirds for the CDA and one third for the development of the PWSC, but by early 1999 both the rival contenders had overspent on the CDA phase. It must be remembered that JSF is not only a common airframe for three different US and the Royal Navy services, but it will utilize a new generation of avionics which will have to be smaller, weigh and cost less, as well as be more capable than current on-board systems.

▼
Boeing's revised JSF PWSC includes swept wings replacing the delta, four tails instead of two, a raked-back low observable inlet, and revised cockpit canopy.

All-aspect radar warning receivers (RWR) and electronic countermeasures (ECM) are being developed along with new compact munitions and a re-programmable cockpit, which will have flexible displays including color helmet-mounted displays (HMD) with an integrated "virtual" head-up display (HUD). The lightweight, active-array radar will have advanced air-to-ground modes featuring high-resolution spot and variable swath synthetic aperture radar (SAR) with moving target indicator (MTI), as used by USAF's J-STARS. An electro-optical (EO) system known as the shared aperture sensor system (SASSY) will provide passive detection of airborne targets, night navigation and ground target acquisition imagery, and missile launch. Virtually every system on the JSF will be new and untried.

While the original aim of the program made a lot of sense in the "new world order" of the post-Cold War era, there remain serious doubts in many quarters about the one-aircraft design formula. It is a fact that in the past several combat aircraft have been operated by more than one US service. The F-4 Phantom II and A-7 Corsair II were both designed for the US Navy but later adopted by USAF. The F-111 was designed for the Tactical Fighter Experimental (TFX) program, a combined Air Force and Navy requirement for an advanced strike aircraft, but in the event was not adopted by the US Navy. Of the two leading competitors for a new Lightweight Fighter (LWF), the General Dynamics winning F-16 Fighting Falcon became USAF's

single-seat tactical fighter, while the losing Northrop YF-17 was developed into the F/A-18 Hornet, the US Navy/Marine combat strike successor to the ubiquitous F-4. In the UK, the RAF Harrier and Royal Navy Sea Harrier are related but are very different aircraft with differing roles.

Designing a common combat aircraft for two services is indeed problematical. Producing one for three services in the US and one in the UK will be a serious challenge, and not only to keep it within budget. Recent operations, such as *Desert Fox* over Iraq and *Allied Force* over the Balkans have highlighted the fact that there may be only a limited requirement for VSTOL Harrier-type aircraft in the future. With the benefit of air refueling, and air superiority having been acheived early in the operations, CTOL and CV attack aircraft have shown they can reach their targets carrying a heavier weapon payload than current VSTOL aircraft, whose main role of providing close air support (CAS) for ground forces from forward operating bases (FOB) over a rapidly moving battlefield is seen as less and less relevant to future limited war and peacekeeping scenarios.

This begs the question, is an ASTOVL version of JSF, the most complex and expensive of the three types, still a reality or could its role be taken over by one of the advanced stealthy attack helicopters currently under development? Pointers to the answer may be found in the following chapter.

▼

Artist's impression of the CV version of Boeing's JSF moving into position on a US Navy Nimitz-class carrier's catapult. It will have a strengthened rear fuselage with arrester hook and landing gear.

CHOPPER WARS

Although the helicopter made its first hesitant appearances over the battlefields of World War II, the technology was in its infancy and its roles were restricted to observation and search and rescue. During the Korean War, the helicopter's true potential first became apparent with the deployment of military versions of the piston-engined Bell 47 and Sikorsky S-55 which were widely used throughout the conflict. US Marine Corps and Air Force Sikorsky helicopters transported troops to the front line and recued downed airmen from behind enemy lines. US Army Bell H-13s flew thousands of wounded soldiers to Mobile Army Surgical Hospitals, the famed MASH units. However, it was a decade later in Southeast Asia that three of the most important types of military helicopter entered service.

The jet-powered Bell Huey, Sikorsky's S-61, and the Boeing Chinook were all deployed to Vietnam by the early-1960s and were remain in service for the next three decades. The development of jet turboshaft plants increased the helicopter's power to weight ratio, reduced fatigue-inducing simplified maintenance. These attributes enabled the Bell UH-1, a 15-seat copter, to become one of the most successful aircraft, with more than 7,000 single and twin-engined variants being delivered between 1960 and 1999.

The Sikorsky S.61, originally designed as an anti-submarine warfare (ASW) helicopter, was deveolped into a very successful combat search and rescue aircraft for service in Southeast Asia where it was known as the "Jolly Green Giant" which will be described in detail in Chapter Ten.

Developed as the world's first all-weather heavy-lifting helicopter for service with the US Army in Vietnam, the twin-rotor Chinook, capable of airlifting

▶

"Apocalypse Now" re-enacted by Canadian Forces Twin Pac Huey utility transport helicopters in pine forests of Quebec Province in the late 1980s.

▼

Vietnam "vets," US Army "Big Windy" Chinooks, parked in a field close to the East German border at the height of the Cold War, waiting for the start of a NATO exercise.

equipped troops at speeds of up to 190mph (305kmh) over 125 miles (200km), remains in production at the beginning of the 21st Century.

However, it was in response to the US Army's Advanced Aerial Fire Supression System (AAFSS) requirement to develop a dedicated armed helicopter for service in Vietnam that led to the Cobra. Using the engine, gearbox, and rotors of the ubiquitous Huey, the Bell AH-1 featured a slim profile fuselage seating a pilot and gunner in tandem. The AH-1G's primary armament was two M134 7.62mm Miniguns fitted in an M28 chin turret, although 2.75in M20 rocket launchers and 40mm M129 grenade launchers could also be carried under the HueyCobra's stub wings.

Some 2,000 Cobras have been produced since 1965, including the navalized SuperCobra for the Marine Corps, and the type set the benchmark for all future battlefield helicopter designs other than those developed in the former Soviet Union. In June 1960, the classic Mil Mi-8 "Hip" multi-role transport helicopter made its first flight and compared well with its Western counterparts. Designed to carry up to 28 fully equipped troops, the Mi-8 featured pressed spar rotor blades with an electrothermal de-icing system for all-weather operations, main rotor hydraulic dampers, four-channel autopilot, and twin-engine safety.

It soon became the Soviet workhorse from which was developed the Soviet Navy's amphibious ASW Mi-14 "Haze," the uprated Mi-17, and the formidable "Hind" multi-role combat helicopter. Along with the MiG-21 fighter, the ferocious-looking Mi-24 "Hind" came to represent the "Red Menace" to many in the West and, like the US Army's Huey in an earlier conflict, became a symbol of the Soviet Union's involvement in the Afghanistan war. With a crew of three and a cabin for eight troops, the "Hind" was designed as an armed assault helicopter with a secondary anti-tank and close air support (CAS) capability.

◄

Developed from the Huey, the AH-1 Cobra was the world's first dedicated attack helicopter, armed with anti-tank missiles, unguided rockets, and an M197 three-barrel 20mm cannon.

CHOPPER WARS

The United States concentrated on the development of an advanced anti-armor attack helicopter. Designed in the early 1970s for the US Army's Advanced Attack Helicopter (AAH) requirement, the Hughes (later McDonnell Douglas) AH-64A Apache was selected to replace the Cobra. Following a protracted eight-year development, the Apache finally entered service in 1983. The rugged AH-64 was built to survive the harsh conditions of the Cold War battlefields in northern Europe. It had IR-suppressed twin turboshaft engines, comprehensive electronic warfare (EW) systems, armor-plated fuselage, and flat plate canopy for protection against 12.7mm rounds with crew seats and systems designed to survive 23mm caliber shells. The multi-layer stainless steel/glassfiber rotor blades will take hits from ground fire, and the long-stroke non-retracting tailwheel landing gear was designed to cushion crash landings.

The Apache is armed with a chin-mounted, 1,200-round M230A1 30mm chain gun, 16 Hellfire anti-tank missiles, or 76 2.75in (70mm) rockets. Its $1 million "eyes" comprise the target aquisition designation sight with the pilot night vision sensor (TADS/PNVS) with forward looking infra-red (FLIR) night sensor, and a TV/optical daylight system which feeds information to the cockpit displays and to the crew's integrated helmet and display sight system (IHADSS). More than 1,000 of these formidable, all-weather, day/night attack helicopters have been produced to date and, despite its high price tag, it remains at the head of the pack.

▼

Developed from the "Hip," the heavily armed and armored Mi-24 "Hind" multi-role combat helicopter carries a crew of three plus up to eight fully equipped troops in the main cabin.

▶

One of the world's most prolific multi-role helicopters was the Russian Mil Mi-8. Seen here is the latest attack/minelaying version of the "Hip," the Mi-17TB.

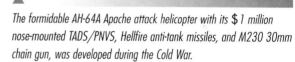

An AH-64 Apache in the air-to-air mode firing Sidewinder missiles. More than 1,000 Apaches are operated by nine countries.

The formidable AH-64A Apache attack helicopter with its $1 million nose-mounted TADS/PNVS, Hellfire anti-tank missiles, and M230 30mm chain gun, was developed during the Cold War.

Its main competitors in the attack helicopter market are the Franco-German Eurocopter Tiger, Italy's Agusta A129 Mangusta, and South Africa's heavyweight Denel Rooivalk. Russian contenders include the successor to the "Hind," the Mi-28 "Havoc," which represents the zenith of Soviet helicopter technology. It first flew in 1982 and was followed closely by the heavily armored, co-axial, single-seat Kamov Ka-50 "Hokum."

Both these Russian helicopters are powered by two 2,200 shp Klimov turboshafts, have a maximum speed of almost 200mph (322kmh), and are armed with 30mm cannon, a full range of anti-tank and air-to-air missiles, and unguided rockets. Despite their advanced designs, neither entered service with the Russian forces and the small batch prototypes have been used to test uprated engines and new night/all-weather systems and nav/attack avionics. A two-seat version of the "Hokum," the Ka-52 "Alligator," flew for the first time in 1997 and is being offered to export customers along with the single-seat "Werewolf."

By the very nature of the machine, the helicopter is easier to hear, see, and electronically detect than

▼

An AH-64D Longbow Apache with mast-mounted millimeter wave fire control radar carries out a "pop-up"' maneuver to acquire a target from behind a treeline mask.

The Franco-German Tiger attack helicopter is produced in two versions, the French anti-tank variant with mast-mounted sight (MMS), and the German close support variant with nose sight.

Bearing a superficial resemblance to the Apache, the advanced Mi-28 "Havoc" all-weather attack helicopter has failed to attract production orders from the cash-strapped Russian forces.

other faster, higher-flying aircraft. The large-span main rotor is noisy and creates distinctive Doppler radar returns, while engine exhausts and large canopies reflecting sunlight attract infra-red homing missiles. A helicopter in the hover is literally a sitting target for ground fire of any type.

To improve survivability, several simple measures were adopted by manufacturers and operators in the 1980s. Redesigned rotor blades using composite materials, and the repositioning of tail rotors, reduced rotor "slap," while flat plane canopies and baffled exhaust suppressors break up the helicopter's IR signature. Mast-mounted sights (MMS) enable attack helicopters to use treelines and other natural features for masking when assuming the classic ambush position. More basic precautions, such as application of dull, flat camouflage schemes and low-viz markings for both visual and IR protection, armored crashworthy crew seats, and nap of the earth (NOE) flying techniques have all improved battlefield survivability. Electronic protection systems such as radar warning receivers (RWR), electronic surveillance measures (ESM), infra-red countermeasures (IRCM) pulsed active jammers combined with chaff/flare dispensers have further enhanced the helicopter's capabilities.

However, the real impetus for stealthy attack helicopter operations came with the development of night vision goggles (NVG). These are image intensifiers that operate at short wavelengths of optics using available light. In order to be able to read the flight instruments, the cockpit has to be NVG-compatible, emitting only enough illumination to be clearly seen by the crew wearing NVGs, and without any highlights which would flare their vision.

A successful night operation against Iraqi radar posts by Apache attack helicopters was the first action of the Gulf War and was followed by a series of devastating night raids against Iraqi armor during the short ground war phase. The Apaches' crews used its unique IHADSS to prosecute the night attacks and the system is being refined for the future generation of battlefield helicopters.

The first of this new generation is the Boeing Sikorsky RAH-66 Comanche, winner of the US Army's Light Helicopter Experimental/Scout Attack (LHX/SCAT) competition. Several "black" programs were involved in developing advanced technology for LHX, including the Sikorsky "X-wing" Rotor Systems Research Aircraft (RSRA), as well as overt projects such as the Bell's Advanced Rotorcraft Technology Integration (ARTI) — a modified Cobra with fly-by-wire (FBW) flight controls — and the Sikorsky S-75 and Bell D292 Advanced Composite Airframe Programs (ACAP).

The Comanche low observable (LO), armed reconnaissance helicopter, which first flew in January 1996, was designed to replace the US Army's AH-1 Cobra, OH-6, and OH-58. It is a tandem two-seat, all-composite construction helicopter powered by two 1,334 shp T800 turboshafts. Its LO characteristics are enhanced by a composite five-shrouded blade, bearingless main rotor, canted fantail or fenestron enclosed anti-torque system, multi-faceted fuselage, and internal weapons bay. The Comanche has a built-in IR suppression system that ducts exhaust through long, thin slots and mixes it with cool ambient air from inlets in the helicopter's spine.

The two crew sit in identical "glass cockpits" each equipped with six 8in (200mm) multifunctional displays and a wide-angle helmet-mounted display. The Comanche's Aided Target Detection/Classification (ATD/C) system enables the helicopter to pop-up from a terrain mask and "grab" images from which the crew can detect and annotate targets as the helicopter returns to cover. It utilizes the AH-64D Apache's millimeter wave low probability of interception (LPI) fire-control radar (FCR), fitted in a nose-mounted LO radome, and this affords the crew greater stand-off ranges and adverse weather capability.

Four active radar AGM-114L Hellfire fire-and-forget anti-tank missiles and two AIM-92 Stinger air-to-air missiles can be carried in the internal weapons bay, while more can be carried externally on the stub-wing pylons. A stowable, chin-mounted, lightweight Lockheed Martin M-197 three-barrel 20mm Gatling gun was designed specifically for the Comanche and has a rate of fire of up to 1,500 rounds per minute.

The Comanche is designed to be a major element of the US Army's "digital battlefield" plans and to that end is fitted with digital radios with automatic link establishment software, and advanced data modems. Target information and sensor images acquired by the Comanche's integrated target acquisition system (TAS) and global positioning system (GPS) navigator can be transmitted to stand-off "shooters" in brief digital databursts from the safety of a terrain mask, bouncing the non-line of sight (NLS) communications off the ionosphere.

VARIETY OF TODAY'S BATTLEFIELD HELICOPTERS

1   Another innovative Russian attack helicopter, the heavily armed, single-seat Kamov Ka-50 "Werewolf," features a coaxial rotor and pilot ejection seat.

2   The heavily armored Apache, its steel/glassfiber rotor blades designed to withstand 23mm hits, shows its baffled "Black Hole" infra-red-suppressed engine exhausts.

3   Russia's five-bladed Mi-28 "Havoc" carrying anti-tank missiles and rockets under its stub wings and also armed with a chin-mounted 30mm cannon, shows its distinctive curved-down IR exhaust suppressors.

4   More than 1,000 Mi-24 multi-role "Hinds" remain in service with the Russian forces. Some are being upgraded with new rotors and avionics developed for the Mi-28 "Havoc."

5   The OH-58D Kiowa Warrior scout helicopter with its all-weather, day/night, electro-optical mast-mounted sight (MMS) with visible and infa-red capability.

6   AN/ALQ-157 infra-red countermeasures (IRCM) pulsed jammers fitted to US Army combat helicopters. This emits a modulated intense heat source designed to cause heat-seaking missiles to break lock.

7   The Eurocopter company pioneered the use of the fantail anti-torque system, or fenestron tail rotor, with its Gazelle light anti-tank helicopter and, here, the stealthy, composite Panther scout/utility helicopter.

8   The world's first truly low observable (LO) combat scout, the Boeing Sikorsky RAH-66 Comanche was the winner of the US Army LHX competition to replace the Cobra and OH-58D.

9   The futuristic, composite-constructed LO Comanche features internal weapons bays, integrated IR suppression, and a unique canted fantail anti-torque system and "T" tail.

10 A worthy successor to the ubiquitous Huey, more than 2,000 air assault/utility, medevac, search and rescue, and electronic warfare (EW) Black Hawks have been built since 1978.

Although the RAH-66 Comanche will be the world's most advanced military helicopter when it enters US Army service in 2005, Japan has flown a smaller and slightly less sophisticated aircraft to fulfill the same role. The twin-engine Kawasaki XOH-1 armed scout is an LO helicopter of composite construction with a four-blade, bearingless main rotor, a fantail anti-torque rotor, and roof-mounted sight. The XOH-1 is being developed to replace Japan's Ground Self Defense Force (JGSDF) OH-6 light scout/attack helicopters in 2005.

While the Sikorsky S-61 family has largely been replaced by its stablemate, the Black Hawk/Seahawk in the US services, the veteran CH-47 Chinook soldiers on into the new millennium. The US Army's heavy-lifter is being upgraded yet again to Improved Cargo Helicopter (ICH) specification with improved engines to reduce airframe vibration, and the fitting of "glass cockpits" with basic digitization capabilities.

The only production transport helicopter that outperforms the Chinook is Russia's Mi-26 "Halo." The world's largest operational helicopter, the "Halo" has a crew of five and can accommodate up to 85 fully equipped troops or carry a 44,000lb (20,000kg) payload. Mi-26s wearing UN markings became a familiar sight during the 1990s in the former Yugoslavia, where they were deployed to support peacekeeping operations in the region.

Other advanced battlefield utility helicopters have been developed in Europe, including the three-engined Anglo-Italian EH101 Merlin and the twin-engined multi-national NH-90. The stealthy NH-90 features a faceted composite fuselage, sheriflex composite four-blade rotor, "glass cockpit," FBW controls, and FLIR. Meanwhile, the United States forces have a Joint Transport Requirement (JTR) to replace US Army Chinooks, Navy CH-53 Super Stallions, and USAF HH-60H Hawks in 2020, a contender for which may be the projected Titan.

Titan

The Titan has been designed to be capable of meeting the US requirement for a new heavy-lift VTOL vehicle. As such, the design proposed has a maximum payload of 60 tons+ and can accommodate two AFV25 vehicles in its payload bay. It could also carry a very significant defensive/offensive armament, comprising forward and rearward cannon turrets and air-to-air missiles (AIM-9L and AIM-120).

To improve the combat effectiveness of the vehicle its operational range can be extended by air refueling (AR) while the aircraft is operating in conventional mode with the X-wing stationary. The main role envisioned for Titan is that of a heavy-lift transport capable of using VTOL at both ends of the route. Its cruise speed should be as high as possible and should definitely exceed that of existing heavy-lift helicopters such as the Chinook and Super Stallion. This benefits the field commander by not only providing quicker placement of troops and equipment, but also allowing a greater number of sorties to be performed in a given time frame.

The prinicipal features of the design are a relatively conventional fuselage to house the payload, crew, systems, and some of the fuel. Its fuselage is more streamlined than that of existing heavy-lift helicopters, since the vehicle is designed to be capable of a cruise speed in excess of 300mph (483kmh) in airplane mode.

An innovative gas-driven X-wing rotor would provide VTOL lift in the same way as a conventional helicopter rotor, but would be driven by high-pressure air bled from the twin turbofan engines. The air would exit the blades through nozzles located at the blade tips, causing them to rotate. The rotor could be brought to rest to allow the vehicle to fly like a conventional aircraft, with the stationary rotor blades performing the same function as the wing on a fixed-wing aircraft. With the blades stationary, no bleed air would be taken from the engines, hence all the air entering the engine would be used to provide forward thrust for flight.

In order to provide large payload capability (especially when operating in VTOL mode) and high speed cruise it is essential to keep the helicopter's empty weight to a minimum. For this reason, advanced composite materials, mainly carbon/epoxy, would be used for Titan's primary structure wherever possible. Production and maintenance procedures for composites have matured rapidly and their use as the primary structural material for a new aircraft does not represent a significant technological risk. Conversely, their advantages over metals, such as low weight, high strength,

▲

The latest version of the Black Hawk battlefield support helicopter, the UH-60L carries Hellfire anti-tank and air-to-air Stinger missiles under its stub wings.

▼

The world's largest operational transport helicopter, the Russian Mi-26 "Halo" can carry a similar size and weight payload to that of a C-130 Hercules.

improved fatigue resistance, damage tolerance, and negligible corrosion, make them ideally suited to the proposed vehicle and its likely operating environment.

X-Wing

The X-wing is comprised of four rotor blades at 90 degrees to each other with a length times chord of 62ft x 6ft (19m x 1.9m). These blades have a bi-convex section to allow them to produce equal lift with either the leading edge or trailing edge facing the oncoming flow. In VTOL mode, the X-wing operates like a conventional helicopter, with the blades rotating to provide a relative airflow and hence lift.

In forward flight (conventional aircraft mode), the blades are brought to rest at 45 degrees to the longitudinal axis of the craft. In this mode they essentially form a tandem wing arrangement, with the forward pair of wings swept forward and the rear set of wings swept aft. This configuration combines some of the best features of rotary and fixed wing aircraft. The rotor disc has a large lifting capacity, thereby catering for VTOL flight with maximum payload. In addition, with the rotors stopped, the high aspect ratio blades form effective lifting surfaces, which are augmented by the fixed wings at the nose and tail of the fuselage.

The X-wing has a number of advantages over direct drive using turboshaft engines. These are:

1. The gas drive system does not result in a torque reaction against the rotor which causes the fuselage to rotate in an opposite direction to the rotor; therefore an anti-torque system is not required. Any small amount of drag in the air bearing would easily be overcome by the reaction control system used for maneuvering at low speed. This system would use the same principle as that of the BAe Harrier, where high pressure jets at the extremities of the vehicle produce the required moments about the center of gravity, thus eliminating the anti-torque system and reducing the weight, complexity, and life cycle cost of the vehicle.

2. The rotor blades are of large chord and a relatively high thickness to chord ratio. This results in a large internal duct, hence pumping losses for the gas drive are reduced and consequently the propulsive efficiency of the system is increased. In addition to this, the rotation of the blades produces a centrifugal pumping effect which tends to offset the losses due to the boundary layer on the walls of the duct.

3. The rotor diameter is large—125ft (38m). Therefore in VTOL mode the lift is generated by imparting a relatively small change in velocity to a large mass of air, which results in improved propulsive efficiency, thereby the X-wing would consume less fuel in VTOL mode than a craft with smaller diameter rotors. This leads to improved range and endurance.

4. The gas passing through the blades is bled from the engine compressors and is therefore hotter than the ambient air. This provides a built-in de-icing system that eliminates the need to design and install a purpose-built system. By reducing the number of systems in the vehicle, this again reduces weight, complexity, and life cycle cost.

5. Gas passing through the blades would also be used for boundary layer control, thereby allowing attached flow to be maintained to much higher cyclic limits. This allows the VTOL payload requirement to be met without resorting to an excessively large main rotor X-wing.

▲
The Anglo-Italian EH101 Merlin is being produced in three variants—an ASW version for the Italian and Royal Navies, a search and rescue version for Canada, and a medium-lift version for Britain's RAF.

▼
Using technologies developed in "black" rotary wing programs, the X-wing Titan would be a contender for the US Joint Transport Rotorcraft (JTR) which is wanted by 2025.

Twin turbofan engines

The X-wing is powered by two high by-pass ratio turbofans. As described earlier, the X-wing/rotor is driven using air bled from the engines' compressors. This results in a reduced forward thrust from the engines, which is desirable since it makes VTOL flight easier. In VTOL flight, any residual thrust is eliminated by deflecting the exhaust eflux downward and to the sides of the vehicle using cascades, which double as IR suppressers (to reduce the threat from IR homing missiles).

Turbofans are used rather than turboshafts since the absence of the free power turbine means that a large thrust is produced when the gas drive to the rotors is inactive. This produces the thrust required for forward flight. High-bypass turbofans provide the best combination of characteristics for this type of vehicle and propulsion system. These are a source of high pressure air to drive the X-wing in VTOL mode and a compact powerplant capable of generating the thrust required to propel a vehicle of this size and weight. The turbofan/gas-drive system does not require special components or systems in the event of an engine failure (unlike the tilt-rotor nacelle concepts, which have a large and heavy prop-shaft running between the engines).

Air bearing

Bleed air used to drive the X-wing in VTOL mode also feeds an air bearing at the rotor hub. This performs the function of a bearing by injecting high-pressure air between the mating surfaces, thus keeping them apart. The air bearing eliminates the need for a rotor hub lubrication system and hence reduces weight, complexity, and life cycle cost. It also suppresses the transmission of vibration from the rotor to the vehicle, and thereby reduces fatigue and improves the life of the vehicle.

Fuselage

The fuselage primary structure is made of composite material wherever possible, in order to keep the empty weight fraction low and maximize the payload. The payload bay is of rectangular cross-section in order to give the best possible packing efficiency; the fuselage is sized to give a payload bay capable of taking two AFV25s and their associated equipment. Loading/unloading is by a rearward opening ramp/door.

Fuel tanks

The vehicle c.g. must be in line with the rotor axis to allow VTOL flight; therefore variable masses such as fuel and payload must be placed such that their own center of mass is in line with the rotor axis. In the case of payload, this is the responsibility of the loadmaster. Fuel is located in the rotor hub fairing and conformal tanks along the lower sides of the fuselage. These locations allow the vehicle's c.g. to be maintained in line with the rotor axis.

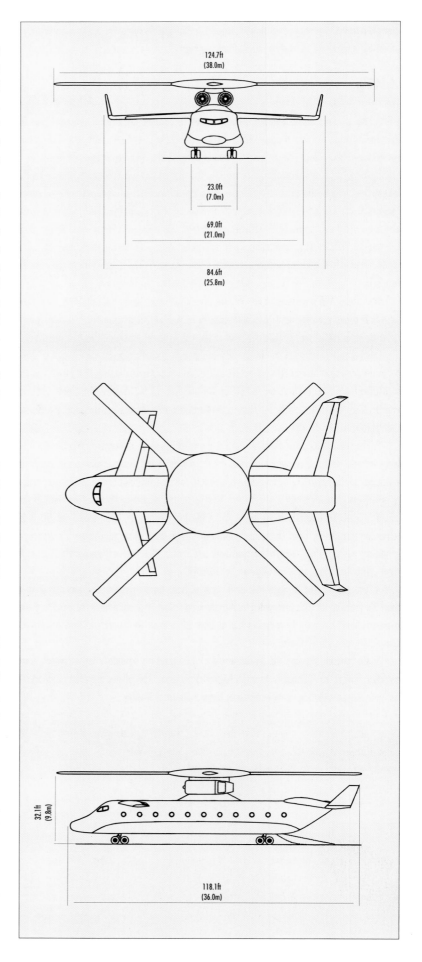

Tandem wings

To allow aerodynamic control of the aircraft when it is operating in conventional aircraft mode, elevons are mounted on the forward and rear wings. In addition, directional stability and control are provided by all-moving fins attached to the tips of the rear wing. Tandem wings reduce the load on the X-wing which is optimized for VTOL operation. They also provide additional fuel tank volume and provide hard-points for armaments. At the same time they simplify CTOL operation.

On-board systems

The leading edges of the rotors contain multi-element phased array radars with electronic beam steering. This provides the crew with 360 degree radar coverage while the X-wing is rotating. With the X-wing stationary, 360 degree coverage is still maintained because each blade can cover a 90 degree scan zone. The data obtained from the radar could be datalinked from the vehicle to AWACS or JSTARS aircraft, or direct to other friendly forces. In essence, the aircraft is capable of performing reconnaissance, SIGINT or ELINT operations while carrying out its transport mission.

The aircraft would employ a fly-by-light flight control system which gives improved performance and reduced weight compared to a conventional mechanical system. In addition, the control laws can be tailored to the unique control requirements of such a vehicle. The best example of this would be the seamless transition between rotating and stationary X-wing flight which is accomplished by giving the pilot a speed controller rather than the conventional throttle which controls engine speed directly.

With the lever fully retarded, the FCS performs all the required functions to bring the aircraft to a hover from forward flight and vice versa. For example, to enter a hover from forward flight, the airbrakes are deployed, the rotor gas drive is brought into operation, and the aircraft c.g. is adjusted as required by pumping fuel fore or aft. As the rotors accelerate they provide the braking force and the airbrakes are retracted. As the aircraft enters a hover this process is transparent to the pilot and hence control of the vehicle is made easy. This is particularly important considering the hazardous environment encountered when transporting equipment to the battlefront.

Canard Rotor Wing

While the X-wing has many advantages over the pure helicopter, especially in the heavy-lift transport role, another advanced hybrid is being developed as a potential replacement for the US Marine Corps' AH-1W SuperCobra attack helicopter. The Canard Rotor Wing (CRW) is being developed at Boeing's Phantom Works in St Louis in response to a US Defense Advanced Projects Agency (DARPA) program.

The principle of the CRW is very similar to that of the X-wing. It has a rotor for VTOL operation which can be stopped and locked in forward flight to act as a conventional wing at high cruise speed. It is powered by a low-bypass turbofan from which exhaust and bypass gases are ducted to nozzles near the rotor/wing tips to maintain rotation. It differs from the X-wing in that it has only a two-blade rotor. Large foreplanes and a narrow tailplane with canted tips, both fitted with high-lift flaps for take-off and landing, plus the stopped rotor acting as a main wing, will give the CRW a top speed of 450mph (725kmh) in conventional flight mode.

The concept will first fly as an unmanned aerial vehicle (UAV) in 2001. The 17ft (5m) long UAV will have a 12ft (3.7m) diameter rotor and is aimed at a US Navy requirement for a ship-borne reconnaissance/surveillance UAV with a 150 mile (240km) range carrying a 200lb (91kg) payload, and having mid-mission loiter of three hours. The US Marine Corps is considering a manned version of the CRW as a replacement for its twin-engine SuperCobra fleet that is currently undergoing a major upgrade to AH-1Z specification, which includes new avionics, communications suite, and active countermeasures systems. Due to join the Corps in 2004, the AH-1Z will remain in service until at least 2015 by which time development of X-wing and CRW designs will have reached maturity.

Attack helicopters of the future may be Canard Rotor Wing (CRW) designs which use a stopped two-blade rotor as a conventional lift aircraft wing for high speed flight.

◀

Designed as a potential replacement for the US Army's CH-47 Chinook and the Navy's CH-53 Sea Stallion, the AVPRO X-wing Titan will combine VTOL with the cruise speed of conventional aircraft.

CASPIAN SEA MONSTERS TO MARAUDERS

O ne of the Soviet Union's most closely guarded secrets during the Cold War was the development of giant "wingships," the Russian word for which is *ekranoplan*. These hybrid craft, a mix of flying ship and low-flying air vehicles, had their origins in World War II when the Soviet Union had experimented with hydrofoils which were boats supported by slender struts mounted on submerged wings. When such a craft accelerates through the water these wings generate the same lift as aircraft wings during take-off, and the hull is raised out of the water, reducing drag to a minimum.

I n the late1950s the late British designer Christopher Cockerell developed the first practical hovercraft, or air cushion vehicle. Part boat, part aircraft, the hovercraft lifts the craft completely out of the water by engine power fed into a flexible skirt suspended from the hull. Other engines mounted above the hull provide forward speed. Large military hovercaft were adopted by the Soviet Navy and US Marine Corps in the 1970s although their speed was limited by the skirt mechanism and they proved difficult and expensive to maintain.

The Soviet *ekranoplan*, designed to transport hundreds of troops over long distances at high speeds, was virtually a warship with stub wings that enabled it to "fly" over the water at up to 50ft (15m). Pilots of conventional aircraft had been aware of ground effect since the dawn of flying. When throttled back on landing, an

▼

The KM-8 ekranoplan, *a prototype of the 540 ton "Caspian Sea Monster" powered by eight starting engines on stub wings behind the flight deck, plus two more in the rear fuselage for cruise propulsion.*

aircraft will "float" along the runway as it flares until drag overcomes power and it will sink to the ground. Wing in ground effect occurs when vehicles producing lift are in close proximity to a surface, most commonly water, land, or ice floes. It reduces the drag caused by the generation of lift, thereby increasing the vehicle's performance. The chief designer of the Soviet *ekranoplan* program, Rostislav Alexiev, exploited this phenomenon to produce some of the largest flying machines ever built. It was in 1967 that a US spy satellite first revealed the existence of a huge *ekranoplan* docked at a Soviet naval facility on the shores of the Caspian Sea.

Larger than a B-52 and weighing more than a Boeing 747 "Jumbo Jet," the KM was promply christened the "Caspian Sea Monster." It was 345ft (106m) long, had a wingspan of 130ft (40m), weighed 540 tons, and was powered by ten turbojet engines—eight for take-off and two for cruising at 250mph (400kmh). It was designed to carry up to 500 troops over a range of 1,900 miles (3,000km). A total of eight "Caspian Sea Monsters" were built between 1965-75 although at least two crashed in bad weather, while a slightly smaller development, the Lun, or Harrier, entered service with the Soviet Navy in 1987. Designed for anti-submarine warfare, the Lun was equipped with three pairs of retractable launchers capable of firing the SS-N-22 "Sunburn" cruise missile as well as other conventional, anti-ballistic or even nuclear missiles.

However, as a fleet of these Sea Monsters was ordered, the Soviet Union imploded and production ground to a halt, although a number of A-90 naval transports with three-engines, two turbojets for take-off and a single turboprop for cruising, have continued to be operated spasmodically over the Caspian by the Russian Navy. At the end of the Cold War, a successor to the Lun, the upgraded Spasatel search and

A Russian Navy 400 ton Lun (Harrier) anti-submarine warfare (ASW) ekranoplan *firing a salvo of "Sunburn" cruise missiles from its six retractable launchers while cruising over the Caspian Sea.*

rescue *ekranoplan*, was under construction at the Volga shipbuilding plant. Ten years later there were plans to complete the craft as a high-speed mobile hospital that could be deployed to major disaster areas anywhere in the world under the auspices of the United Nations.

The Russian flying boat manufacturer Beriev built a number of research *ekranoplans* designed by R. L. Bartini in the 1970s and the company had a number of *ekranoplan* projects up to a 1,000-ton, 450mph (700kmh) giant with a range of 5,000 miles (8,000km). In 1993, the once-powerful MiG Design Bureau, which was the Cold War's most prolific jet fighter constructor, designed a four-seat "wing in ground effect" (WIG effect) amphibian, the TA-4, which could travel over any surface using an air cushion landing system at speeds of up to 160mph (260kmh). It was never built.

More successful was the seven-place Aero-RIK, designed by a team led by the Sokel production plant which produced the MiG-29 "Fulcrum" and MiG-31 "Foxhound." It was another multi-role, amphibious WIG craft designed to operate over any surface using an 850shp Pratt & Whitney Canada PT6A turboprop for propulsion plus a 250shp TVA turboprop to provide the cushion effect. With a maximum speed of 200mph (322kmh) and a range of 500 miles (800km), the Aero-RIK first "flew" in 1995 and limited production was reported to be underway two-three years later. However, it was clear that there would be no substantial funding for many of these projects in Russia and several "Caspian Sea Monster" designers and technicians have moved to California where AeroSea Innovations are currently designing a 1,500 ton, 1,000 passenger trans-Pacific *ekranoplan*.

But the military species is by no means extinct. Lockheed-Martin is undertaking low-key research programs into the potential of small and medium scale *ekranoplans* as landing craft and special forces platforms in the future. The US Marine Corps has a requirement for a fast, stealthy WIG effect craft for special missions and has tested two small FlareCraft Corporation designs. Several state-of-the-art *ekranoplans* are currently being developed in Australia and China, while a British company has revealed a number of concepts aimed at NATO requirements.

The Manta and Marauder are a pair of ground effect craft developed by Avpro U.K. Ltd. These two craft differ in size and role. The Marauder is the smaller of the two and can fly "out of ground effect" (OGE) as a conventional aircraft. By contrast the much larger Manta is intended to be used solely "in ground effect" (IGE).

▶

A pair of Russian Navy A-90 Orlyonok (Eaglet) transport ekranoplans *cruise over the Caspian Sea at 250mph (400kmh) powered by a 14,800shp NK-12MK turboprops as used in the Tu-95 "Bear" bomber.*

▼

A single-seat Russian UT ekranoplan *powered by a single 160hp Czech Walter piston engine is used to train Russian Navy* ekranoplan *captains in the art of "flying" in ground effect.*

Powered by two 3,300lb (1,495kg) thrust AI-25 turbojet starting engines in the nose, and an An-26-type 2,800shp AI-24 propulsion turboprop, the SM-6 was able to climb to higher than other coastal patrol ekranoplans.

The 140 ton naval transport version of the A-90 parked on a beach. It has two 22,050lb (10,000kg) thrust Nk-8-4K turbofan starting engines in the nose and a cruise turboprop mounted on the fin.

MARAUDER

Two basic versions of the stealthy Marauder are proposed. The first can be operated in the same way as the Manta, "flying" a few yards above the water surface, but it can also be operated out of ground effect as a conventional flying boat. The second version operates as a conventional aircraft out of ground effect but cannot be operated on the surface of the water as it does not have the hull of the combined capability version. Both versions of the twin-turbofan-powered craft are based on a common airframe of composite construction. The design of the Marauder is modular so that it can be reconfigured according to the required role—for example, an anti-submarine warfare (ASW) version equipped with a sea-going hull can be converted to a strike aircraft by replacing the hull with a bomb bay. Other potential roles are as follows.

The amphibious combined-capability Marauder, which can operate in the airborne early warning (AEW) role from an aircraft carrier, transit in ground effect (IGE), and land on water to refuel.

Airborne Early Warning (AEW)

An aircraft carrier or assault ship could be used to provide AEW coverage for surface fleets. Two vehicles would provide continuous coverage. When the endurance of the on-station vehicle is exhausted, the replacement craft could rapidly transit to the search area, minimizing its fuel burn by cruising in ground effect. This also has the advantage of reducing the chances of detection by ship-based enemy radar as the craft would be at low level, hence over the horizon (OTH) until within relatively short ranges. It could then take up its search station while the other craft used its surface operation capability to be refueled by any surface vessel of sufficient size or by submarine, or it could return to its launch vessel.

Anti-Submarine Warfare (ASW)

The craft could rapidly transit to the search area in ground effect. It could then drop sonar buoys from the air and/or land on the water and lower a dipping sonar device on a cable. On detection of enemy submarines it could then deploy the appropriate ASW weapon and transmit the location of the enemy to friendly forces via a datalink. The ability of the craft to land on water means that it could remain on active search for very lengthy periods, perhaps several days, the energy requirements being fuel to run generators and supplies for the two/three-man crew. If the craft were detected its high performance would allow rapid relocation or retreat.

Search and Rescue (SAR)

The craft could operate at altitudes used by conventional search and rescue aircraft such as the P-3 or Nimrod, thereby allowing the search of a large area. However, the Marauder has the advantage that it can land on the water and pick up survivors immediately rather than directing slower surface vessels to do so.

Fire-Fighting/Oil Pollution at Sea

In its fire-fighting role the craft would pick up water from any suitable source which it could then carry to the location of the fire at high speed. In the second role it could operate in ground effect in close proximity to the spill which would allow more accurate placement of the dispersant than is currently possible with conventional aircraft operating at higher altitudes.

Special Forces Landing Craft

Marauder would make a highly effective landing craft. In addition to two crew, the Marauder is intended to carry up to 12 fully equipped troops in a bay inside the hull. The ability of the craft to approach a beach at low level and high speed would reduce the probability of detection and the exposure of the crew/troops. In addition, because of the ground effect, a high speed approach to the drop zone would be terminated by cutting the throttles and allowing the craft to glide/ride, hence reducing acoustic signature and making detection by the enemy less risky.

The second basic version of the Marauder does not have the hull of the combined capability version and therefore could not be used as a surface vessel but could be utilized as a conventional aircraft.

GROUND ATTACK/CLOSE AIR SUPPORT

The ability of the Marauder to fly as a conventional aircraft allows it to be used as a relatively simple subsonic ground attack/strike aircraft performing a similar role to that of the A-4 or Jaguar. Its relatively small size combined with its ability to be configured to carry a wide range of modern stand-off stores would also make it an effective close air support (CAS) craft in a similar role to that of the A-10.

AWACS/STAND-OFF TARGET ACQUISITION

The hull of the combined capability version would be removed and replaced with infra-red (IR) and electro-optic (EO) sensors, and a laser designator. This would allow it to detect targets and to provide this data directly to friendly aircraft via a datalink. It would also allow it to guide "smart" weapons launched by other aircraft.

INTERCEPTOR

Although the configuration of the Marauder is not suitable to close range dogfighting it could carry stand-off air-to-air missiles such as the AIM-l20 and the proposed FMRAAM, allowing it to be used as an interceptor.

▲

The ground attack version of the Marauder used to launch cruise missiles is capable of flying in and out of ground effect even over desert terrain when ingressing and egressing the target.

▼

Powered by two advanced turbofans, the two-seat conventional flight Marauder would be an ideal stealthy maritime strike or close air support platform.

A future combined operations assault force would comprise unmanned reconnaissance aerial vehicles (URAV), hydrofoil armored personnel carriers (APC), and wing in ground effect (WIG) landing craft.

Powered by four turbofan engines, the Manta landing craft WIG could travel at speeds of up to 350mph (565kmh) carrying a 60-ton payload up to 350 nautical miles.

THE MANTA

The Manta is a wing-in-ground effect vehicle proposal with a wide variety of applications, both civil and military. Currently, its principal intended use is as a large landing craft capable of performing a similar mission to the Landing Craft Air Cushion (LCAC) of the US Marine Corps and Japanese Navy.

The craft would fly over the sea at an altitude of approximately 15ft (4.5m). At this altitude, the velicle operates in ground effect, essentially floating on a cushion of air. The vehicle configuration proposed in this study is designed to carry a 60 ton payload over a range of 350 nautical miles at 350mph (565kmh). It can operate in sea states up to level 5.

These specifications make the vehicle suitable for roles other than as a landing craft. For example, the craft's large payload bay and ability to operate in rough seas allow it to be used for search and rescue/medevac duties. Its cruise speed is significantly higher than that of helicopters and therefore it could reach the scene of a maritime accident more quickly. It could also be used as a high speed transporter.

A further requirement for the Manta is that it should be capable of operating from an internal bay of a base ship such as a Marine Assault ship. The vehicle has been laid out with folding wings, canards, and tails so that it can fit in an internal bay whose dimensions are 50ft wide x 46ft high x 150ft deep (15.25 x 14 x 46m).

Manta is equipped with an air cushion skirt like that of a hovercraft which allows it to be driven on to beaches, or to prevent the craft colliding with underwater obstructions. One configuration has four propfan engines. These are better suited than turbofans to the cruise speed and low speed maneuvering requirements of the Manta. At the current time, there is no Western propfan of the required 7,500lb (3,40kg) shp rating. The craft could probably be made to work satisfactoriiy using high by-pass ratio turbofans but the long term solution would be either to develop a new engine or modify an existing turbofan.

The Manta would include a digital fly-by-wire (FBW) or fly-by-light (FBL) flight control system to provide a safe and controllable vehicle while maximizing the benefits of the WIG effect. The fuselage is of rectangular cross-section to provide maximum usable payload volume. The front and rear of the vehicle are open to provide access to the payload bay. The rear door is a ramp type, hinged at the bottom, while the front doors are hinged at the sides and open outwards.

Although ground effect will occur when the craft is at low altitude over any surface, its main operating environment would be over water. However, the craft could operate over ice floes, snow, and beaches if required. The Manta has to compete with conventional landing craft, heavy-lift helicopters, and transport aircraft, so why should it be developed?

Firstly, it combines some of the best elements of all these vehicles in a single craft. It is large enough to carry payloads as large as those carried by heavy-lift aircraft. For example, the maximum payload of

▶

Having unloaded troops and equipment on the beachhead, Manta landing craft could be used as helipads for attack and support helicopters involved in the operation.

▼

As a Royal Navy Manta approaches the beachhead at low speed, it is escorted by Royal Marine Commando WAH-64D Apache helicopters and Fleet Air Arm Marauder combined-capability attack WIGs.

A version of the Manta offered to the US Marine Corps would be capable of operating from the internal dock of a Marine Assault ship and become a mini-carrier for helicopters on the beach.

the C-17A Globemaster III is 77 tons and that of the Manta in 60 tons.

In addition, it can be ship-based like a helicopter and provide the ability to mobilize rapidly and project a large amount of the ship's fighting force at ranges of up to 350 nautical miles. The Manta offers the versatility of the hovercraft to operate over water, and to be driven on to beaches, flood planes, and so on, to give commanders a maximum tactical advantage in the placement of troops and equipment.

The Manta has been laid out to utilize the power augmented ram (PAR) effect whereby the slipstream from the engines is directed under the inboard wing. The flow decelerates under the wing which increases its pressure and hence lifts the vehicle up in the water. For the Manta, the PAR effect would be used to reduce the take-off run. This would be particularly useful at high gross take-off weights (GTOW) since this reduces the vehicle's exposure to damaging wave strikes and slam loading. However, it is not proposed that the PAR effect should be exploited to the extent that the vehicle is completely lifted out of the water.

Roles for which the Manta is being proposed include the following.

HIGH SPEED MARITIME TRANSPORT

The ability of the Manta to carry large payloads at high speed would allow it to compete with both aircraft and hovercraft in both military and civil applications. The main internal bay of the military version would carry both troops and equipment. Taking operations in the seas of Europe as an example, the high performance of the Manta would allow it to reach mainy European ports in a time that would make it competitive with medium transport aircraft. In this respect, when compared to hovercraft, the superior speed and range of the Manta give it an advantage.

SEARCH AND RESCUE/MEDEVAC

Due to its larger size and payload capability, the Manta would be more useful than the Marauder in the rescue and treatment of survivors of a large maritime accident. It could carry more survivors, would allow extensive medical facilities to be carried, and its high performance would allow it to reach the target quicker than either surface vessels or helicopters.

LANDING CRAFT

The Manta would perform this role in a similar way to that proposed for the Marauder. However, the greater payload capability of the Manta means that it can land vehicles and a greater number of troops. The current configuration proposed for the Manta has bow doors that allow heavy vehicles including main battle tanks (MBT) and armored personnel carriers (APC) to be driven directly on to the !anding site and allow the rapid disembarkation of froops.

Both the Manta and Marauder have operational advantages over more conventional craft when used in the above roles. The first is the flexibility offered by the ability to operate as surface craft and in the air. This is particularly the case for the Marauder, which has an additional capability over the Manta in that it can operate in OGE as a conventional aircraft. Because of this flexibility, a single craft can perform a number of roles. This allows a single common design to be adopted to a specific requirement that would require separate vehicles if a more conventional approach were used. In addition, since the uses outlined previously can be met by reconfiguring the common basic design this reduces development and production costs and overall project risk.

The vehicles are competing in an under-developed market. Until recently the wing-in-ground (WIG) effect concept has not been successfully exploited in military applications, at least in the West. As we have seen, the former Soviet Union probably carried out most of the modern research in this field and produced a number of craft for the Russian forces. These vehicles were of a different configuration to the Manta and

The NauticAir 400 is an innovative design that combines WIG with a conventional high performance aircraft using a tunnel hull with a retractable step in the sponsons.

The NauticAir's tunnel hull/sponson design in water landing and take-off configuration.

A heavyweight armed version of the Manta powered by four advanced 7,500shp propfan propulsion engines would utilize power augmented ram (PAR) to increase lift and gross take-off weight (GTOW).

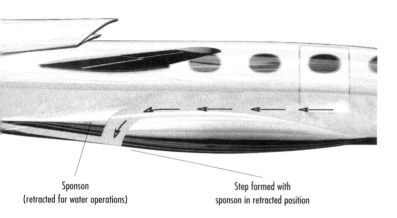

Sponson
(retracted for water operations)

Step formed with
sponson in retracted position

▼

The twin-engined tunnel hull forward swept-wing (FSW) NauticAir 450 would be a capable platform for maritime patrol, search and rescue, anti-drug, and special operations roles.

Marauder. They resembled a conventional aircraft fuselage with a tandem wing arrangement. This provides an inherently more stable configuration than those of the Marauder and Manta but at the expense of weight and performance.

In an extension of the WIG effect, Dr G. Leonard Gioia, an instrument-rated pilot of mutli-engined aircraft, with over 3,500 hours in light twins, started flying amphibians. While enjoying the freedom of water take-offs and landings, he realized amphibians were just not aerodynamically clean enough to be efficient at high speeds. After working with the aeronautical engineering department of the University of Daytona Beach, Florida, he decided that a conventional deep-"vee" amphibious hull would cause too much drag for a high performance jet. After trials at the Langley NASA high subsonic wind tunnel in Virginia, Dr Gioia developed a sponsored tunnel-hull fuselage which produced unprecedented hydrodynamic stability as well as relatively low drag high-speed aerodynamic performance. It also provides a relatively shallow draft of less than 18 inches (0.45m), making operations possible in shallow water.

As Dr Gioia began work on a prototype, he teamed up with former Grumman chief engineer Roy LoPresti to develop the NauticAir 400 using his patented hydrodynamic design. Wing floats are not necessary as sponsons with retracting "steps" and a tunnel hull are designed to provide exceptional water and land take-off performance. The NauticAir also features a forward swept wing (FSW) which gives excellent low speed handling combined with a high cruise speed. Constructed mostly of composite materials and powered by two 2,300lb (1,043kg) thrust Williams/Rolls-Royce FJ44-2 turbofans, the NauticAir will cruise at over 500mph (800kmh) and have a range of 1,800 miles (3,000km). Able to carry up to eight troops, the NauticAir 450 is in the same class as the flying boat version of the Marauder for maritime patrol, search and rescue, drug surveillance, and special forces roles, while its designers foresee the development and production of much larger aircraft, even of the C-130 category, utilizing their tunnel-hull sponson concept.

The future of water-borne military aircraft for special missions in the 21st Century is full of innovative possibilities even though the "Golden Age" of the flying boat was considered to have ended with World War II.

CHAPTER SIX

AEROSTATS AND SUPERBLIMPS

The military potential for lighter-than-air balloons has been realized for more than 200 years. Together with rigid and non-rigid airships, they have been used in a variety of roles in warfare, including reconnaisance, bombing, anti-submarine warfare (ASW), search and rescue (SAR), and transport. As a result of advances in materials and systems, there is a revival of interest in their use over the battlefields of the future.

When the superpowers became locked into the Cold War following the Berlin Airlift and Korean War, the United States reverted to the most basic of aerial reconnaissance platforms, the gas-filled balloon. Between 1956 and 1980 some 10,000 surveillance aerostats were drifted across the WarPac countries. As part of a program codenamed "Moby Dick," a covert CIA/USAF Air Resupply and Communications Command operation, 48ft (15m) diameter converted weather observation balloons were released from Giebelstadt in Germany, Incirlik in Turkey, and Eielson AF Base in Alaska to drift freely on the prevailing winds through Soviet and WarPac airspace. Although their official role was to drop propaganda leaflets over Iron Curtain countries, many of the balloons carried radio monitoring devices or automatic cameras programmed to take a photograph every six minutes. These cameras held enough film to record a track 40 miles (65km) wide by 3,100 miles (5,000km) long, but few were recovered intact. More than 4,000 were detected over the Soviet Union and nearly 800 shot down by high-flying Soviet interceptors and SAMs. Man's earliest form of flight was finally superseded by space-age satellites.

Shooting down balloons was a hard habit to break for Russian air defenses even after the end of the Cold War. On September 12 1995, a balloon was spotted by the crew of a Belarus Air Force Mi-24 "Hind" attack helicopter as it drifted over the Polish border and was seen to be heading for a prohibited military region near the Belarus capital Minsk. Following the break-up of the Soviet Union, its air defenses were taken over by separate members of the post-Cold War Commonwealth of Independent States (CIS) but communications between many of these states was virtually non-existent.

What the Belarus Air Force did not known was that their target was an American-crewed hot-air balloon taking part in the long-distance Gordon Bennett International balloon race which had strayed into Russian airspace. Despite urgent requests by the race organizers for permission from the Russian government in Moscow to allow the hot-air balloon to continue overflying the country unimpeded, disaster was about to strike near Minsk.

The Mi-24 was ordered to intercept it. The balloon's crew assumed that the helicopter had been sent up to escort them out of the area and were horrified when it turned and fired a salvo of unguided rockets at the fragile but brightly colored nylon envelope. The balloon immediately burst into flames and plummeted almost

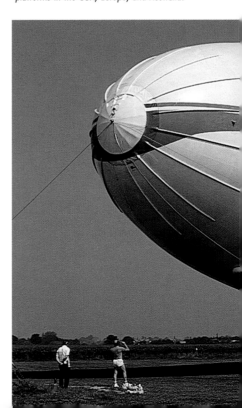

▲ *Seven Goodyear "blimps," developed from the US Navy's World War II K-class non-rigid airships, are used as Goodyear's global fleet of aerial TV camera platforms in the USA, Europe, and Australia.*

10,000ft (3,050m) to the ground near the border town of Brest, killing the two American aeronauts. The crew of the Belarus "Hind" were later decorated for their valiant efforts in the defense of their country.

The above incident involved a civilian balloon flight, but at the beginning of the 21st Century balloons are perceived as having a military role. One example concerns unmanned helium-filled balloons which are still operated as a potent tool of the South Korean Intelligence and Security Service (KISS) in its ongoing propaganda war against Communist North Korea. After drifting over the border, the balloons are programmed to explode over the famine-hit North scattering leaflets promising defectors free houses, cash, employment—and food.

The United States has also carried out extensive research into the use of airships as military craft. By the 1970s, fixed wing aircraft and increasingly helicopters had taken over the US Navy's ASW role; looking for alternatives, the service undertook a series of benchmark studies to re-examine the airship concept and its potential. Surveillance and communications, command, and control (C_3) operations carried out over long endurance and with proven reliability seemed to point the way to a healthy future for the airship. However, owing to a series of technical and funding problems, the US Navy finally called a halt to its airship operations after 60 years of continuous service.

At the same time, an innovative new airship design, featuring composite materials such as glass-fiber and Kevlar for both the envelope and gondola, fly-by-light (FBL) control system, and vectored thrust propulsion was being developed by the UK company, Airship Industries. A series of 194ft (70m) long AI Skyship 500/600 non-rigid airships were produced in the 1980/90s, several of which were evaluated by the military. In the late 1980s a Skyship 600 became the first airship to wear French Navy colors since the ill-fated *Dixmude* more than 60 years earlier. Fitted with a MEL MARAC II Sea Searcher maritime surveillance radar mounted within the envelope, an Aerospatiale Atal high-resolution camera pod and infra-red sensors, the Skyship was capable of detecting surface vessels at a range of 50 miles (80km) from a height of 2,000ft (620m). Although the trials were successful, cuts in French naval budgets prevented deployment of the system.

▼
The UK Airship Industry's composite-construction, helium-filled non-rigid Skyship 500, powered by vectoring thrust engines, revived interest in airships in the 1980s.

▼
Vectoring-thrust cowled propellers gave the Skyship 500/600 airships the capability of controlled near vertical take-off and landing and improved maneuverability.

However, the performance of the Skyships continued to impress. In September 1990 one of the British airships powered by two cowled, vectored-thrust Porsche auto engines, which gave it a maximum speed of 70mph (112kmh), remained airborne for more than 50 hours, and a major breakthough came a year later when the US Federal Aviation Authority (FAA) certified the Skyship to operate in the United States.

This enabled Airship Industries to team up with Westinghouse to develop a new advanced long-range maritime airship for the US Navy which awarded the company a $169 million contract to design and build the YEZ-2A. This would be an operational development of the Westinghouse Airship Industries (WAI) Sentinal 5000, a 425ft (127.5m) long, helium-filled, composite-construction craft with a fly-by-light system. It would be the largest non-rigid airship ever to be constructed.

Powered by two vectored-thrust 800hp PPB marine diesel engines plus a 1,750shp GE CT7-9 turboprop for forward thrust, the Sentinel 5000 would have a top speed of 100mph (160kmh) and an endurance of 60 hours at 50mph (80kmh). Its 82ft (25m) long double-deck gondola could accommodate up to 15 crew and an APS-138 radar as used in the Grumman E-2C Hawkeye.

In 1991, WAI flew a privately funded half-scale Sentinel 5000, the Sentinel 1000, a 220ft (66m) long development of the Skyship 600 designed to a US Drug Enforcement Agency requirement for a radar surveillance platform. It was planned to use this airship to renew the US Navy's skill at airship operations. However, disaster struck when the Sentinel 1000 was destroyed in a fire at its World War II "blimp" hangar at Weeksville, North Carolina, following which Westinghouse decided to withdraw from the airship program. Added to the fact that the USA had changing priorities in the new "downsized," post-Cold War age, the YEZ-2A fell victim to US Navy defense cuts.

But all was not yet lost for the airship revivalists. The British Ministry of Defence (MoD) had been involved in a "black" airship program for some considerable time while denying any interest in such craft. In 1998, the British Army's Airship Trials Unit at the Army Air Corps Centre, Middle Wallop in Hampshire, completed five years of trials with a heavily modified Skyship 600. Fitted with advanced electronic systems from almost every leading British defense contractor, the airship was used to develop operational mission packages for surveillance and counter-terrorism roles initially in Northern Ireland, but later in the Balkans.

▶
Projected to fly in 1994, the 425ft (130m) long Sentinel 5000, the US Navy's prototype YEZ-2A, would have been the largest non-rigid airship ever built.

▶▼
A mock-up of the two-story YEZ-2A gondola, designed to accommodate a 10-man crew, in the WAI facility at Weeksville. It was also destroyed in the fire that finished the US Navy's advanced airship program.

▼
The two-man flight deck of the Airship 600 shows the aircraft-type yoke and excellent visibility afforded from the all-composite gondola.

▼
A sight not seen in the UK since the 1930s, two advanced airships, a Skyship 600 trailing its mooring lines with a Skyship 500 in the background.

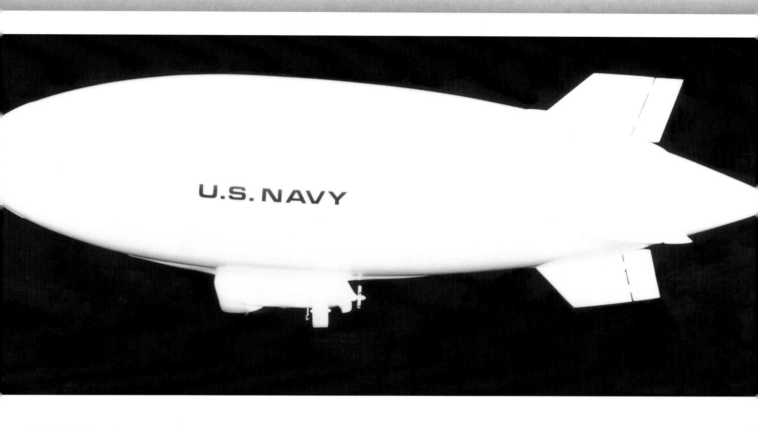

The British Army has announced its intention to operate a fleet of advanced technology airships capable of carrying up to 30 tons of equipment or military personnel. Quiet and cost effective, they will be required to operate in areas where conventional fixed and rotary-wing aircraft cannot. Unlike a helicopter, which uses large amounts of fuel when it hovers, an airship simply throttles back and floats in one position at altitudes between 2-4,000ft (720-1,080m), depending on the wind, for as long as is required. The composite envelope would be filled with hundreds of small helium-filled honeycomb cells, and it is believed that bullets or even a missile would pass straight through with little loss of gas.

Although its main role is seen as that of a stealthy "spy-in-the-sky," a number of more specialized mission are also being seriously considered. These include airborne early warning (AEW), radio relay over mountainous regions such as the Balkans—where communications are often disrupted—maritime and landmine countermeasures, and as large floating field hospitals. Despite their bulk, gas-filled airships have a low radar signature and with state-of-the-art radar warning receivers (RWR) and electronic countermeasures (ECM) sensors, the airship should be assured of a high rate of survivability.

There are several contenders for the future British Army airship including AI successors, Airship Technologies, which is proposing its 270ft (82m) long AT-04. Fitted with advanced rotating or fixed phased array UHF radar and powered by three 450hp Diesel Air Ltd engines, two with vectoring ducted propulsors mounted on the gondola and one fixed in the stern, the all-weather, day/night AT-04 has a maximum speed of 100mph (160kmh) and a ferry range of over 3,600 miles (5,750km) unrefueled at 50mph (80kmh), plus an in-flight refueling capability.

The AT-04 has also been chosen for testing the RAF's E-3 Sentry system upgrade program in 2003, which includes UHF sensors. There is also growing support for using a small fleet of AEW airships to

▶ ▶

The advanced-technology "glass cockpit" of the US Navy's YEZ-2A airship, designed during the Cold War as a platform for airborne radar to counter supersonic cruise missiles.

▶

Evaluated by the French Navy in the early 1990s, the Skyship 600 would have been fitted with maritime surveillance radar, camera pods, and infra-red sensors.

supplement the RAF's heavily committed fleet of seven Sentry AEW.1s. The AT-04 could also become a contender for the Royal Navy's Future Organic Airborne Early Warning (FOAEW) system and, in view of naval task forces becoming increasingly involved in littoral operations, this could be combined with a command and control platform. Meanwhile, Australia is evaluating the AT-04 for a coastal surveillance requirement.

Another company that was invited to take part in the British Army's airship evaluation was the American Blimp Corporation. The small, three-seat Lightship A-60+, fitted with the WESCAM system, took part in UK MoD trials at the beginning of 1997 as a surveillance platform with a special operations forces role. The company is currently developing the Spector 30, a 10-man A-100 powered by twin vectoring Renault diesel engines, and is aiming at the military market.

Advanced unmanned surveillance airships are already widely deployed around the world and others are under development. The US TCOM company has designed and manufactured more than 100 advanced tethered aerostat systems, the most successful of which is the Low Altitude Surveillance System (LASS). Operated for the US Coast Guard by USAF, 16 of the 120ft (36m) long tethered aerostats, fitted with ventral blisters that house radar antenna, are flown at altitudes from 3,000 to 20,000ft (909 - 6,060m) to form an unbroken counter-drug surveillance line across the southern borders of mainland USA and out to sea to the Bahamas and Puerto Rico. The LASS radar can detect small, low-flying aircraft up 200 miles (320km) away. LASS has also been acquired by the Kuwait Air Force to provide round-the-clock 200 mile (320km) surveillance against surface vehicles, low flying aircraft, and off-shore marine threats.

▶

Another small, stealthy, non-rigid airship, the American Blimp A-60+ is seen here carrying a stabilized heli-tele camera system in front of the gondola during trials with British MoD in the late 1990s.

▶▼

The unmanned TCOM Low Altitude Surveillance System (LASS) is operated by the USAF for counter-drug operations and by the Kuwait Air Force for patroling the country's border with Iraq.

▼

The British Army carried out highly classified trials with Skyship 600 ZH762 over a period of five years, evaluating a wide range of cutting-edge technology surveillance systems.

A dedicated maritime system developed from LASS in TCOM's Maritime Aerostat Tracking and Surveillance System (MATSS) is equipped with fully coherent I/J-band radar and can be mounted from a flatbed trailer, deployed from a ship, or towed behind a helicopter. Communications from the LASS and MATSS with the surface is via the latest fiber-optic technology embedded in the umbilical tether.

At the beginning of the 21st Century, the spirit of Count von Zeppelin is not dead. In fact, a new Zeppelin airship, the first for more than 60 years, has already taken to the air. The Zeppelin Luftshifftechnic company, headed by one of the count's descendents, Albrecht Graf von Brandenstein-Zeppelin, is developing a 14-seat LZ NO7 airship powered by twin vectored-thrust engines.

For the first time since the *Graf Zeppelin II* was launched in 1938, the German government is backing the development of a giant heavy-lift airship, the CargoLifter CL160. Almost 800ft (245m)

◀

The air-refuelable Airship Technologies AT-04 designed as a multi-role platform is seen here configured for land mine countermeasures with the United Nations.

◀

The AT-04's gondola showing its twin vectored-thrust ducted propulsors, an electro-optical laser sensor in the cabin floor, and a remote-controlled mine detector ready to deploy from the rear ramp.

▶

In the maritime role, with rotating maritime radar fitted above the gondola within the hull envelope, the AT-04 could carry special forces teams for insertion and combat search and rescue missions.

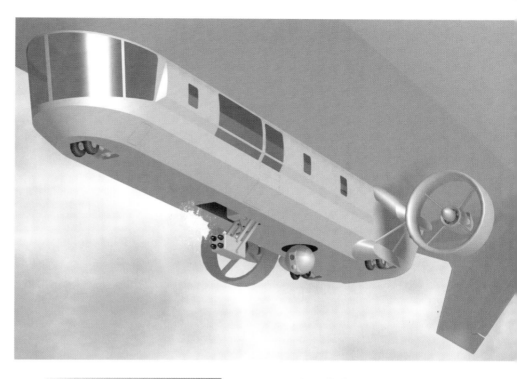

The unmanned mine detecting vehicle is controlled by an operator aboard the AT-04 which has excellent low-speed performance efficiency and outstanding low altitude performance.

In the day/night surveillance role, the AT-04 can be equipped with a comprehensive suite of rotating or phased array radars, electro-optical laser sensors and IR/LLTV cameras.

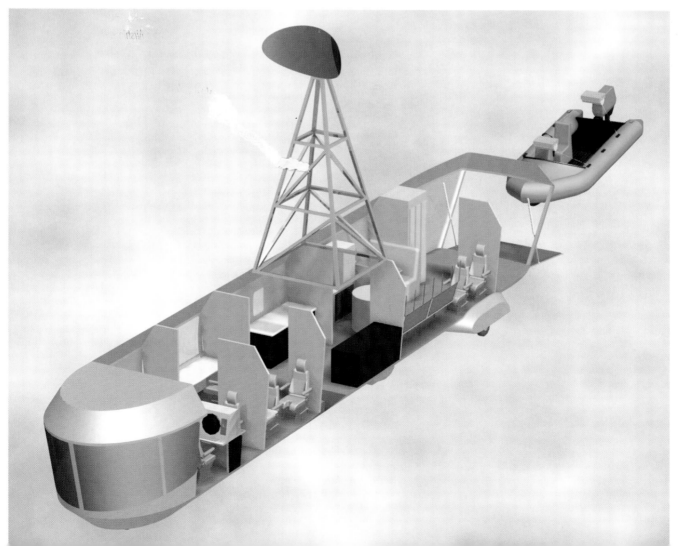

long, the semi-rigid CL160 is powered by four low-speed, vectored-thrust diesel engines with bow and stern spacecraft-type thrusters for additional maneuverability. Although primarily aimed at the commercial market, the CL160 will have a 160 ton payload, as its designation suggests, and would be an ideal military strategic transport. With a cruising speed of 50-60mph (80-100kmh), the CargoLifter has a still-air range of 6,000 miles (10,000km).

Its unique integrated winch system enables the CargoLifter to station itself over pickup or delivery points and remain airborne during cargo on- and off-loading. Ground support is kept to a minimum and comprises a football-pitch-sized operating zone, four tie-down anchor points, and water for its computer-controlled ballast tanks. Water, along with fuel, can be pumped aboard using ground-based systems. No mooring mast is required. The CL160 is optimized to carry a 164ft (50m) long "multibox" container which could carry up to 500 fully equipped troops, three main battle tanks (MBT) or Apache helicopters, or 36 standard commercial FEU containers.

Work is well advanced on the construction of a CL160 assembly hangar at Brand, 15 miles (25km) south of Berlin. Able to house two CargoLifters side-by-side, the air-conditioned building will be 1,000ft (360m) long, 660ft (210m) wide, and some 330ft (107m) high. The maiden flight of the immense CL160 is scheduled for 2001, and the first series production of up to four or five a year will begin in Germany and the USA in 2004.

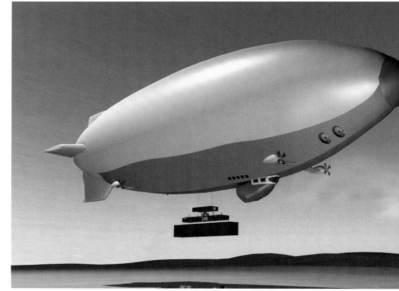

Another heavyweight contender is being developed by the Lockheed Martin "Skunk Works." The US Aercraft, known as "Superblimp," is being designed under a "black" program with the British company Airship Technologies, which is developing the AT-04 for the British Army. Of a similar length to that of the CL160, the Aercraft will resemble a giant conventional aircraft with four advanced turboprop tiltrotor engines mounted on stub wings and a rigid cargo bay able to carry up to 500 tons of equipment such as 10 MBTs or 1,500 troops.

The upper sections of the "Superblimp" will comprise a helium-filled composite envelope which will enable the craft to take-off vertically using its tiltrotors for propulsion before transitioning into the level flight mode and accelerating the Aercraft to a cruising speed of some 140mph (224kmh).

With the recent problems experienced in the rapid deployment of the UN/NATO K-For peace-keeping force in Kosovo, advanced heavy-lift airships are being seen as a practical, safe, cost-effective, and essential asset in any future out of area operations.

The airship is also going into space, or at least on its fringes. The exciting new unmanned High-Altitude Long-Endurance (HALE) airship designed by the UK-based Lindstrand Balloons and Germany's Daimler Chrysler Aerospace will be unique in that it will be solar-powered. With the development of cheap, flexible solar cells that can produce power for the airship's computers, payload, and 98kW stern-mounted electric engine, the 600ft (216m) long helium-filled aerostat, built of lightweight composite materials, would operate at 70,000ft (25,200m) where there is no weather, few winds, and little humidity.

The HALE would be an ideal platform for a stratospheric communications platform, capable of handling up to 100,000 communications simultaneously within a 400 mile (640km) radius. Two or more HALE platforms linked together by microwaves could cover an area the size of the UK. Electricity generated by the solar cells could also be used to produce water ballast which would allow the HALE to be easily recovered to a base to be reconfigured in the AEW or surveillance role.

The HALE designers are confident that their pollution-free stratospheric airship could revive the US Navy's interest in lighter-than-air platforms, and the US company Sky Station, set up by General Alexander Haig, the former US Defense Secretary, is one of a number of international aerospace companies exploring future military roles of solar-powered airships.

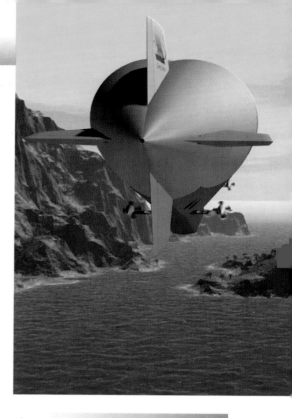

◀

The CargoLifter CL160 will be capable of deploying large numbers of fully equipped troops, main battle tanks, and attack helicopters to out of area operations.

◀

Fly-by-light flight control system, computerized maneuvering, and an integrated loading and unloading system make the CargoLifter an ideal strategic transport.

◀ ▼

The semi-rigid, helium-filled CargoLifter has a keel constructed of ultra-light bonded carbon fiber and multi-laminated skin on which to anchor the 160 ton payload "multibox" container.

▲

A military version of the CargoLifter could be used for supporting peace-making and peace-keeping operations in remote and inaccessible regions of the world.

▼

A contender for the world's largest flying machine will be the Anglo-US tiltrotor Aerocraft, christened "Superblimp," being developed under wraps at Lockheed Martin's "Skunk Works."

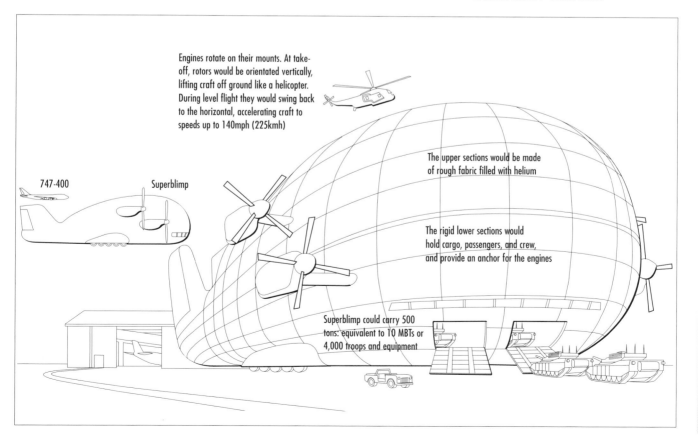

Engines rotate on their mounts. At take-off, rotors would be orientated vertically, lifting craft off ground like a helicopter. During level flight they would swing back to the horizontal, accelerating craft to speeds up to 140mph (225kmh)

747-400   Superblimp

The upper sections would be made of rough fabric filled with helium

The rigid lower sections would hold cargo, passengers, and crew, and provide an anchor for the engines

Superblimp could carry 500 tons: equivalent to 10 MBTs or 4,000 troops and equipment

CHAPTER SEVEN

FUTURE AIRCRAFT CARRIERS

There can be few military assets that are as impressive and valuable as the aircraft carrier. Whether it is providing close air support (CAS) to ground forces or combat air patrols (CAP) to protect surface ships, the despatch of an aircraft carrier to back up diplomacy is a powerful tool in foreign policy, as was demonstrated during the 1990s in the Gulf region against Iraq.

The modern aircraft carrier is a highly sophisticated platform for operating both aircraft and helicopters in ever more demanding operational environments. This has led to more and more countries either joining or having the desire to belong to the world's growing number of carrier fleet operators.

The basic shape of the aircraft carrier has altered little since World War II. However, this is all about to change. As the benefits of carrier operations increase, the desire to build faster and more capable ships has led to many countries looking for new and innovative carrier designs. The modern demands for "stealth" and lower manpower requirements have led to a complete rethink on the design of the aircraft carrier.

The United states, the world's biggest carrier operator, is looking at smaller designs that are comparable in size to the British anti-submarine Invincible-class carriers currently in service with the Royal Navy. The current US Nimitz-class carriers are truly awesome in their

size and performance, operating over 100 fixed-wing aircraft and helicopters and carrying a crew of several thousand personnel. It is ironic that the US Navy has decided to look at smaller carriers just as the UK Royal Navy has announced its intention to procure two larger carriers each capable of operating an air wing of 50-plus aircraft. The program is known in the UK as the CV(F) project and has attracted considerable overseas interest not least because of the decision yet to be made as to what aircraft it will operate. This decision is of key importance because until it is made the design of the carrier cannot be finalized. Should it be a STOVL (Short Take-Off and Vertical Landing) or CTOL (Conventional Take-Off and Landing) design, or a mixture of both types?

The UK experience of operating mini-carriers with the Sea Harrier aircraft has inspired many other countries to adopt the concept, including Spain, Italy, and Thailand. Although It is beyond the scope of this book to look into the recent history of the carrier, it is important to understand the criteria that an operational carrier of the future will need to meet and the complex issues that have to be addressed before a navy makes the decision to procure a new carrier.

At present the USA and the UK are looking at many different innovative designs and concepts. The carrier of the future will be a quantum leap in capability over the current generation of carriers. The US CVX carrier replacement program is one of the most detailed and far reaching studies ever carried out, with nothing ruled in or out. Indeed the US has recently commissioned the giant oil rig constructor Kavaerner to carry out a detailed study into the feasibilty of building man-made islands, known as Mobile Offshore Bases (MOB) to carry aircraft and stores. In time of conflict these giant structures would be towed to a theater of operations to provide air support and docking facilities for ship and troop operations without the need to use land bases where their deployment may be politically sensitive.

The size of these MOB structures will allow the use of large capacity transport aircraft such as the Boeing C-17A Globemaster, with complete refueling and support services available. Although likely to be

▼

The five United States Navy conventionally powered aircraft carriers, such as CV-63 USS Kitty Hawk seen here, may be replaced by a future CVX design.

▼

Two large UK CV(F) Conventional Take-Off and Landing (CTOL) carriers will replace the Royal Navy's three Invincible-class short take-off and Vertical Landing (STOVL) carriers, one of which is seen here.

well protected by air and sea, these relatively static structures would be prime targets for an adversary with sophisticated ballistic missile capabilities. The disadvantages aside, there are many positive aspects to the MOB concept. Such a structure would give the US armed forces flexible operating bases around the world that could be semi-permanent in position allowing more reliable deployments to be made, without the normal political negotiations needed to allow foreign troops to operate overseas. The US in particular has found itself adopting the role of global policeman and the need for it to have reliable and effective support facilities is paramount for the success of its overseas foreign policy.

US CVX Program

The Nimitz-class carriers date back to the 1960s, yet still remain effective and flexible in adapting new technology. Some will even remain in service well into the 21st Century working alongside the new generation of US carriers. The first of these new generation carriers is due to enter service in 2013 and will incorporate much new technology in respect of command, control, communications, computers, and Intelligence (C_4I) capability and launch and recovery systems. The USA has not been involved in the design of a carrier for almost 30 years, and is currently engaged in numerous studies to identify new concepts that will keep the future carrier modern and flexible enough to engage new technologies as they develop. One example is the Navy's commitment to developing new, more efficient aircraft launch systems. It is currently looking at the use of electromagnetic rail systems that will offer faster launches than possible by the current generation of steam catapults, and will be more reliable for continuous operations.

However, the key area of debate at present is that of the air wing to be embarked on the future carrier. Nimitz-class carriers currently carry a typical combat air wing of 80 aircraft, some having specialist

Five nations operate STOVL carriers including Italy. Here is the ITS Garibaldi in the Mediterranean with HMS Invincible. Others, including China, may soon follow.

roles such as airborne early warning (AEW) and electronic warfare (EW). The new carriers will be smaller in size, and will operate with a reduced air wing. There is justification for this, as new generation aircraft such as Joint Strike Fighter (JSF) enter service. They will bring with them greater firepower effectiveness and better use of their capabilities due to Intelligence-driven operations that will become the norm with the "digitized battlespace" of the future.

The increased usage of conventional air launched cruise missiles (CALCM) and other tactical assets will also alleviate the pressure currently felt by carrier operators during long term out of area (OOA) operations. The carrier of the future will almost certainly operate uninhabited air vehicles (UAV) for roles such as reconnaissance and suppression of enemy air defenses (SEAD) missions. These air systems are expected to play an increasing part in future operations and in due course smaller, purpose-built carriers will operate UAVs as their only air system.

Having decided which its next generation of carrier-borne aircraft will be, the US Navy will also have to make a decision on the design of the carrier. This design will be either a CTOL or STOVL carrier and, since the Navy has tremendous experience with CTOL carriers and their operations, it will be cautious toward operating a STOVL carrier as it has little experience of this design. The choice of carrier propulsion will also be examined in great detail for issues of signature and reliability. The conventional choices include steam, gas turbine, or all-electric, or to opt again for nuclear power. One thing for sure is that the US Navy has a long an proud history of carrier operations and will continue to protect US interests in an effective way during the 21st Century, regardless of what carrier system it eventually deploys.

▼

The Mobile Offshore Base (MOB) concept, which could operate large aircraft such as the C-17A Globemaster III, and accommodate up to 10,000 troops and their equipment.

UK CV(F) PROGRAM

Like the USA, the UK is also currently engaged in several detailed studies to evaluate potential designs for its future CV(F) program. The current UK Invincible-class carriers will come to the end of their useful working lives around 2010 and will by then have served the Royal Navy for over 30 years.

The UK's current carriers have seen action during the Falklands and Gulf wars. In the case of the Falklands conflict, they, together with the Commando carrier HMS *Hermes* (now sold to the Indian Navy) acted as the operating bases for the Sea Harriers which provided the UK Task Force with most of its air support.

The Invincible-class carriers were originally designed for anti-submarine operations and have through constant upgrading served in roles that were never envisaged for the original design. The 1990s crisis in the Gulf, however, highlighted a number of operational shortcomings that have impacted on operational efficiency. These performance issues provided the justification for a new carrier program.

UK foreign policy is heavily dependent on maritime assets and this factor was taken into account in the Strategic Defence Review of 1998 in which the decision to procure two new 35-40,000 ton carriers was formally announced, The design of these new carriers will be dependent on the outcome of a seperate UK requirement, the Future Carrier Borne Aircraft (FCBA). This requirement could be fullfilled by the Joint Strike Fighter, F/A-18E Super Hornet, France's Rafale, a navalized version of Eurofighter Typhoon, an upgraded Sea Harrier/Harrier, or a completely new design. As seen in a previous chapter, the JSF program is a collaborative effort with the USA and is currently seen as the favored solution.

The new UK carrier will embark an air wing of some 50 aircraft during operations, and have a significant command and control (C_2) capability for OOA operations. There are many areas of common interest in both the US CVX and UK CV(F) programs, particularly with propulsion. Both countries are working together on integrated full electric propulsion (IFEP) as the favored option. The UK carrier profile options are also very similar to those of America's CVX, being either a CTOL or STOVL platform. The winner of the FCBA contest will be the deciding factor as to which carrier design the Royal Navy will operate.

FUTURE CARRIER CONCEPTS

AIR SUPPORT CATAMARAN (ASCAT)

The UK company AVPRO carried out a series of studies looking at the navy of the future and its requirements. It became apparent in the study that there are numerous countries which desire the capabilities of an aircraft carrier but cannot afford the enormous investment that operating such an asset requires. AVPRO set about designing a small craft known as an Air Support Catamaran (ASCAT) to provide a limited air support capability for low-intensity conflicts, where a ground attack, reconnaissance, or air defense capability would be desirable.

Although the concept was targeted at smaller naval operators, it became obvious that such a system would have a great benefit to larger navies where the use of a large carrier would be wasteful in terms of manpower and aircraft in small scale out of area operations, where only limited air support capability would be needed.

AVPRO is developing the uninhabited combat air vehicle (UCAV) concept for the UK Future Offensive Air System (FOAS) requirement (see Chapter Eight), and these craft will eventually provide a credible alternative to manned aircraft, as well as being suitable for operations on the ASCAT concept.

The mini-carrier concept has attracted interest throughout the world and it is conceivable that such systems will enter service in quantity during the early 21st Century, since they would be cost effective and require only minimal manpower levels.

STEALTH TRIMARAN AIRCRAFT CARRIER (STAC)

As part of the UK CV(F) program, several concepts that were fed into the original design stage pre-feasibility studies are being developed. One of these studies, the Stealth Trimaran Aircraft Carrier (STAC), created considerable interest worldwide when it was first revealed. The concept impressed the US Navy who consider that the STAC could be the carrier of the future after CVX. In the UK the Trimaran concept is being taken very seriously and the UK Defence Evaluation Research Agency (DERA) has commissioned the building of a Trimaran research vessel, known as the R V Triton. This ship will evaluate the benefits of the Trimaran form and will if successful create the necessary confidence to build a Trimaran aircraft carrier in the future as a possible successor to the CVX and CV(F) programs.

The STAC concept has a very low radar cross section (RSC), its profile being that of a small ship, making it extremely difficult to detect. The stealth aspects of the design are meticulous, with every part of the ship's design being scrutinized for maximum effect. To contribute to its low RCS, even the integrated mast on the carrier's superstructure has no exposed moving parts, while the exhaust from the ship's engines is vented through the sides of the inner and outer hulls, considerably reducing thermal signature.

▲ Air Support Catamaran (ASCAT) mini carriers could operate STOVL aircraft, helicopters and unmanned combat/reconnaissance aerial vehicles (UC/RAV) close to beachhead.

▼ A radical British design for a future aircraft carrier is the Stealth Trimaran Aircraft Carrier (STAC) which will be faster, longer, and more stable than Royal Navy CTOVL carriers.

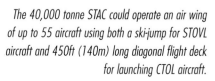

▶ The 40,000 tonne STAC could operate an air wing of up to 55 aircraft using both a ski-jump for STOVL aircraft and 450ft (140m) long diagonal flight deck for launching CTOL aircraft.

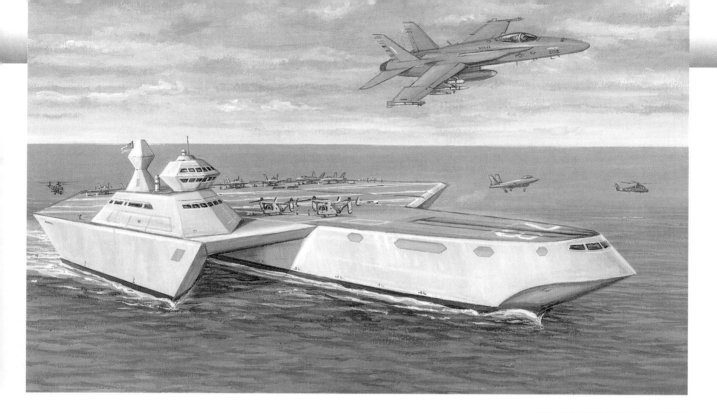

The STAC has a major advantage over conventional designs in that it can operate all types of aircraft including CTOL and STOVL designs. This capability is possible due to the STAC's unique design. Its central hull flight deck features a ski jump as currently fitted to the Invincible-class carriers, which enables aircraft like the Harrier and proposed JSF to take off from shorter flight areas. The portside flight deck is equipped with an electromagnetic rail launch system for CTOL aircraft operations which will enable aircraft such as Typhoon, Rafale, and F/A-18E to be carried. At the stern of the ship there is a rotating flight lift, known as Skyracker, for rapid re-arming and stowing of aircraft, similar in operation to automated car parking systems currently being used in Europe and Japan.

Survivability is paramount to the success of any naval operation, and the carrier is usually the best protected asset in the fleet. The STAC concept features separate landing areas which make recovery of aircraft possible even if the ship is seriously damaged. The Trimaran platform offers many advantages over conventional carriers in terms of speed and stability. It would be capable of speeds in excess of 40 knots, not currently possible with single hull carriers. This speed would enable rapid deployment to conflict areas, and make targeting of the STAC extremely difficult.

One of the main advantages of the Trimaran form is that of stability. The most dangerous part of any carrier operation is the approach and recovery of fixed-wing aircraft and helicopters due to pitching and rolling frequently experienced during operations. The Trimaran platform provides stability in high seas, making flight operations considerably safer than currently possible.

The STAC concept has generated a number of new and significant improvements in carrier design, many of which will be fed into more current requirements such as CVX and CV(F).

▲

Equipped with an electro-magnetic rail launch system and circular rotating Skyracker aircraft lift, the STAC could be a contender for the US CVX requirement.

▼

A new aircraft launching system to be used on the STAC would consist of a onetime strop mounted on a cylinder that is "fired" along a tube below the flight deck, so dispensing with heavy steam catapults..

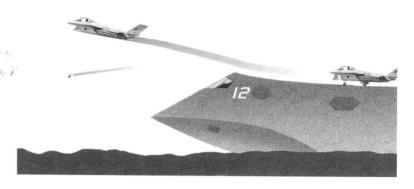

▶

A new aircraft launching system to be used on the STAC would consist of a one-time strop mounted on a cylinder that is 'fired' along a tube below the flight deck, so despensing with heavy steam catapults.

WING ASSISTED TRIMARAN (WAT)

One of the most interesting carrier concepts to be put forward recently is the Wing Assisted Trimaran (WAT) concept which is in development for commercial operations. However, the Italian consortium behind the WAT concept recognizes that it has significant military applications and one of the proposed design concepts is for a mini-aircraft carrier. The WAT concept is in a class of its own, being a cross between a wing in ground (WIG) effect vehicle (see Chapter Five) and a hydrofoil, and originally was referred to as a surface piercing wing (SPW) in ground effect vehicle. The concept has been put forward as a solution to the demands of the world's navies for faster, safer, and more economical means of rapidly deploying forces to areas of conflict, and then patrolling them in a more effective way. Designed to reach a speed of 200 knots, the WAT is the only other craft that can travel at comparable speeds to the larger WIGs.

There are, however, some doubts over its stability and safety at high speeds. The designers of the WAT feel that their concept is safer due to its revolutionary layout which consists of a traditional trimaran configuration, supporting a wing. At low speed the three hulls keep the vessel floating; when the craft operates at speeds of 35 knots or above the wing works in ground effect creating enough aerodynamic lift to support the displacement of the craft. It has fins that are submerged in water to provide maneuverability, and propulsion by means of highly powerful waterjets. The WAT combines a cross fertilization of aerodynamics and hydrodynamics and features highly sophisticated sensors to enable it to operate in sea states as high as 7 in complete safety.

The carrier version of this concept would embark a small air wing of up to three strike aircraft. A small elevator will be fitted to move the aircraft from the central body to the flight deck. Its high cruising speed would enable aircraft to launch and recover within a few feet without any assistance such as catapults and arrester cables. With the current interest in the mini-carrier concept the WAT has a lot to offer, and it will be interesting to see if it enters service in the 21st Century.

At the end of the 20th Century there were several significant carrier commissionings. In 1998 the new French nuclear-powered carrier *Charles de Gaulle* was launched. It is a CTOL carrier designed to operate an air wing of 40 Rafale and E-3 Hawkeye AEW aircraft. A second new French carrier is due in service within the next decade, but its design has yet to be decided. The French may wait to see the outcome of the US CVX and UK CV(F) requirements or even collaborate in a European carrier program.

Another significant event was the deployment of the new British Royal Navy Helicopter carrier LP(H) HMS *Ocean*, which was commissioned in 1998. This purpose-built carrier will provide the Royal Marines with air support during out of area operations, and will be a great asset to the Royal Navy as it will be capable of operating the UK's new Sea Harrier/Harrier strike force known as Joint Force 2000 (JF2000). During the new carrier's work-up period, a natural disaster struck parts of South America, and HMS *Ocean* was deployed to assist with helicopters and on-board medical facilities, illustrating just how valuable these assets are in peacetime and war.

The only other naval power to operate large CTOL aircraft carriers is Russia which struggles to maintain its first and only conventional carrier, the 40,000 ton *Admiral Kutznetsov* with an air group of 50 aircraft. These include the navalized version of the "Flanker," the Su-33, and SAR, ASW, AEW, and assault versions of the Kamov Ka-27/31 helicopters. Fitted with a ski-jump but no catapults, the carrier was one of four planned before the end of the Cold War. One was cancelled before it was built, a second was scrapped before being completed while an incomplete third, the *Varyag*, was offered to the Indian Navy in 1999 free of charge, provided that they purchased Russian aircraft as part of a defense package. The Indian Navy, which also has a requirement for a smaller carrier known as an Air Defense Ship (ADS), has up to now had to use secondhand carriers and a carrier of this quality would be a major asset.

▶

France's new nuclear-powered carrier Charles de Gaulle *uses new generation weapons such as the ASTER ship-to-air missile for point and area defense at sea.*

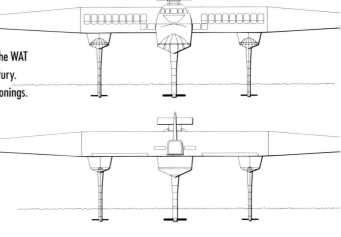

▲

The Italian Wing Assisted Trimaran (WAT) concept design to operate at speeds of up to 200mph (320kmh) could become a future mini-carrier platform for STOVLs and UAVs.

CTOL AND VTOL CARRIER AIRCRAFT

As seen in Chapter Three, both the CTOL and STOVL versions of the JSF are contenders for the UK Future Carrier-Borne Aircraft (FCBA) requirement and the Royal Navy and BAe are both heavily involved in its development. While upgraded Sea Harriers/Harriers could be used in the CTOL/STOVL roles, several other types that could fulfill short take-off but arrested landing (STOBAR) requirements include Typhoon, Rafale M, and the Super Hornet. However, a number of new FCBA concepts are being proposed by UK companies, two of which are described here. They are intended to form part of the air-to-air and air-to-ground capability of the next generation of carrier aircraft. Both vehicles allow a CTOL or VTOL variant to be built from a common airframe, the primary structural components of both variants being virtually identical, and hence they could be built on the same production tooling to allow lower unit production costs.

Both vehicles are also intended to perform the same mission. CVTOL-1 represents a more expensive, higher technical risk option but is more stealthy, can carry a greater payload, and has greater survivability because of its twin engines, than CVTOL-2. Each aircraft would be capable of performing the roles of the US Navy's F/A-18E Hornet and the Royal Navy's V/STOL Sea Harrier. However, both are much more capable aircraft in terms of performance, payload, and systems

▼
The UK's Future Carrier-Borne Aircraft (FCBA) could be an upgraded version of the BAe Sea Harrier multi-role combat aircraft which proved its worth in the 1982 Falklands War.

capability. Their role would be to provide airborne defense for the carrier and would also give a strike capability against enemy shipping or ground targets.

CVTOL-1 and -2 would both be equipped with conformally mounted LPI phased array radar with electronic beam steering. This has a number of advantages over the conventional moving flat scanner type. It conforms to the contours of the airframe and therefore eliminates the need to compromise the aerodynamics of the forebody. The multi-element phased array radar is lighter and more damage-tolerant than conventional radars. Failure of a single element does not result in a total loss of radar coverage, which degrades only gradually with element failures. Both concepts share imaging infra-red and low-light TV (IRLLTV) which provide passive target detection and tracking both night and day in all weathers.

The concepts use optical signaling of the flying controls which is more stealthy than electrical signaling or fly-by-wire (FWB) since no electro-magnetic (EM) fields are produced by the passage of light through fiber optic cable, unlike electrical cables. An optical databus has greater resistance to the EM pulse produced by the detonation of thermonuclear weapons, thus giving added protection to onboard systems. The CVTOL's high-speed, large bandwidth, digital datalink allows secure transmission of data to and from the aircraft from several sources including J-STARS and AWACS. Data is fed directly to the onboard computers to provide improved awareness of enemy forces or to allow the aircraft to target enemy aircraft without using their own radar which may betray their position. In addition. it is also possible for the CVTOL aircraft to extend the reach of AWACS or J-STARS by relaying data back from their own sensors via the datalink. The datalink also allows two or more CVTOL aircraft to pool their resources, thus enabling one to act as a stand-off target acquisition and guidance system for a number of allied aircraft if they are datalinked together.

The twin-engine CVTOL-1 has a blended double-delta fuselage with an internal weapons bay which not only gives a low RCS but produces large amounts of vortex lift at high angles of attack, enhancing maneuverability. The large plan area presented by the fuselage allows the aircraft to generate large amounts of fountain lift when operating as a VTOL aircraft. This is generated by the efflux from the lift nozzles being reflected by a solid surface—carrier flight deck or runway—and being brought to stagnation on the lower surface of the vehicle. This results in a higher-than-atmospheric pressure on the underneath of the aircraft, thereby producing a vertical force, or lift.

▲

A leading contender for the FCBA is the naval version of Rafale which entered service on the French carrier Charles de Gaulle in 1999.

▼

The Super Hornet, with a 40 percent greater range than the F/A-18C, and capable of carrying 20 percent more external stores from "dumb" bombs to Stand-Off Land Attack Missile Expanded Response (SLAMER), is another FCBA contender.

Another advanced carrier-borne multi-role fighter to enter service in 1999 was the Boeing F/A-18E Super Hornet which began to replace the F-14 Tomcat.

▲

A navalized version of the Eurofighter 2000 Typhoon, capable of short take-off but arrested landings, could be in contention for the UK's Future Carrier-Borne Aircraft (FCBA) role.

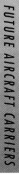

FUTURE AIRCRAFT CARRIERS

Among the most novel features of the CVTOL-1's design are its all-moving wingtips which eliminate control reversal. At high supersonic speed, conventional ailerons cause the wing to twist in such a way that it opposes the desired rolling motion. This happens because the load on the aileron acts aft of the wing's flexural axis and hence causes it to twist. By contrast, the load on the all-moving wingtips acts close to the wing's flexural axis. With careful flight control systems (FCS) programming the tips on the aft wing can be made to deflect downwards as the aircraft's angle of attack increases, which keeps the flow over the tips attached and allows the control effect to remain even when the flow over the rest of the aircraft has separated. The tips on both forward and aft wings can be deflected upwards to act as high-lift devices and hence improve take-off and landing performance for the CTOL version.

CVTOL uses two-dimensional thrust vectoring nozzles which when deflected symmetrically are used to augment pitch authority, while assymmetric deflection augments roll authority. Nozzle deflection is handled automatically by the FCS according to the pilot's stick inputs and information obtained from the aircraft's air-data sensors. The trailing edges of the nozzles are aligned with the edges on the remainder of the wing trailing edge which scatters incident radar energy in only two directions, thereby reducing the probability of enemy detection.

The more conventional design of the CVTOL-2 reflects the resurgence of interest in forward-swept wing (FSW) design that was adopted by Sukhoi for its S-37 Berkut which surprised Western observers when it made its first appearance in September 1997. There are several advantages in the FSW concept. The forward-swept wing stalls first at the root and spreads outboard with increasing angle of attack. This means that compared to a straight or aft swept wing it has vastly superior high angle of attack roll control, which is obviously an advantage in high "g" dogfight situations. The wing leading edge root extensions (LERX) also generate a large amount of vortex lift at high angles of attack, thus enhancing the aircraft's maneuverability.

FSW features leading edge slats, inboard trailing edge flaps and outboard flaperons which can be used to improve maneuverability, reduce landing speed—

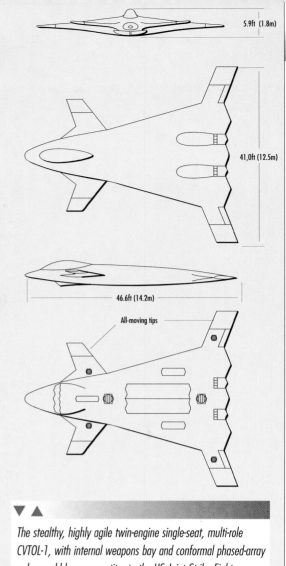

5.9ft (1.8m)

41.0ft (12.5m)

46.6ft (14.2m)

All-moving tips

▼ ▲

The stealthy, highly agile twin-engine single-seat, multi-role CVTOL-1, with internal weapons bay and conformal phased-array radar, could be a competitor to the US Joint Strike Fighter.

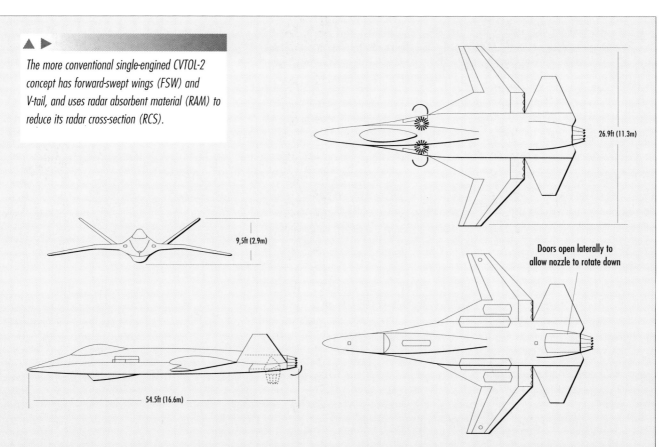

The more conventional single-engined CVTOL-2 concept has forward-swept wings (FSW) and V-tail, and uses radar absorbent material (RAM) to reduce its radar cross-section (RCS).

26.9ft (11.3m)

9,5ft (2.9m)

Doors open laterally to allow nozzle to rotate down

54.5ft (16.6m)

FUTURE AIRCRAFT CARRIERS

113

particularly important for CTOL carrier operation—and also supersonic wavedrag by reducing the wing's camber. Although the inboard trailing edge flaps butt to the fuselage at right angles, which is not desirable for low RCS, they have radar absorbent material (RAM) inserts to minimize the reflected energy. The main reason for having flaps with the hinge at 90 degrees to the fuselage is that they have the greatest lift increment per unit deflection when compared to flaps with a swept hinge line. If CTOL carrier operations are envisaged then it is important to have the most effective flaps possible.

CVTOL-2 also features a V-tail that eliminates tailfin/rudder surfaces. This results in a lighter and less expensive solution to pitch and yaw control than a conventional tailplane-and-fin. A V-tail is more stealthy than a conventional tailplane-and-fin configuration because in the latter these surfaces are usually at or close to 90 degrees to each other, resulting in a strong specular reflection component of incident radar energy and hence making the aircraft easier to detect. V-tails on CVTOL-2 are at an angle of significantly greater than 90 degrees to each other and therefore the specular reflection component is eliminated.

The jetpipe is elliptical which means that, when cut at a specific angle, a circular cross-section is formed that allows a number of segments of the jetpipe to be rotated relative to each other. By using a number of segments and the correct cut angle, the jetpipe can rotate through 90 degrees to allow the engine thrust to be used for lift during VTOL operation without significantly affecting the engine's performance in forward flight. However, the elliptical jetpipe system would result in a heavier engine, but this would be true for any VTOL engine when compared to a non-CTOL type.

▶

Lockheed Martin is also exploring the concept of advanced assault ships to operate the CTOL and STOL unmanned naval strike aircraft for the US Navy.

Affordable mini-carriers dedicated to operating VTOL
UC/RAVs from shallow waters in out of area (OOA)
deployments are being considered by the Royal Navy.

CHAPTER EIGHT

UK FUTURE AIRCRAFT PROGRAMS

During the next decade, the United Kingdom's Ministry of Defence (MoD) has to replace a number of the RAF's frontline aircraft to meet the ever changing requirements of the 21st Century. Apart from Eurofighter, which will replace the RAF Tornado F.3 ADV air defense fighter and the Jaguar attack aircraft, the most important program is the Royal Air Force's Future Offensive Air System (FOAS) concept which has been conceived to replace the UK Tornado GR.4 multi-role strike and reconnaissance aircraft at the end of its service life around the year 2017. The FOAS concept rules nothing in and nothing out, and it will greatly enhance the RAF's commitment to NATO's operational capability for the next 50 years.

One proposal for the FOAS requirement is the modification of manned multi-role aircraft such as the Tornado or, as here, the F-16 to an unmanned combat aerial vehicle (UCAV).

The British Future Offensive Air System (FOAS) program will replace the RAF's multi-role strike fighter, the Tornado GR.1/4, seen carrying ALARM anti-radar missiles in its suppression of enemy defense (SEAD) role.

The solution is likely to be a mixed force of air vehicles—manned aircraft, unmanned air vehicles (UAV), and conventionally armed air-launched cruise missiles (CALCM)—operating in the future "digitized battlespace." Although primarily a UK project, the FOAS concept is likely to be viewed with close interest by other NATO members, not only other Tornado IDS operators such as Germany and Italy, since they face similar operational demands around the same period. British Aerospace (BAe), which was awarded a £35 million ($57.5 million) contract in 1998 for a FOAS feasibility study into new and emerging technologies, sees the program as a springboard for further collaboration in Europe and has already benefited from an Anglo-French agreement for a co-operative technology demonstration program for future weapon systems.

FOAS platforms will need to operate deep behind enemy lines with minimal risk, and with greater operational flexibility than is currently possible. As we shall see in detail in the following chapter, the use of unmanned combat air vehicles (UCAV) now being developed in the USA and UK will become of growing importance within the next decade for such roles as suppression of enemy defenses (SEAD) and as arsenal support aircraft, both missions currently undertaken by NATO Tornado IDS aircraft.

One FOAS proposal is to modify existing Tornado airframes into unmanned aircraft flown in formations with a manned "mother" airplane. Using voice recognition and advanced radar technology, these robojets would be directed to attack programmed targets by the "backseater" of an accompanying manned Tornado fighter-bomber. By removing heavy cockpit equipment and the two-man crew, more fuel and weapons can be carried, and the Tornado's computerized engine control system would make it ideally suited to conversion into an unmanned vehicle.

In whatever form it takes, FOAS will benefit from the development and introduction of a new class of weaponry, some of which may be those designed for the Joint Strike Fighter (JSF). An example is Proteus, a projected modular multi-role (MRR) weapon concept designed to perform multiple profiles using a common airframe fitted with interchangeable weapon modules. This will significantly reduce development costs and provide improved tactical flexibility for strike aircraft and attack helicopter operations.

FOAS-1

Two of the FOAS concepts for manned platforms that MoD planners will have to examine in the near future are state-of-the-art vehicles which would use extensively automated and integrated on-board systems. The single-seat FOAS-1 has been conceptualized assuming greater financial and engineering resources than FOAS-2, which has a pilot and a weapons systems officer (WSO), to allow development of the onboard systems to a greater extent such that the roles of both pilot and WSO can be performed by a single crew.

The purpose of the FOAS program is essentially to develop a successor to the Tornado IDS and replace this aircraft in the deep penetration strike role, operating mainly at medium to high altitude, including weapons delivery phases. It would avoid detection due to stealthy configurations and the use of an automatic emissions control (EMCON) system as fitted to the Lockheed-Martin F-22 Raptor. The FOAS-1 aircraft concept would be capable of sustained Mach 2 supercruise (i.e., without afterburner) and a high Mach 2+ dash speed. High speed reduces the amount of time that the aircraft is exposed to enemy defense systems and makes enemy interception more difficult. The aircraft would be equipped with a retractable refueling probe to increase the range and hence its combat effectiveness.

In addition to its high and medium altitude missions, the aircraft has also been designed to be effective at low altitudes. The slender delta configuration of FOAS-1 has a low-lift curve slope and is therefore less responsive to gusts and ground effects than high aspect ratio aircraft with low wing loadings. This is an important consideration for high-speed low-level attacks, as the uncommanded aircraft movements due to gusts can prevent accurate weapons aim and release and are uncomfortable, hence distracting, for the crew.

The configuration and performance capabilities of both aircraft concepts are also well suited to the reconnaissance role. Aircraft on a strike mission would be datalinked together and back to an AWACS aircraft to provide real-time images for battlefield commanders. These images could be used to update ingress routes to the target for a following wave of aircraft, for example if a previously undetected SAM battery had been encountered by the first wave.

▼

BAe's vision of future air wars includes several FOAS assets, including manned and unmanned combat and reconnaissance aircraft and CALMs launched from the RAF's Future Transport Aircraft (FTA).

The aircraft would be capable of carrying approximately 17,650lb (8,000kg) of ordnance in a single internal weapons bay. The unrefueled combat radius would be 1,850 miles (3,000km) with a full weapons load. As the aircraft's role is deep penetration strike it is of the utmost importance that all its weapons carried hit their target. Therefore, weapons capable of surgical precision would be used. The FOAS-1 concept aircraft could be capable of carrying four Storm Shadows, and six ALARMs, or four AGM-65 Mavericks, while up to six GBU-16 and -24 laser guided bombs (LGB) could also be carried. The internal weapons bay of both concepts has been designed to allow safe launch of the weapons at high speed. However, internal weapons bays usually suffer from extreme turbulence due to flow separation at the forward edge of the bay. This turbulence can make released weapons become unstable before they have cleared the aircraft structure, which poses a danger to the launch aircraft and can prevent target destruction if the weapon's flight control system cannot recover control of the weapon and guide it to the target. This cavity-flow problem can be lessened by flying at a lower speed but this is clearly not desirable since it exposes the aircraft and its crew to increased risk. For this reason, a way has been found to eliminate the cavity flow problem. An additional top surface of the bay translates downward with the stores and seals the cavity, while at the same time lowering the stores into the smooth external flow underneath the vehicle.

The advanced design features of FOAS-1 include anhedral canards to augment pitch control and reduce the excessive dihedral effect of the highly swept main wing and large tail surfaces. The canards can be used in conjunction with the tail surfaces to minimize gust response during low-level high-speed flight. They are both deflected in the same direction by the FCS which can be set to cancel out undemanded vertical accelerations. This is a similar but improved version of the low altitude ride control (LARC) system proven by the Rockwell B-1B Lancer.

Control surfaces are positioned as far from the vehicle's center of gravity as possible to give the control forces the maximum possible moment arm to increase their effectiveness and

▲ ▼

How the manned and unmanned strike packages might work are graphically depicted in these scenarios from (above) AVPRO UK and (below) Lockheed Martin, emphasizing how the force mix would capitalize on the strengths of each vehicle type.

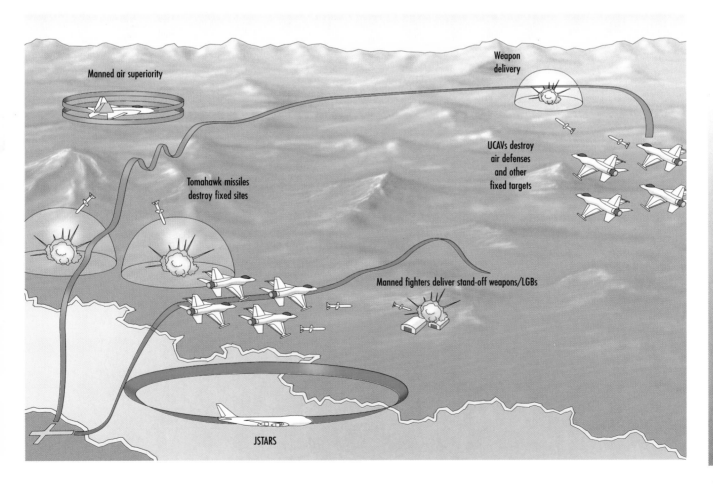

Manned air superiority

Weapon delivery

Tomahawk missiles destroy fixed sites

UCAVs destroy air defenses and other fixed targets

Manned fighters deliver stand-off weapons/LGBs

JSTARS

make the aircraft more maneuverable. The large tail surfaces combine the functions of aileron, elevator, and rudder which eliminates the need for separate surfaces and therefore reduces RCS and wetted area, hence reducing drag.

Positioned above and behind the cockpit is the dorsal inlet. As the aircraft is intended mainly to operate at medium to high altitudes, the primary radar threat will be from below; therefore, positioning the inlet, a large RCS contributor, on the upper surface and out of sight of the enemy radar reduces the chances of detection.

The front fuselage acts as the primary shock ramp. Dorsal-mounted inlets are uncommon due to the fact that they will be in a region of separated airflow at high angles of attack (AoA) on most conventionally configured aircraft. However, on a slender delta, the central portion of the wing has attached flow even at high AoA. This was proved in the 1960s by the Handley-Page HP 115 slender delta research aircraft which had a dorsally mounted engine/intake combination and experienced no inlet problems even at angles of attack up to 45 degrees. As the aircraft is intended to operate at low AoA the RCS advantage of this location outweighs the aerodynamic concern.

FOAS-1's radar is a conformally mounted phased array type. Conformal mounting means that the separate array elements are mounted such that they conform to the shape of the nose contours. Phased array radars feature electronic beam steering which gives better track and scan performance than conventional mechanically steered radars. The fixed portion of the tails have radar arrays in them to give a sidescan capability. This allows the aircraft to scan a greater area of enemy territory which in turn allows greater awareness of the enemy's location and numbers to give the pilot improved situation awareness (SA). The aircraft can feed this data back to base to be used for reconnaissance purposes.

A high capacity datalink will allow the aircraft to send and receive large amounts of data from other FOAS or AWACS aircraft. For example, the FOAS aircraft could receive data regarding enemy aircraft threats from a friendly AWACS which would allow it to turn off its own radar thereby reducing the chances of enemy detection and increasing the probability of mission success. Alternatively, the data link could be used to assign targets to UCAVs flying far ahead of the FOAS aircraft to clear a path through enemy air defenses by engaging enemy fighters or SAM systems.

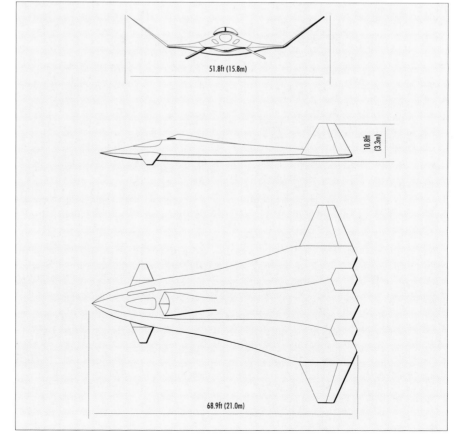

▲ ▲ ▶

AVPRO's FOAS-1 concept could be produced in single-seat manned or unmanned versions, both of which would heavily rely on speed, maneuverability, stealth, advanced on-board systems, and new generation "smart" weapons.

51.8ft (15.8m)

10.8ft (3.3m)

68.9ft (21.0m)

◀

A small, stealthy, single-seat, twin-engined strike aircraft representing a BAe concept of the manned element of FOAS.

FOAS-2

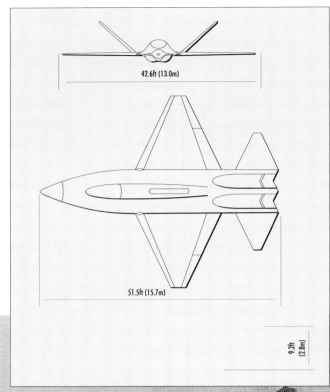

The configuration of FOAS-2 features a large wing area giving maximum lifting capacity, allowing a large fuel and ordnance load to be carried. The wing is equipped with trailing edge fowler flaps and flaperons to give good field performance at high weights and is also equipped with full span leading edge flaps which further improve field performance and enhance maneuverability.

A trapezoidal wing configuration helps maintain a low RCS and the sweep of the leading and trailing edges reflects radar energy from hostile radar systems, especially when the aircraft is viewed head on— the typical orientation when attacking an enemy position—or directly from the rear. The trapeziodal wing is fixed-geometry, which saves weight, complexity, and cost compared to a variable-geometry type. It also allows smooth variation of the cross-sectional area of the aircraft to reduce wave drag at supersonic speeds and hence increases range and endurance for a given fuel and weapons load.

The remaining surfaces, rudderons, exhausts, and beaver tail have been aligned with the wing leading and trailing edges, which dumps incident radar

The more conventional two-seat, twin-engined FOAS-2 could carry a larger weapon payload with a greater radius of combat than FOAS-1 and would act as a package leader.

One of the primary roles of the unmanned element of FOAS, such as the stealthy AVPRO Archangel UCAV, would be SEAD, clearing the way for manned strike aircraft.

energy in two principal directions thus further reducing the probability of enemy tracking. The blended wing/body junction provides good structural depth at the wing root which is the most highly loaded part of the wing structure. The structural depth afforded by the blending makes the wing stiffer and reduces the stress in the structure, giving the airframe a longer fatigue life and hence longer aircraft usage life than a more highly loaded structure.

The wing is smoothly blended into the fuselage to reduce interference drag due to the wing/body junction. This improves the aerodynamic efficiency of the aircraft, which in turn improves its operational effectiveness through greater range and endurance, or the requirement of less fuel, which results in lower life cycle cost.

Chines at the leading edge of the wing root extension provoke orderly flow separation and vortex formation, providing a useful increase in maximum lift and maneuver capability especially at high angles of attack such as may occur when maneuvering to egress the target area after a bombing run or to evade an enemy interceptor. The blended fuselage provides the space to allow side-by-side seating for pilot and the WSO to improve crew co-operation, simplify the internal structure of the aircraft, and allow greater volume for fuel/avionics. However, drop tanks which increase the RCS could be carried if long-range missions were to be performed but they would be dropped before entering areas of high radar threat.

A relatively wide front fuselage has been designed to allow a large radar antenna to be carried in the nose which would have narrower beam widths than those of smaller diameter antenna. This would increase scan resolution for accurate ground mapping from a greater range, giving the crew longer to assess threats close to the target.

Airborne STand-Off Radar (ASTOR)

Often described as a "poor man's J-STARS" (Joint Surveillance and Target Attack Radar system), which has proved an invaluable, but expensive, asset in both large and small conflicts such as the Gulf War and the Bosnian conflict, ASTOR fills a glaring gap in the RAF's ability to monitor the 21st Century's 24-hour all-weather "digitized battlespace."

Since the mid-1970s, the RAF's only dedicated long-range high-altitude reconnaissance assets have been a handful of veteran Canberra PR.9 photo-reconnaissance aircraft and even fewer Nimrod R.1 Electronic Intelligence (ELINT) gathering aircraft. With a proliferation of "local" conflicts that left unchecked could flare into much larger wars that would require a response from the United Nations or NATO, technologically advanced airborne surveillance systems are of growing importance. In the Cold War era, intelligence of known and predicted battlefields and targets was routinely updated and the results fed into NATO databases. In the New World Order, every Third World country is a potential battleground, and therefore the results of surveillance, intelligence gathering, and target acquisition have to be downloaded to commanders in real-time before any ground troops can be committed to a hostile area.

In the mid-1980s, a highly classified research program into synthetic aperture radar (SAR) was conducted by the UK MoD which took the initiative to combine the high resolution SAR with a moving target indicator (MTI) radar. MTI is an airborne radar that can detect, track and isolate high-value ground targets against land clutter. Dual-mode SAR/MTI radar was originally developed in the United States for use in the upgraded U-2S and Northrop Grumman E-8 J-STARS, first deployed in Operation *Desert Storm* in the Gulf War of 1991.

In 1997, the MoD issued an Invitation to Tender for a £750 million ($1,200 million) contract for five airborne platforms, six mobile tactical ground stations (TGS), and two operational level ground stations

▶

In the Raytheon/Bombardier STand-Off Radar (ASTOR) concept the radar on board the Global Express identifies and quantifies hostile forces (1) and transfers the information via secure data links to the Astor ground stations. On board the aircraft (2) the data is developed into visual images and transferred to similar image exploitation equipment on the ground. The ground station can transmit the data to other areas (3) via secure data links, SATCOM and ground networks. The air segment can also operate independently of the ground stations, disseminating data via its communications systems.

▼

In order to provide future battle commanders with a comprehensive intellgence overview, airborne stand-off radar platforms, such as the Raytheon/Bombardier ASTOR, will be vital.

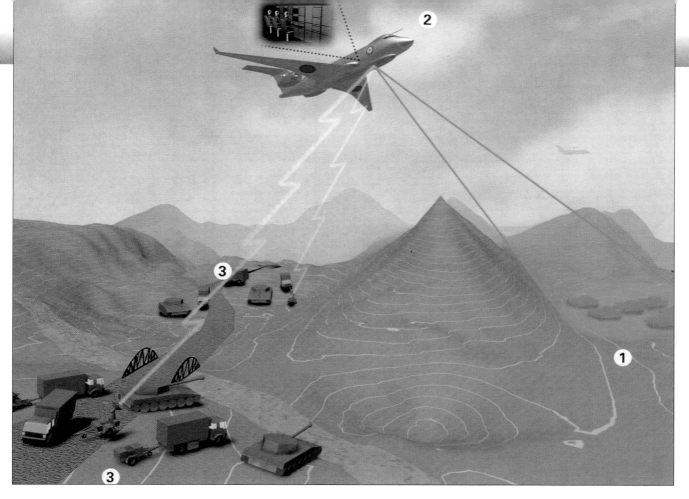

Cutaway of the ASTOR concept proposed by the
Northrop Grumman/BAe "Wizard Team."

(OLGS) to three approved ASTOR teams. Lockheed-Martin's TeamASTOR comprises Racal, Logica, and Marshalls, and will use the Gulfstream GV airframe, while the platform for the Raytheon team which includes New British Aerospace, formerly Marconi, will be based on the Bombardier Global Express corporate wide-body. A strong late contender was Northrop-Grumman, supported by BAe and Gulfstream, which offered its radar technology insertion program (RTIP), a recently declassified "black" project developed for the J-STARS upgrade. Known as "Wizard," the sensor considerably enhances the MTI with use of RTIP technology, enabling coherent tracking of multiple targets such as a Scud launchers traveling on public roads through civilian traffic, in all weathers, and has the benefit of an instant replay capability.

ASTOR will be capable of sharing its intelligence with other airborne platforms including the RAF E-3 Sentry and Nimrod R.1, as well as downloading to ground stations, and supporting three levels of

▼

An RAF ASTOR aircraft on station over enemy territory for long periods could be protected by Archangel UCAVs armed with advanced air-to-air missiles.

Army and RAF commands within the theater's Joint Force Air and Land Control Centers (JFACC/JFLCC). If the Northrop-Grumman team is selected, the "Wizard" system may be compatible with J-STARS and the US Army's U-2S ground stations using its enhanced tactical radar correlator (ETRAC) system. This system is also being offered to NATO as a platform to operate alongside its E-3 Sentry fleet.

Within a week of the end of NATO's Operation *Allied Force*, the UK Ministry of Defence announced that it had selected the Raytheon team for the RAF's ASTOR system. A new unit will be formed in 2005 at RAF Waddington which will become the service's surveillance center, and the ASTOR aircraft will operate alongside the RAF's Sentry AEW.1, Nimrod R.1, and Canberra PR.9 squadrons.

However, should NATO also choose the Raytheon ASTOR systems, US funding for the "Wizard" system could be withdrawn. The stakes in providing battle commanders with a more complete intelligence picture are still high for both the operator and supplier.

▼

A new generation of weapons such as Proteus, a Modular Multi-Role (MMR) stand-off airframe fitted with changeable weapon modules, could be launched from manned and unmanned aircraft.

Future Transport Aircraft (FTA)

Another of the most important projects aimed at NATO for the 21st Century is the seven member nations' (UK, France, Germany, Italy, Spain, Belgium, and Turkey) requirement for a new tactical transport aircraft to replace the C-130 Hercules/C-160 Transall. However, the program has been marked by numerous twists and turns since it was originally announced as Europe's Future Large Aircraft (FLA) by the Euroflag Group comprising Airbus, DASA, CASA, BAe, TUSAS, and Gosselies of Belgium in the early 1990s.

FLA was largely prompted by lack of the Coalition's heavy lift capabilities during the Gulf War, particularly when speed of reaction was vital in the *Desert Shield* build-up phase. Two concepts were initially offered by the Euroflag Group, both wide-bodied designs with shoulder-mounted swept wings — one powered by four advanced turbo-props and the other by four state-of-the-art turbofans. However, early in the 1990s, the German aerospace company DASA decided to break ranks and offer the larger Ukranian Antonov An-70, which first flew in 1994, as an alternative FLA contender.

The position was further complicated by the RAF issuing its own requirement for a Future Transport Aircraft (FTA) in 1998 for which FLA may be a potential candidate. At the same the UK Ministry of Defence recognized that its target in-service date for the FTA of 2005, when the remainder of the RAF's elderly and overworked C-130K Hercules fleet are due for retirement, was not realistic.

It therefore issued a Short Term Strategic Airlift (STSA) requirement in October 1998 which would act as a shortfall solution. Invitations for Tender were issued for four aircraft capable of carrying 1,400 tons of equipment to any conflict zone worldwide within seven days. The aircraft must have an unrefueled range of 3,200 miles (5,150km) and be able to carry WAH-64 Apache, Chinook, and Puma helicopters, the Rapier SAM system, the Warrior Mechanized Combat Vehicle (MCV), and the British Army's Multiple-Launch Rocket System (MRLS) which was deployed for the first time in the Gulf War. Although the original plan was to purchase four STSA aircraft required to be in service by mid-2001, this was later amended to

An unlikely contender for the RAF's Short Term Strategic Airlift (STSA) requirement was the heavyweight Ukrainian An-124 Ruslan fitted with Rolls-Royce turbofan engines.

The Royal Air Force's Future Transport Aircraft (FTA) requirement was almost designed around the USAF long-range and in-theater C-17A Globemaster III heavy cargo airlifter.

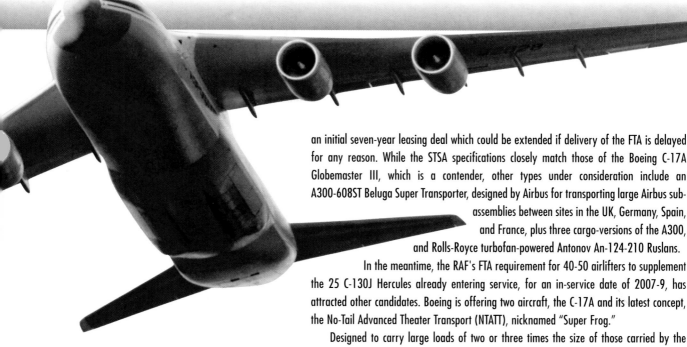

an initial seven-year leasing deal which could be extended if delivery of the FTA is delayed for any reason. While the STSA specifications closely match those of the Boeing C-17A Globemaster III, which is a contender, other types under consideration include an A300-608ST Beluga Super Transporter, designed by Airbus for transporting large Airbus sub-assemblies between sites in the UK, Germany, Spain, and France, plus three cargo-versions of the A300, and Rolls-Royce turbofan-powered Antonov An-124-210 Ruslans.

In the meantime, the RAF's FTA requirement for 40-50 airlifters to supplement the 25 C-130J Hercules already entering service, for an in-service date of 2007-9, has attracted other candidates. Boeing is offering two aircraft, the C-17A and its latest concept, the No-Tail Advanced Theater Transport (NTATT), nicknamed "Super Frog."

Designed to carry large loads of two or three times the size of those carried by the C-130J, the "Super Frog" utilizes a tilt-wing to improve short take-off field performance which will enable it to land on runways as short as 600ft (182m) at a speed of only 50 knots. As Boeing is already teamed with BAe for the STSA bid, the two companies may form a partnership to promote the 'Super Frog' to compete for the European FTA airlifter project.

A consortium of several German aerospace companies continues to back a NATO spec development of the An-70, known as the An-7X or Medium Transport Aircraft (MTA). However, in early 1999, Airbus officially entered the military market by unveiling the

The main contender for a European air forces' requirement for a common tactical airlifter/tanker, previously the Future Large Aircraft (FLA), is now the the Airbus A400M.

A400M military transport. Formerly FLA, the Airbus's new designation denotes that the strategic aircraft is the first of a new series of military transports to complement its existing range of successful Airbus commercial airliners. The A400M will be the only aircraft that fully meets the European Staff Requirement (ESR) for a future military airlifter which represents the harmonized view of the seven relevant NATO air forces including that of Germany, of the design targets for their next generation of military transport aircraft. The requirements include a two-crew "glass cockpit" plus one or more loadmasters to be accommodated in an independent work station to operate, load, and unload the pressurized cargo deck. With Lockheed-Martin expressing interest in joining the European airlifter project (which could also be a contender for the USAF's C-141 Starlifter replacement, although the US company has already proposed an innovative Joint-Wing tanker/transport concept which does away with a vertical tail) there is all to play for on the future

▲

Europe's A400M concept for turboprop-powered, swept-wing tactical aircraft is pitched between the C-130 and C-17 in performance and load carrying capability.

▼

AVPRO's Advanced Future Airlift concept resembles Boeing's short take-off and landing (STOL) tilt-wing No-Tail Advanced Theater Transport (NTATT) known as "Super Frog."

Although 64 C-141C Starlifters were upgraded with "glass cockpits" in 1999, the aging strategic transport which entered service in 1965 will have to be replaced in 2015.

One of the more radical C-141 replacement designs is Lockheed-Martin's Joined-Wing (JW) transport/tanker which has no vertical tail and rear-mounted turbofans.

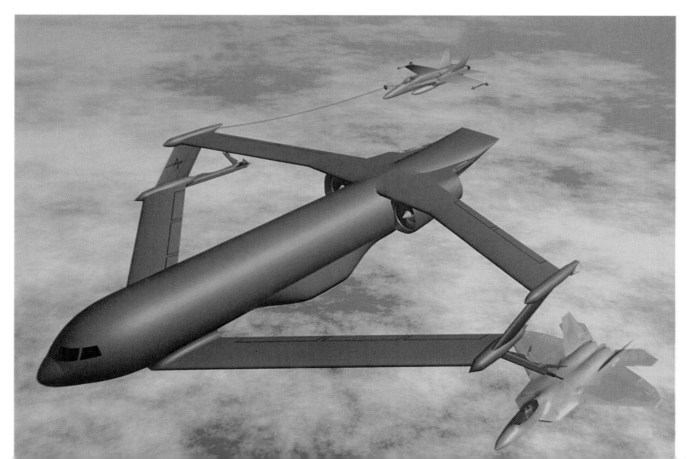

SKY ROBOTS

For many military analysts, the future of military air power will put heavy emphasis on remotely piloted aircraft, both the unmanned reconnaissance aerial vehicle (URAV) and, more controversially, the unmanned combat aerial vehicle (UCAV).

Neither is a new concept. UCAVs were some of the first "black" projects dating back to World War I. Americans Dr Peter Cooper and Elmer A. Sperry invented the automatic gyroscopic stabilizer and carried out tests with their first "aerial torpedoes" at Long Island, New York, in December 1917. They used a converted US Navy Curtiss N-9 biplane trainer powered by a 40hp engine and capable of carrying a 300lb (135kg) bomb load for 50 miles (80km). A more sophisticated unmanned aircraft was designed by Charles F. Kettering of Delco, later General Motors. Known as the "Kettering Bug," it could also carry a 300lb bomb load over short distances.

However, it was not until the next world war that the unmanned "flying bomb" concept was developed into a very efficient "terror" weapon. Germany's first secret weapon, the Fieseler Fi-103, better known as the V-1 "Revenge Weapon," was a pulse-jet-powered aircraft carrying a 2,000lb (907kg) warhead designed to be launched from a ground ramp or from an aircraft. It could cruise at 400mph (645kmh) and be pre-programmed to fly 100-150 miles (160-240km) before its engine cut out and it would fall vertically on to its random target. Nearly 6,000 V-1s fell on British cities between June 1944 and January 1945, killing more than 900 people, mostly civilians.

The highly advanced V-1 was used to develop the United States' post-war missile and UAV programs, the most successful of which was the Ryan Firebee family. Designed originally as an unmanned target drone, the Firebee was developed into a high- and low-altitude surveillance and electronic intelligence (ELINT) UAV during the

▶ *With its ability to pull high "g," the highly maneuverable USAF BQM-34F Firebee fighter UAV could outfly the latest F-15/-16 fighters. One named "Old Red" survived 82 dogfights.*

▶ *The Ryan Firebee was developed into a successful series of high and low level surveillance UAVs during the Vietnam War and later UCAVs armed with Maverick and Stubby Hobo air-to-ground missiles.*

▼ *The first unmanned "flying bomb," Germany's V-1 "Doodlebug" wreaked havoc over southern England in 1944 when 6,000 of them fell on major British cities, indiscriminately killing almost 1,000 people.*

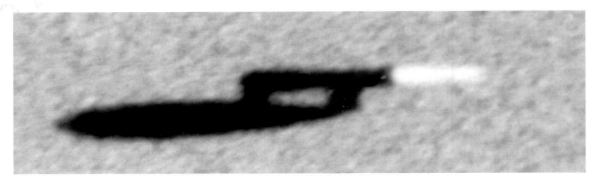

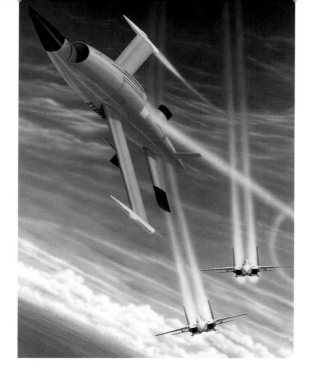

Vietnam War under the code-name "Lightning Bug."

Under another "black" program of the mid-1970s, the Firebee became the first turbojet-powered UCAV when it dropped bombs and launched missiles. Trials were carried out with an armed version of the Firebee, known as Pathfinder, fitted with laser designator and low-light TV (LLTV) cameras in the nose to acquire targets for a variety of air-to-ground weapons ranging from Mk 82 "iron" bombs to Maverick air-to-ground missiles. Guided by operators in its "mother" launch plane, a DC-130 Hercules, the Pathfinder Firebees were able not only to find their targets but to hit them with some accuracy. However, the end of the war in Vietnam also spelt the end of the Firebee.

Other "black" unmanned programs that were spawned by the Southeast Asia conflict were the Mach 3 D-21 reconnaissance drone, which suffered from being in front of the then-known technology, and the ultra-secret Teledyne Ryan Model 154 Compass Arrow, the first high-altitude reconnaissance UAV to have contoured structural shapes that shadowed engine intakes and exhaust ducts with radiation absorbing material (RAM) to minimize its RCS. "Stealth" had been discovered, but it would be another 20 years before stealthy UAVs were back in fashion.

Although small piston-engined surveillance and target acquisition UAVs were developed by Israel in the 1970s and acquired by US forces for use during the Gulf War in 1991, it was the Defense Advanced Research Projects Agency (DARPA) Tier project that introduced a new generation of UAVs which would push known technologies to their practical limits. The first of the USAF's "dream team" of high-tech UAVs was the General Dynamics Predator, developed from a CIA "black" program, the GNAT 750. Officially known as Tier II Medium-Altitude Endurance (MAE) UAV, Predator first flew in June 1995. A year later it was flown operationally over Bosnia in support of the International Force (IFOR) by the USAF's 11th Reconnaissance Squadron (RS) based at Indian Springs in the Nellis complex in the Nevada Desert.

Predator is a conventional design built largely of composite materials and powered by a 44hp pusher piston engine, although it has an endurance of 40 hours at a cruising altitude of 25,000ft (7,620m) carrying a 450lb (204kg) sensor payload. Its larger cousin, the Teledyne Ryan Global Hawk, or Tier II Plus High-Altitude Endurance (HAE) surveillance UAV, which first flew in 1998, is powered by "low burn"

Developed from the GNAT 750 operated by the CIA over Bosnia in 1995, the Predator medium altitude endurance (MAE) UAV flew surveillance missions over the former Yugoslavia, with USAF 11th Reconnaissance Squadron.

The first successful UCAV was the TDR-1, 50 of which were launched by the US Navy Special Task Air Group One (STAG-1) against Japanese shipping around Guadalcanal in late 1944, scoring a 50 percent hit rate with 2,000lb (905kg) bombs.

7,050lb (3,198kg) st Rolls Royce Allison turbofan. The performance of this large UAV— it has a wingspan of 116ft (35.5m)—is impressive. It can remain airborne for more than 40 hours, cruise at 375mph (603kmh) at 65,000ft (1,980m), and has a maximum range of 14,500 miles (23,335km). Its 2,000lb (908kg) payload comprises electro-optical (EO), infra-red (IR), synthetic aperture radar (SAR) sensors, active and passive electronic support measures (ESM), on-board data storage, and real-time transmission. Able to survey an entire country the size of Switzerland in 42 hours, Global Hawk is viewed as an unmanned replacement for the remarkable U-2 "Dragon Lady," an unmanned conversion of which has been proposed by the Lockheed "Skunk Works."

The third, and most unconventional of the three Tier project UAVs was the Lockheed Martin/Boeing futuristic DarkStar. Powered by a Williams FJ-44 turbofan, the stealthy surveillance UAV was designed to loiter unseen over a battlefield for up to eight hours. DarkStar first flew in March 1996, but due to a software problem the prototype was detroyed in a crash only a month later. Although a second DarkStar flew successfully in 1998, the program was cancelled a year later because of budget restrictions, but much of its advanced sensor technology was rumored to have been transferred to another "black" project.

▲

The futuristic Lockheed Martin/Boeing DarkStar medium-range endurance (MAE) UAV makes a dramatic appearance at the "Skunk Works" in 1995.

▼

Designed as an ultra-stealthy battlefield surveillance UAV, DarkStar, powered by a lightweight Williams FJ44 turbofan and capable of carrying a 1,250lb (565kg) sensor payload, was cancelled due to rising costs in 1999.

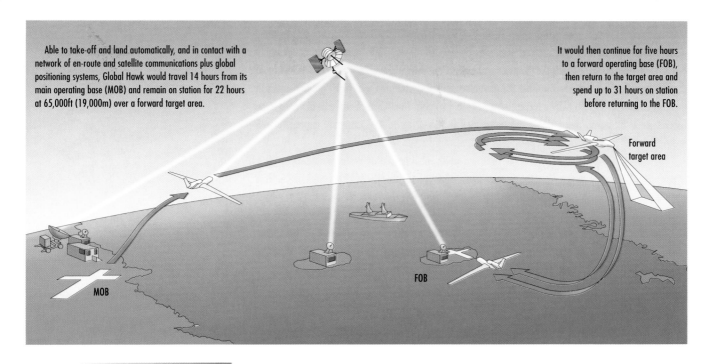

Able to take-off and land automatically, and in contact with a network of en-route and satellite communications plus global positioning systems, Global Hawk would travel 14 hours from its main operating base (MOB) and remain on station for 22 hours at 65,000ft (19,000m) over a forward target area.

It would then continue for five hours to a forward operating base (FOB), then return to the target area and spend up to 31 hours on station before returning to the FOB.

Forward target area

FOB

MOB

The Tier II Plus concept of operations.

Resembling a "blind" reptile, the all-seeing Global Hawk high-altitude endurance (HAE) URAV has a 14,000 mile (22,525km) range, an endurance of 42 hours flying at 65,000ft (19,810m), and can loiter over a target for up to 24 hours.

Unmanned Combat Aerial Vehicle (UCAV)

A logical progression in UAV development is the UCAV, intended to provide a relatively cheap weapon system capable of carrying out high risk missions. Typically the UCAV would be used for suppression of enemy air defenses (SEAD) missions, close air support (CAS) to neutralize enemy armor and ground forces prior to invasion, and reconnaissance. All these missions are high risk and while it is intended that the stealth and EW capabilities of the vehicle would increase its survivability, it is clearly of less military importance to lose a relatively cheap unmanned vehicle than an extremely expensive combat aircraft and its human crew. The UCAV would also be useful for missions where it is difficult for pilots to remain fully alert, such as combat air patrol (CAP) in which role the aircraft is flown in a racetrack circuit for long periods while scanning for enemy aircraft.

SEAD strikes, CAS, and reconnaissance may well be the "dull, dirty, and dangerous" roles usually associated with UCAVs since the recent resurgence of interest in these vehicles. However, by making use of the advances in computer power, artificial intelligence, virtual reality, and jamming resistant datalinks, many other interesting missions for these vehicles are possible. The UCAV could operate autonomously as an interceptor, escort for tankers or AWACS, or as a fighter-bomber, using pre-programmed missions but with the ability to deviate from the planned mission to evade enemy defenses or to actively engage enemy aircraft.

Another scenario is to assign UCAVs to a package of manned aircraft to act as flying weapons dumps. When the manned aircraft has expended its weapons load, it can assign targets to the UCAV and authorize weapon release. UCAVs and manned aircraft could communicate with each other via datalinks to provide pilots and out-of-theater commanders with a more complete picture of the tactical situation than could otherwise be achieved.

Missions that could not be flown by the on-board computer, such as close range dogfights, could be flown remotely by a

U.S. AIR FORCE

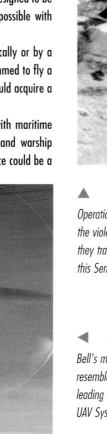

human operator in an airborne AWACS or JSTARS aircraft or from a mobile ground station. Data from the onboard sensors, such as synthetic aperture radar (SAR), electro-optical (EO) and infra-red (IR) systems, would be transmitted back to the control post and displayed on conventional displays or a virtual reality (VR) style helmet enabling the "pilot" to more easily direct the vehicle's sensors. The virtual "pilot" could then engage the enemy aircraft without the physiological limits associated with high "g" maneuvers in manned aircraft, giving the UCAV a tactical advantage in dogfights. The UCAV can easily be designed to be capable of withstanding much higher maneuver load factors of up to 22g, currently impossible with manned aircraft.

Provision can also be made for inflight refueling which could be carried out automatically or by a human pilot via remote control from the boomer's position in the tanker. If a UCAV programmed to fly a CAP mission did not encounter any hostile aircraft by the time its fuel was running low, it could acquire a tanker, refuel and return to its CAP Station.

One area where the UCAV could be particularly effective would be when operating with maritime forces. Apart from launching and recovering UCAVs from conventional aircraft carriers and warship helipads, small aviation support vessels designed to carry a light but lethal URAV/UCAV force could be a

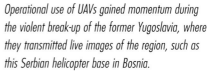

Operational use of UAVs gained momentum during the violent break-up of the former Yugoslavia, where they transmitted live images of the region, such as this Serbian helicopter base in Bosnia.

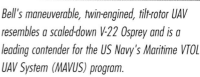

Bell's maneuverable, twin-engined, tilt-rotor UAV resembles a scaled-down V-22 Osprey and is a leading contender for the US Navy's Maritime VTOL UAV System (MAVUS) program.

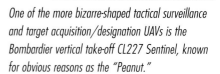

One of the more bizarre-shaped tactical surveillance and target acquisition/designation UAVs is the Bombardier vertical take-off CL227 Sentinel, known for obvious reasons as the "Peanut."

practical proposition for many smaller navies. Even submarines could carry small numbers of specially adapted URAV/UCAVs which could be launched from under the surface in much the same way as Polaris missiles.

As only a few countries have the technological and economic resources to be able to develop and operate practical UCAVs in the foreseeable future, it will come as no surprise to find the United States leading the race. Most of its leading aerospace companies are submitting UCAV concepts to DARPA, while

Lockheed Martin have proposed a concept of UCAVs launched from submarines.

the US services are struggling to grasp their potential. The USAF's Air Combat Command (ACC) is looking forward to building its operational UAV experience when Global Hawk joins Predator with the 11th Reconnaissance Squadron, and is actively studying how UCAVs can be integrated with its future F-22 and JSF fleets. However, at present the US Navy has no validated missions or official requirements for these systems, although the US Marine Corps is close to having some.

It has been reported that British Aerospace (BAe) has already flown prototypes of a large, stealthy, triangular-shaped UAV over the North Sea, utilizing an exotic microwave propulsion system. As we have seen in Chapter Eight, the UK's MoD is putting UCAVs in the frame for its Future Offensive Air System (FOAS) program for which one of the following concepts has been slanted. The other two are intended for maritime operations.

▲

A typical "dangerous and dirty" role ideally suited to the UCAV is that of SEAD, which is graphically illustrated by this lethal anti-radar attack by a "suicidal" Israel Aircraft Industries Harpy mini-UCAV.

The UCAV-1 AVPRO Avenger is a stealthy, VTOL, navalized UCAV with low priority of intercept (LPI) conformal radar, and capability of carrying a heavy weapon payload of air-to-ground and anti-ship missiles.

UCAV-1

UCAV-1 is a stealthy vertical take-off and landing (VTOL) vehicle designed to be operated from the heli-pad of modern frigates and destroyers. Its diamond wing planform gives low wing loading for increased maneuverability combined with a large lifting capacity, allowing for a greater payload. The wing configuration also produces powerful vortices just inboard of the leading edge which produce dominant lift term at high angles of attack and are very stable. This reduces the likelihood of wing drop and nose slice that tend to occur on aircraft with more conventional swept tapered wings, such uncommanded motions of the aircraft marking the point at which realistic weapons aiming is no longer possible. The configuration also provides good longitudinal volume distribution, reducing wavedrag at supersonic speeds and allowing fuel to be pumped fore and aft to control the center of gravity location. This is especially important at take-off and landing when the c.g. must be midway between the jet nozzles.

The wing's anhedral shields the exhaust nozzles and weapons bay doors from radar when viewed from most of the upper hemisphere. Outward-canted winglets give the required projected areas for directional and pitch control, and also keep them out of the worst of the leading edge vortex flow. They are one-piece, all-moving surfaces to give the largest possible control surface area, providing good control effectiveness at both high and low speed.

The vehicle has two weapons bays located one each side of the aircraft centerline to allow the engine to be mounted centrally, which is essential for a four-nozzle VTOL engine where the c.g. must be midway between the forward and rear nozzles. The weapons bay doors would be opened during take-off and landing to maximize the fountain lift produced by the engine eflux impinging on the ship's deck, and this permits higher all-up take-off weights. UCAV-1 has a full-authority digital engine control (FADEC) system to keep the engine within safe operating parameters, which is especially important for an unmanned vehicle where a skilled pilot is not present to take corrective action.

The upper surface of the vehicle is equipped with a retractable probe for air refueling of the probe-and-drogue type. On-board systems include low probability of intercept (LPI) conformally mounted phased array radar, with air-to-air and air-to-surface modes. Synthetic vision, including night vision, allows real-time video data to be transmitted from the UCAV to a ground station or the ship; this system could be used to allow man-in-the-loop control of the vehicle. Global Positioning System (GPS), a high capacity digital datalink, imaging infra-red (IIR) passive detection and tracking, and laser-range finder and guidance systems are also carried.

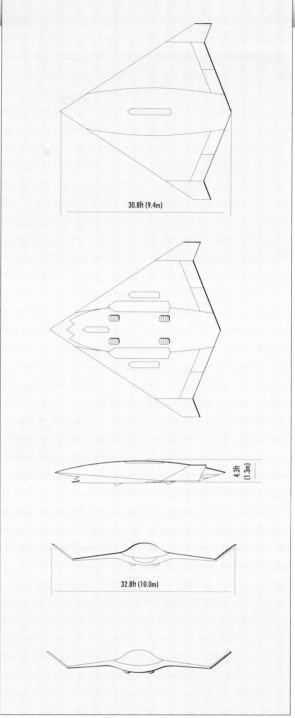

30.8ft (9.4m)

4.3ft (1.3m)

32.8ft (10.0m)

UCAV-2

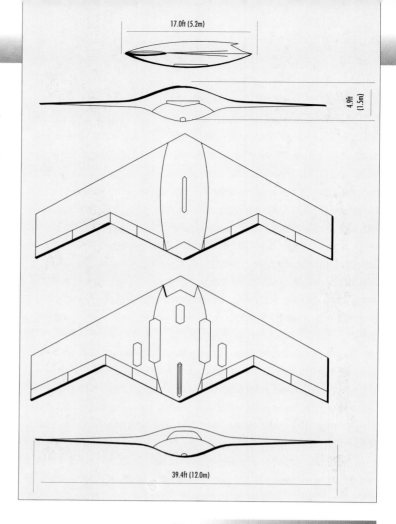

The role of this vehicle is essentially the same as that of UCAV-1. It is a maritime-based vehicle capable of performing air-to-air, air-to-surface, and air-to-ground attack as well as reconnaissance missions. UCAV-2 would be operated from an aircraft carrier, therefore the design of the vehicle exploits the rolling take-off and landing capability made possible by the flight deck of these vessels.

The aircraft is a high aspect ratio flying wing which is a good shape for low RCS, as displayed by the Northrop B-2A Spirit. Vertical surfaces such as winglets are not required as the flight control system (FCS) would provide artificial stability about all axes. It also produces a lightly loaded structure which means very high maneuver loads can be achieved without resorting to excessively heavy structures.

As the aircraft is intended to make conventional landings on a carrier flight deck that may be pitching and rolling, it is essential that the aircraft is stable on its wheels. A wide track undercarriage provides this desirable stability and, for this reason, the main gears are located outboard of the large weapons bays. The provision for rocket-assisted take-off (RATO) allows a conventional rolling take-off which eliminates the requirement for a vectored thrust engine with its associated design compromises. Using RATO to attain take-off speed allows a larger weapon payload or fuel load to be carried compared to a VTOL aircraft of similar dimensions. This in turn permits longer range and endurance together with a greater attack capability. The RATO pack would be jettisoned after take-off.

To allow the UCAV to make a conventional approach and landing it is fitted with an arrester hook and the aircraft would be brought to rest by both the arrester cable and wheel braking. Although current British Royal Navy aircraft carriers do not feature arrester cables, they would be very easy to install and would be standard equipment on the planned CV(F).

Another naval UCAV concept, the UCAV-2 is a conventional take-off, stealthy flying wing design capable of undertaking air-to-air, air-to-ground, and surveillance missions from aircraft carriers.

UCAV-3

UCAV-3 is a land-based system to be used for reconnaissance, SEAD strikes, and CAS to neutralize enemy armor and ground personnel prior to the insertion of friendly ground forces. All these missions are high risk and the stealth and EW capabilities of the vehicle are designed to give it increased survivability. Intended as one segment of the RAF FOAS program, it would nevertheless share many of the on-board systems of its maritime cousins, although it would have a considerably larger weapons bay to accommodate a vast range of state-of-the-art air-to-air and air-to-surface weapons on NATO's inventory. These would include ALARM, ASRAAM, Sidewinder, and Sea Eagle anti-ship missiles, and AGM-65 anti-armor missiles. The deep roots of the trapezoidal wing provide plenty of space for the installation of a cannon such as the M61-A1 Vulcan or the RBK-27 Mauser.

The trapezoidal wing allows the aerodynamic center of the vehicle to be located close to the c.g. This is important since it reduces the trim change in the weapons release phase of the mission. It also allows excellent stealth characteristics while retaining good aerodynamic performance. Only two angles are present in the whole vehicle, including the canard, intake, wing, exhaust, weapon bay doors, and undercarriage doors. Therefore incident radar energy is reflected in two principal directions—both away from the enemy radar.

UCAV-3 is packaged in a trapezoidal wing design that provides a large wing area, thus increasing the lifting capability and consequently the weapons payload, and therefore allowing heavy air-to-surface weapons to be carried. Conversely, in the air-to-air role where the payload is likely to be less, it gives a low wing loading which allows very high maneuver loads to be achieved. It is important to exploit the UCAV's ability to generate higher maneuver loads than manned aircraft since it is not subject to a pilot's

▼

Conceived as an element of the RAF's FOAS program, UCAV-3 AVPRO Archangel has a large weapon bay capable of carrying state-of-the-art air-to-air, air-to-ground, and anti-shipping missiles.

5.45ft (1.66m)

23.5ft (7.16m)

24.6ft (7.5m)

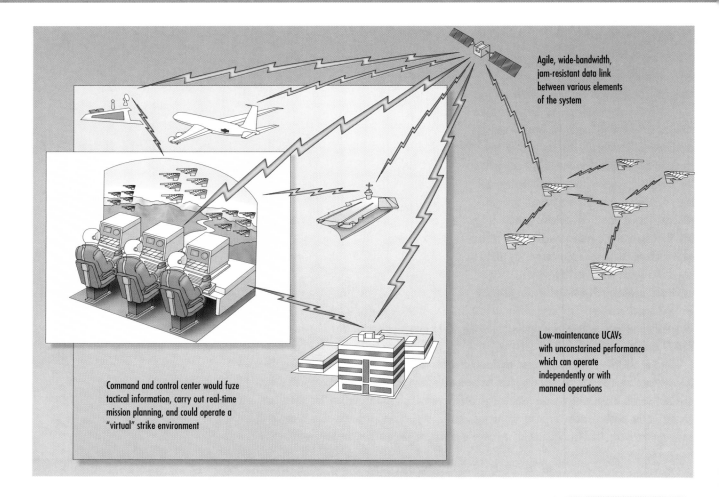

Agile, wide-bandwidth, jam-resistant data link between various elements of the system

Low-maintencance UCAVs with unconstarined performance which can operate independently or with manned operations

Command and control center would fuze tactical information, carry out real-time mission planning, and could operate a "virtual" strike environment

physiological limits, and this will give it a tactical advantage over manned opponents.

Relatively low leading edge sweep increases the lift curve slope of the wing and, in combination with canard foreplanes, this results in very low landing speeds, particularly important for recovery on temporary or damaged runways. It also makes the landing less demanding for the computer or ground-based human pilot. Most UCAV failures are in the take-off and landing phases of a mission.

The canard foreplanes also give the vertical area required for yaw control and yaw stability. As the vehicle is unmanned it would clearly have some form of automatic control which would easily generate artificial stability to overcome the inherent instability of the configuration. Since the canards also destabilize the vehicle in both pitch and yaw the configuration is more maneuverable, because the stability that has to be overcome to initiate and sustain maneuvers is lower. Trim drag is also reduced, which increases the aerodynamic efficiency of the vehicle and hence overall performance.

UVAC-3's inlet has been designed to provide a significant overhang that allows the conformally mounted radar to see downward, as well as upward and forward, to give it a look-down shoot-down capability against targets at much lower altitudes than itself. As the engine is located above the center of the weapons bay it prevents enemy radar from seeing the engine face which is a large contributor to the vehicle's low radar cross-section.

A number of factors stimulated the development of the unmanned aerial vehicles at the end of the 20th Century. The most obvious was the escalating costs of new manned combat aircraft and their pilots. The ever increasing number of potential "hot spots" around the world mean that the "dull, dirty, and dangerous" missions are increasing, along with the requirement for support assets such as combat search and rescue (CSAR) and mine tracking and clearance, two more roles that could be carried out by UAVs in the near future.

Advanced on-board systems such as GPS, inertial navigation system (INS), FADEC, and LLTV are becoming smaller, lighter, and cheaper "off-the-shelf" items, while more sophisticated avionics are being developed and produced for fourth and fifth generation manned fighter programs. Along with a new family of miniaturized weapons being developed for the Joint Strike Fighter program and for deployment in future of combat aircraft in space, the adoption of the UCAV can be seen as a logical progression in future aerial warfare.

The Lockheed Martin UCAV system concept.

A future USAF or NATO air warfare package concept from Lockheed Martin that combines manned and unmanned air-refuelable strike aircraft. It is being considered for the FOAS system.

P. Benson

Micro-UAV

At the other end of the UAV technology and size scale is the micro-unmanned aerial vehicle designed to be part of the back-pack of every platoon leader or member of a special forces unit. It will be just six inches (152mm) long, stay in the air for 30 minutes, fly at 30mph (48kmh), and ounce-for-ounce be one of the most effective surveillance aircraft ever depolyed.

Fantasy or fact? In a very few years' time, hyper-technology will produce a family of highly capable micro-UAVs which will be cheap, expendable, and extremely difficult to detect. The program was initiated by the US Defense Advanced Research Projects Agency (DARPA), whose mission is to develop imaginative, innovative, and often high-risk research ideas offering a significant technological impact that will go well beyond the normal evolutionary development approaches—and pursue these ideas from the demonstration of technical feasibility through to the development of prototype systems. The micro-UAV fits

▼

In this Lockheed Martin concept, two 20ft (6m) long low observable (LO) UCAVs get close to an enemy airfield to ensure accuracy with advanced penetration weapons.

these criteria. But what is the micro-UAV, what is its role, and what are the problems associated with its development?

The soldier of the future will have his own mechanical "bird" which will provide him with pictures, sounds, and even smells of what is inside a target building or bunker. Controlled by a handheld computer, it will have a maximum range of about three miles (5km). Locked in its tiny brain will be a complete floor plan of a target building which will enable it to home in on one particular place, such as the battle planning room. There it would scan documents, wallcharts, maps, and computer screens, relaying the data back to its controller in real time.

Although initially the micro-UAV's role was viewed as part of a conventional battlefield, it did not take long to recognize the fact that it could be extremely helpful in an increasingly common and deadly environment for the soldier in the 21st Century—the urban battlefield of the Third World, and so-called

An LO Lockheed Martin UCAV concept superecruises over a landscape that resembles the former Yugoslavia. It will have an appreciable impact on an integrated battlefield of the 21st Century.

peacekeeping operations. A typical mission scenario may include the checking of a building for a sniper, using video cameras and infra-red sensors or detecting sophisticated booby-traps by sniffing explosives. It may be possible for the micro-UAV to laser a target from co-ordinates relayed from a soldier's satellite location device. Other roles could include searching for bomb survivors with acoustic and heat sensors threading their way through the debris of collapsed buildings.

The first step to designing a practical micro-UAV that could undertake these specialized tasks is being taken as part of an advanced technology DARPA program. It is to create a vehicle with a six-inch wingspan, a weight of only 4 ounces (113 grams), and the capability of operating autonomously for up to 30 minutes—and cost less than $3,000 each.

Two US companies are already flying protoype technology demonstration vehicles, AeroVironment Inc. of California, and Lockheed Martin/Sanders. AeroVironment's Black Widow weighs less than 16oz (453gm) and is powered by a 0.25oz (7gm) direct current brush motor delivering 4,000 milliwatts of power and using a 0.92oz (26gm) lithium battery. The gearbox, propeller, control actuators, and airframe together account for only another 0.28oz (8gm), while its payload is made up of a 0.04oz (1gm) receiver, a 0.11oz (3gm) downlink transmitter, a 0.04oz magnetic compass, and a 0.07oz (2gm) black and white video camera! The AeroVironment micro-UAV will be developed to carry an airspeed indicator, GPS, and a color video camera by the year 2003, when lithium batteries will be replaced by a solid oxide fuel cell that will have two-to-three times the energy output.

The Sanders MicroSTAR designed by the "Skunk Works" (responsible for its larger relative, the super-stealthy DarkStar), will be powered by a 7 watt electric engine developed by General Electric, with the complete system using just 11 watts of power, about twice that used by a bedside clock/radio. Some of the devices being used to navigate the MicroSTAR come from the auto industry, including the accelerometer which is used to trigger air bags.

Also involved in DARPA's program is the University of Toronto which is developing a six-inch ornithopter micro-UAV powered by electrostrictive polymer artificial muscles. Meanwhile, the Vanderbilt University is working on mimicking the insect's flight mechanism, using piezoelectric actuators to resonate metallic structured "wings." AeroVironment, together with the California Institute of Technology (CIT) and the University of California, have been awarded a $1.8 million contract to study the possibility of flying a 0.35oz (10gm) flapping "microbat" that could carry miniature microphone arrays for acoustic homing on sounds.

These are just the first of a series of incredible developments of future micro-UAVs that one day may land on the enemy's computer and literally "suck" out the data or inject it with a virus—or crawl into a darkened, "sealed" control bunker and release a lethal gas to kill all inside....

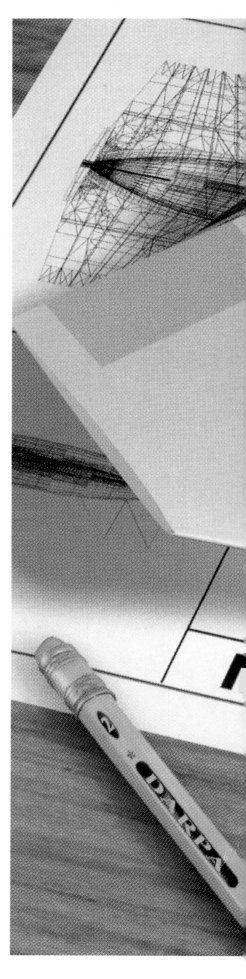

▶
A new concept for the future battlefield—capable and sophisticated micro-UAVs, such as the Lockheed-Martin MicroStar, that will be standard equipment for ground troops in the 21st Century.

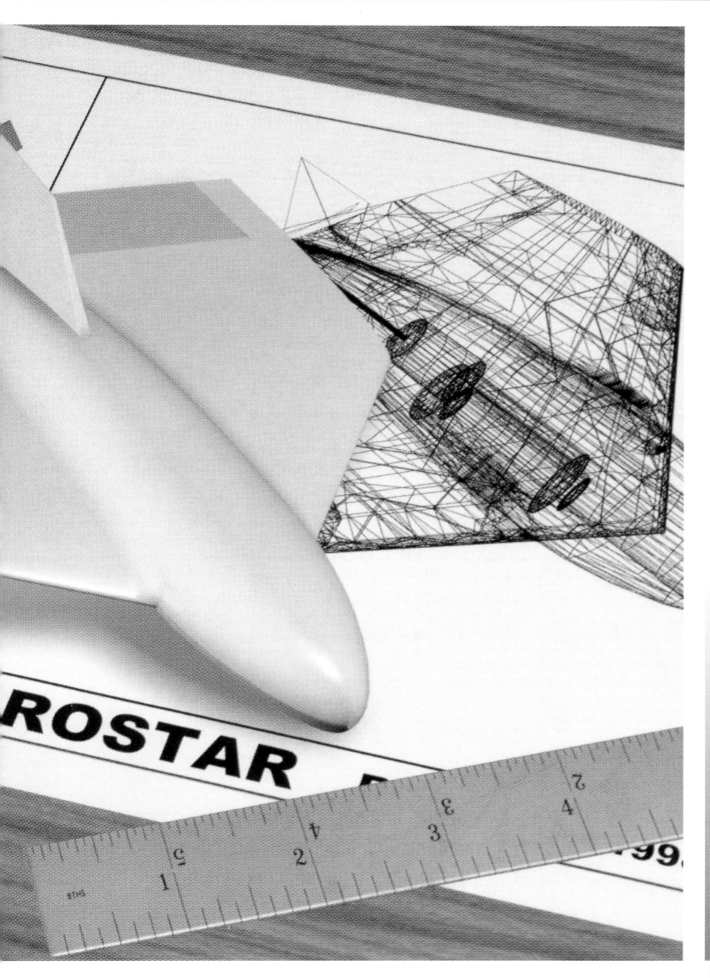

ROSTAR

INSERTION AND RECOVERY

I n post-Cold War conflicts, the importance of two key roles have grown out of all recognition—special operations (SO) and combat search and rescue (CSAR). Covert operations carried out by small specialist units of the three main services of most of the combatant nations became an increasing feature of World War II. Early in the war British Special Service Brigades carried out commando raids against the German U-boat base at St Nazaire, France, and the Norwegian port of Vaagso; Italian Navy commandos attacked British warships at Gibraltar with min-subs; and special detachments of US Marines raided Japanese-held Pacific islands after Pearl Harbor.

B ritain's Special Operations Executive (SOE) and the US Office of Strategic Services (OSS) operated in occupied Europe supported by dedicated RAF "black" squadrons of Whitley and Halifax night bombers and STOL Lysanders, while the Luftwaffe's famed KG 200 operated a mixed fleet of more than 50 aircraft including captured B-17 and B-24 bombers for dropping secret agents into western Europe, the Soviet Union, and the Middle East. Leading exponents of irregular warfare, including Major-General Orde Wingate and his "Chindits" operating behind Japanese lines in Burma, and Major David Stirling's Special Air Service (SAS) group, relied heavily on air support for insertion, supply, and recovery.

While the SAS survived the end of World War II, the SOE was disbanded, as was the OSS which was revived as the Central Intelligence Agency (CIA) on the outbreak of the Cold War in 1947. Although its primary role was to provide the White House with up-to-date human intelligence (HUMINT), the CIA was also responsible for operating covert spyplanes over the Soviet Union and its satellites. This role was

▼

USAF forged one of the most enduring teams of SOF/CSAR aircraft during the 1960s in Vietnam, with the HH-3 "Jolly Green Giant" (shown here) and HC-130 Combat Shadow.

exposed during Operation *Overflight* when a CIA Lockheed U-2C high-altitude reconnaissance aircraft piloted by Gary Powers was shot down near Sverdlovsk by an SA-2 surface-to-air missile (SAM) on May 1, 1960.

Although this event caused the cancellation of a US/Soviet summit meeting, the CIA moved its U-2 detachment to Taiwan before an even more potent "black" reconnaissance aircraft came within the Agency's sphere of operations. As the world's first operational Mach 3 combat aircraft, the A-12 had been developed in the early 1960s by the Lockheed "Skunk Works" with 12 aircraft being delivered to the CIA in 1964. Deployed to Kadena Air Base at Okinawa, Japan, in May 1965, CIA A-12s flew Operation *Black Shield* missions over China, North Korea, and North Vietnam until June 5, 1968. Their role was then taken over by the USAF SR-71

Blackbird, a two seat development of the A-12. The Agency continued in the covert reconnaissance business with the Project Tagboard until 1971. Tagboard was a supersonic drone carried "piggy back" on the A-12 but it was cancelled after only four partially successful missions over China.

While the CIA continued its airborne activities by operating the largest airline in the world at the time, Air America, to cover its spying operations in Southeast Asia until the fall of Saigon in May 1975, the US Army Special Operations Forces (SOF) became more involved in counter-insurgency (COIN) missions in Vietnam. Created at Fort Bragg in the early 1950s, the Special Forces, known as the "Green Berets" because of their distinctive headgear, were "bloodied" in action during the Korean War. Special Forces came of age in Southeast Asia, where they were known as "Sneaky Petes," and took part in numerous high profile operations such as the Son Tay raid.

In November 1970, USAF HH-3 "Jolly Green Giant"' and HH-53 "Super Jolly Green Giant" helicopters air-refueled by MC-130 Combat Talons and escorted by A-1 Skyraiders flew a 50-plus strong SOF assault force more than 400 miles (645km) in an attempt to rescue US PoWs from a North Vietnamese prison camp at Son Tay. Although the prisoners had been moved days before the raid, Operation *Ivory Coast* showed that a large SOF force could be successfully inserted and recovered from behind enemy lines.

Another version of the "Jolly Green Giant," which gained its nickname from the jungle green camouflage scheme worn in Southeast Asia, was the CH-3 which was used throughout the Vietnam conflict for infiltrating and extracting SOF teams behind enemy lines and, during Operation *Buffalo Hunter*, for

A USAF CH-3 Mid-Air Retrieval System (MARS) returning a Firebee drone following a reconnaissance mission over North Vietnam during Operation **Buffalo Hunter**.

recovering unmanned Ryan Firebees returning from clandestine reconnaissance missions over North Vietnam and China.

US Air Force special forces, known as Air Commandos, were deployed as pilot "advisers" to the South Vietnamese Air Force, and as combat air controllers (CAC)—to direct close air support from covert ground positions. However, the USAF's main SOF role remained that of insertion and recovery of US Army "Green Berets" and would remain so for the next two decades.

Created in 1962 as an independent group capable of undertaking covert counter-insurgency operations, the US Navy SEALs deploy by sea, air, and land. Although trained mainly for offensive warfare, SEALs are used for covert reconnaissance, along with USMC "Recon" Marines, to monitor potential amphibious landing sites and move inland to seek out enemy defenses and troop deployments. The favored mode of air transport for SEALs and "Recon" Marines is the three-engined CH-53E Super Stallion heavy-lift helicopter.

Inspired by British SAS, US Special Forces Operational Detachment Delta, known as "Delta Force," was established in November 1977 as a specialist anti-terrorist hostage rescue group. One of "Delta Force's" first missions was Operation *Eagle Claw*, the attempted rescue of American hostages held in the US Embassy in Teheran by Iranian militants in April 1980. In the event, the mission was a disaster. With "Delta Force," US Army Special Forces, SEALs, US Navy and Marine helicopters, and USAF MC-130s involved, command and control was a nightmare. Three MH-53s went unserviceable en route to a desert rendezvous and another collided with a Hercules on lift-off from the airstrip Desert One. The operation was cancelled.

As a direct result of the failure of Operation *Eagle Claw*, the US Joint Special Operations Command (JSOC) was established to provide a single command body for covert operation units of all US services. At the same time the Counter-Terrorist Joint Task Force (CTJTF) came into being at Fort Bragg, bringing together elements of "Delta Force," US Navy SEALs, USAF 1st Special Operations Wing (SOW), and the US Army's ultra-secret 160th Special Operations Aviation Regiment (SOAR).

The first real test of these new organizations came with Saddam Hussein's invasion of Kuwait in 1990. Teams of US Special Operations Forces and Britain's SAS were inserted into Kuwait and Iraq months before Operation *Desert Storm* commenced. "Recon" Marines were inserted along the Gulf coast to scout for potential landing sites for Marine Assault Groups (MAG). They all helped to build a detailed intelligence

AFSOC's MH-53H "Super Jolly Green Giants" have been upgraded to MH-53J Pave Low III Enhanced standard with advanced avionics and ECM suites for special operations behind enemy lines.

picture of the enemy forces and their deployment, while the SAS took part in mobile "Scud" missile launcher hunts and designating targets for Coalition attack aircraft with their portable laser designators.

The SAS was also tasked with watching vital road links between Baghdad and Kuwait City. Having bolstered its already formidable reputation with a series of daring operations during the Falklands conflict in 1982, typical of which was the raid on a remote Argentinian airstrip on Pebble Island when 11 enemy aircraft were destroyed in 15 minutes before the force was recovered by Royal Navy helicopters, the Iraqi road watch patrols were some of the most dangerous operations the SAS had ever undertaken. During Road Watch North, codenamed Bravo Two Zero, an SAS team was inserted by an RAF Special Forces Chinook some 100 miles (161km) north-west of Baghdad. After being sighted, the eight-man team fought their way north to Syria, killing some 250 Iraqis en route for the loss of three of their own. SAS soldiers were the first British troops to reach a liberated Kuwait City when they were dropped into the British Embassy compound by RAF SOF Chinook and Puma helicopters at the end of February 1991.

A flight engineer looses off a 1,600-round burst with his M134 7.62mm minigun from the side door position of an AFSOC "Super Jolly Green Giant" to provide suppressive fire during CSAR missions.

In addition to inserting and recovering SOF, aircraft of the recently established US Air Force Special Operations Command (AFSOC) at Hurlburt Field, Florida, flew both active and passive roles in the Gulf War. EC-130E Commando Solos of the Air National Guard (ANG) Special Operations Command (SOC) flew psyops missions, interrupting Iraqi TV and radio stations and broadcasting Coalition news and propaganda. Special Operations Wing MC-130 Combat Talons actually dropped 15,000lb (6,800kg) BLU-82 bombs on Iraqi Republican Guard armored units.

Yet another variant of the ubiquitous Hercules, the fearsome AC-130A Spectre gunship operated by AFSOC's 16th Special Operations Squadron (SOS), undertook clandestine attack missions against enemy positions. Armed with two fixed 20mm Vulcan cannon, a 40mm cannon, and a trainable 105mm howitzer, the Spectre possessed a heavy punch. Unfortunately, one was shot down down by a SAM-7 off the Kuwait coast, killing the 14-man crew, USAF's worst casualty of the Gulf War.

A para-jumper launches himself from the open rear ramp of an AFSOC MH-54 Pave Low III during a practice combat rescue mission, while a crewman mans the rear minigun.

As related in Chapter One, no sooner had the Gulf War finished than the Balkan wars began. Almost a decade of conflict in the former Yugoslavia, which began in Slovenia and spread to Croatia, Bosnia, and Kosovo and eventually ended up at the gates of the Serbian capital Belgrade, taxed NATO's Special Operations Forces to the limit. As soon as NATO began supplying UN Protection Forces in Bosnia in October 1993, teams of special forces, including the "Green Berets" and SAS, were infiltrated into the region.

Although the UN approved NATO air strikes against Bosnian Serb military assets in August 1993, it was two more years before Operation *Deliberate Force* commenced. Allied aircraft attacking Bosnian Serb positions surrounding Sarajevo used "smart"' weapons against targets designated by SOF on the ground using portable laser designators. By the end of 1995, the Dayton Peace Agreement was signed and the war in Bosnia came to an end, supervized by a 60,000-strong NATO peace-keeping force. But the SOF units did not leave.

The "new" Yugoslavia had now shrunk to only two republics, Serbia and Montenegro, and the neighboring province of Kosovo. In 1992, Kosovo's ethnic Albanians, who comprised 90 percent of the population, voted to secede from Yugoslavia but their effort was thwarted by Serbian military forces directed by President Slobodan Milosevic. Six years later actions by the embrionic Kosovo Liberation Army (KLA) provoked swift and bloody reprisals by the Belgrade-led internal security forces. By September 1998 NATO was warning Milosevic of a phased air campaign against his forces in Kosovo. After a series of warnings and failed diplomacy, Operation *Allied Force* was launched on March 24, 1999.

Before air strikes began, NATO's special operations assets, US AFSOC MC-130H Combat Talon II, HC-130P Combat Shadows, and MH-53J Pave Low III helicopters, were deployed to Brindisi in Italy with forward detachments to Bosnia, Macedonia, and Hungary. Psyops EC-130E Commando Solos soon joined the action, flying from Ramstein in Germany, while AC-130H Spectres were held in reserve waiting to support any NATO ground troops if and when they were deployed.

Although AFSOC's primary mission is to provide unconventional warfare, direct action, special reconnaissance, and counter-terrorism support to US Special Operations Command (SOCOM), combat search and rescue (CSAR) is almost of equal importance in contemporary out of area (OOA) operations.

Ever since Lt Carter Harman landed his prototype Sikorsky YR-4 in a Burmese jungle paddy field behind enemy lines in April 1944 to rescue the pilot and three wounded soldiers aboard an L-1 Vigilant that had force-landed in the jungle, the helicopter has been the military's preferred CSAR platform. Up to that point, search and rescue had been the domain of the amphibious flying boat such as the famed Catalina and Grumman Goose, but during the Korean War this role was shared by the Goose's larger successor, the HU-16 Albatross, and the precocious rotary-wing newcomer.

In Vietnam, the veteran HU-16s of the USAF Air Rescue Service (ARS) were credited with more than 50 rescues of downed American aircrew, many from behind enemy lines, but four of these amphibians were lost in action before they were replaced by HC-130 Hercules and air-refuelable Sikorsky HH-3 "Jolly Green Giant" helicopters in 1967. It was during the Vietnam conflict that use was made of rescue packages of search and rescue task forces (SARTF) made up of forward air controllers (FAC), combat air patrols (CAP), helicopters, tankers, and rescue escorts—A-1 Skyraiders codenamed Sandys. Teams of para-jumpers were inserted by helicopter to carry out limited surface operation (LSO) searches for downed pilots or other "friendlies" who had been forced to escape and evade. The Sandys gave close air support to the mission while Air Force fighters provided top cover to the force.

SARTFs remain the core of AFSOC's CSAR operations, although fully night-capable MH-53J Pave Low III and MH-60G Pave Hawk helicopters have replaced the HH-3 "Jolly Green Giants." During the Gulf War, a SARTF MH-53J rescued a downed US Navy F-14 Tomcat pilot 30 miles (48km) from Baghdad in broad daylight, with A-10 Warthogs playing the Sandy role. During the UN Operation *Restore Hope* in Somalia in1993, MH-60 Pave Hawks assigned to the US Army's 160th Special Operations Aviation Regiment (SOAR) rescued surviving crew of two Army Black Hawks bought down by rebel militia ground fire.

The prompt safe return of downed aircrew, preferably before capture, is a military priority. This was graphically illustrated on June 2, 1995, when USAF F-16 pilot Capt Scott O'Grady was shot down by a

US Marine CH-53E Super Stallions were flown in the daring dawn mission to rescue USAF Capt Scott O'Grady, whose F-16 was shot down by a Serb SAM over Bosnia in 1995.

Capt Scott O'Grady arrives on the flight deck of the US Marine assault carrier USS Kearsarge *following his dramatic rescue six days after his shoot-down over Bosnia.*

An RAF Chinook HC.2 heavy transport helicopter firing flares over Bosnia during Operation Deliberate Force *as protection against Serb SAMs.*

Bosnian Serb SAM during Operation *Deny Flight*. Having evaded capture for six days, Capt O'Grady's transmissions from his digital personnel locator system (PLS) were interrogated by an AWACS aircraft, and a successful combined service CSAR mission was undertaken, comprising a pair of USMC CH-53s escorted by Marine Corps AH-1W SuperCobra Sandies with top cover from F/A-18D Hornets and EA-6B Prowlers for suppression of enemy air defenses (SEAD).

NATO CSAR assets were again in action in Yugoslavia in the opening days of Operation *Allied Force*. On the night of March 27, 1999, the USAF lost its first F-117A Nighthawk, brought down by Yugoslav SAMs 45 miles (70km) north-west of Belgrade. The pilot ejected successfully and landed some 5 miles (8km) from the crash site. Almost immediately a combined CSAR mission swung into action with eight helicopters led by two AFSOC MH-53J Pave Low IIIs from their forward base at Tuzla in Bosnia. Top cover was provided by F-15s and F-18s, while a back-up CSAR package of French Navy Super Frelon helicopters was deployed to Ploce in Croatia. Although it was some seven hours before a textbook recovery of the pilot was completed, it was the use of his advanced hand-held PLS (which allows a downed pilot to burst transmissions of his position to searching CSAR helicopters and, when closer, speak directly to the helicopter or MC-130H Combat Talon CSAR command aircraft) that made it possible.

On May 2, a USAF F-16 suffered an engine failure and crashed during a night mission over north west Serbia. The pilot again ejected successfully and was rescued 11 miles (18km) east of Kozluk by an Allied CSAR team only two hours later.

The Balkan conflicts have brought special operations forces and CSAR operations into focus as never before, and many NATO members are now looking to upgrade their forces' clandestine capabilities. While the Italian Air Force continues to rely on the elderly FLIR-equipped HH-3F Pelican helicopters in its CSAR role, several European air forces, including those of France, Germany, Spain, and Britain's RAF, use the Eurocopter Puma or its development, the Cougar, for CSAR and SOF operations. For long-range/loiter mission profiles, the French Navy uses the venerable three-engined Super Frelon, while the RAF is taking delivery of a small force of specially configured Chinook HC.3s based on the US Army's special operations MH-47E. The Royal Navy also operates the Commando assault variant of the Sea King, known as "Junglies," for limited special operations/CSAR missions.

Among new rotary wing aircraft being considered as potential replacements for many of these CSAR/SF helicopters, the stealthy, multi-national NH90 leads the pack. Having been ordered by Germany's Luftwaffe, the Italian Air Force, and French Navy, the composite-construction NH90 will have integrated FLIR slaved to its tactical navigation suite, and a tail ramp for rapid deplaning of SOF teams or the airdrop of para-jumpers. The heavyweight EH101 Merlin is being considered for a Future Amphibious

Support Helicopter (FASH) replacement for the Royal Navy/Royal Marine Commando force Sea Kings in 2002.

The US AFSOC is looking forward to the next generation of special operations aircraft to supplement its existing Pave Low and Pave Hawk helicopters—the CV-22 Osprey. Bell-Boeing's unique tiltrotor, multi-misson Osprey combines the V/STOL characteristics of helicopter with the dash speed and long range of a conventional fixed-wing aircraft. The CV-22 will fulfill AFSOC's requirement for a high-speed, long-range V/STOL aircraft capable of low-visibility, clandestine infiltration/extraction of denied areas in adverse weather.

Developed from the Marine Corps MV-22 amphibious assault mission Osprey, the CV-22 can accommodate up to 18 SOF troops over a combat radius of 500 miles (805km) at a speed of 400mph (645kmh), enabling it to accomplish its mission in less than 4.5 flight hours or during one period of darkness. Its cockpit is fully NVG-compatible and the aircraft is equipped with a multi-role terrain-following/terrain-avoidance (TF/TA) radar in addition to a turreted FLIR. Cockpit situational awareness during high-speed low-level night flight is enhanced with a head-up helmet-mounted display (HMD) that projects flight symbology over FLIR or NVG imagery.

Radar signature-reduction features of the CV-22 include a low-noise, low-flicker prop-rotor system, low-IR paint, low-contrast color schemes, advanced engine IR suppressors, and cockpit electronic emissions control. The Osprey's high speed lessens its exposure to Triple-A and missile threats by reducing acquisition, lock-on, and firing opportunities. The CV-22's survivability is further enhanced by a comprehensive suite of electronic countermeasures (ECM).

The US Navy's Osprey variant, the HV-22, will conduct strike rescue missions out to a radius of 500 miles (800km) without refueling, and will provide naval forces with the capability to deliver, remove or replenish SOF teams. The Osprey is scheduled to become fully operational in 2005.

US Army rotary wing SOF assets operated by the clandestine 160th Special Operations Aviation Regiment include small numbers of long-range, air-refuelable, and armed MH-60K/L Black Hawks, a development of AFSOC's Pave Hawk, and MH-47E Chinook transports fitted with IR linescan and weather radar in an enlarged nose. First fielded by the SOAR in the mid-1980s was a fleet of AH-6 and MH-6 "Little

▲
The pilot in the night vision goggles (NVG) compatible cockpit of an RAF Chinook, the system that has enabled most SOF mission to be flown at night in comparative safety.

▼
About to enter service with AFSOC and the US Navy, the unique Bell-Boeing Osprey tiltrotor combines the VTOL capabilities of a helicopter with the dash speed of a fixed-wing aircraft.

Bird" helicopters developed from the Army's Hughes OH-6A Cayuse Light Observation Helicopter.

Prototypes of the small but nimble "Little Bird" were used for covert CIA operations in North Vietnam a decade earlier, and attack and utility variants of the more powerful Hughes (later McDonnell Douglas and now Boeing) Model 500 Defender were later adopted. Both versions have self-sealing tanks, inlet particle filters, and IR-suppressing exhausts. The AH-6J Nightfox gunship fitted with a nose-mounted, laser-augmented FLIR can be armed with a 7.62mm minigun, 70mm rockets, and Hellfire anti-tank missiles. Utilized for the insertion/recovery of small SOF teams into denied areas, the MH-6J can carry four fully equipped troops in addition to the two-man crew in the main cabin, and can be rigged with external pods for SOF assault missions.

Under the Mission Enhanced Little Bird (MELB) program, the SOAR AH/MH-6 fleet is being upgraded with more powerful Allison turboshaft engines with Full Authority Digital Electronic Control (FADEC), a six-blade rotor system, and four-blade tail rotor. The less noisy No Tail Rotor (NOTAR) anti-torque system was trialed for the MELB upgrade but, due to the fact that it used more power and was heavier than a conventional tail rotor, it was considered unsuitable for SOF operations.

Fixed wing aircraft used for US SOF missions are mainly derivatives of the ubiquitous C-130 Hercules. USAF AC, HC, and MC-130s plus RAF Hercules C.3s are the backbone of NATO long-range SOF operations, while a small force of USAF C-141 Starlifters is dedicated to low-level special operations. Part of USAF's 16th Airlift Squadron (AS) based at Charleston AFB in South Carolina, nine C-141B SOLL II (Special Operations Low-Level II) aircraft are equipped with chin-mounted FLIR, ALR-69 Radar Warning Receivers (RWR), AAQ-17 IR-detection sytem, chaff/flare dispensers, and SATCOM, together with an NVG-compatible cockpit.

As SOF and CSAR operations are set to take center stage, albeit covertly, air forces are looking at new equipment to replace many types that have been in service since the Vietnam War. Most of the C-130 types are likely to be replaced by more of the same—the re-engined, re-winged, new-generation Hercules, the C-130J.

One of the few fixed-wing types being considered by AFSOC for covert unconventional warfare missons to unprepared landing surfaces is the C-27J Spartan. Lockheed Martin is building an advanced development of the Italian twin-turboprop STOL Alenia G222, ten of which were operated by USAF's 310th AS at Howard AFB in Panama. At the other end of the scale, Boeing is offering USAF a variant of the C-17A Globemaster III modified for special operations as a potential replacement for the C-141B SOLL II.

A French SOF team boards a French Navy Super Frelon through its open rear ramp on the flight deck of the carrier Foch *steaming off the coast of the former Yugoslavia.*

It could be that a more likely long-term replacement for SOF C-130s will be a VTOL type such as the X-wing Titan described in Chapter Four. The stealthy Titan would replace both the rotary-wing MH-47 Chinook and the fixed-wing MC-130 Combat Talon for night/adverse weather, low-level, deep penetration tactical SOF missions.

Yet another hybrid aircraft viewed with interest by SOF operators is the VertiJet under development by the Taiwanese helicopter manufacturer Modus. An aircraft in the MH-60 class, the VertiJet has a circular wing housing two sets of contra-rotating retractable rotors. When the rotors are fully extended the aircraft takes off vertically like a conventional helicopter. With contra-rotating rotors, the VertiJet has no need of an anti-torque system. Once airborne the landing gear is retracted, the disc hub tilts forward, and the aircraft accelerates to 100mph (160kmh) at which point power to the rotors will be cut and the blades retracted into the disc/wing. Two turbofans positioned at the roots of an inverted "V" tailplane, which have combined rudders and elevators for control authority, will give the VertiJet a maximum speed of over 400mph (645kmh). X-wing and Canard Rotary Wing (CRW) technology are likely to be introduced into the US Army's RW-X rotorcraft program to replace the SOAR's "Little Birds" in 2015-18.

Other specialist technology that will be bought to bear in future SOF platforms includes that being developed for the British Marauder and American Nauticair 450 flying boat designs described in Chapter Five. The wing-assisted amphibious Marauder and wing-assisted hull-lifting Nauticair are both powered by two advanced turbofans fitted above the wing/fuselage for low radar cross-section (RCS) and would be ideal platforms for infiltrating SAS-size teams onto beaches and inland waterways behind enemy lines or conducting strike rescue missions.

Other water-borne aircraft bear a closer relationship to the Russian "Caspian Sea Monsters." The

AVPRO's innovative low observable (LO), jet-powered, amphibious Marauder could be used for inserting/extracting small teams of special forces on hostile beaches or inland waterways.

Various configurations of the EXINT pod.

American FlareCraft Corp is building a series of small, stealthy, wing in ground (WIG) effect craft, constructed of composite materials and propelled by low-powered piston engines. With a range of some 400 miles (640km), the low observable, five-place FlareCraft could deliver a small SOF team from the well deck of a Marine assault ship to hostile beaches over the horizon.

One of the most exciting pieces of kit that could revolutionize future CSAR/SOF operations is EXINT. Designed by the UK company AVPRO, EXINT (Extraction/Insertion) is an aircraft pod which can be used for the speedy recovery of downed aircrew, or the insertion/extraction of SOF personnel, using the unique VTOL capability of the AV-8 Harrier. The EXINT is a one-man pod of some 13ft (4m) in length fitted with internal equipment such as radio, air conditioning, and GPS. An equipment bay also allows small arms and other personal equipment to be carried. A state-of-the-art parachute and airbag system, developed from the Marslander spacecraft program, will allow the pod to make a soft landing should it be released from the aircraft in an emergency situation.

The pod is fitted on the outer weapon pylon of a Harrier in the same way as a munition is, without any modification to the aircraft. In an SOF role the pod would be released at high altitude from the carriage aircraft, which could be a tactical transport or fast jet such as an F-15 or Tornado. Due to the EXINT pod's extremely low RCS and composite construction, it would be very difficult to detect. Once released, the SF soldier in the pod would release a steerable parachute and float down to the drop zone (DZ). The pod's internal oxygen supply would allow for many hours of flight at high altitude. Windows on each side would enable the occupant to see out, thus eliminating claustrophobia. The EXINT pod's parachute system would be fully steerable: the soldier would input the DZ's map co-ordinates into the pod's integrated computer and it would steer by means of a GPS accurate to within a yard. The soldier could take manual control at any time to change course if required.

In maritime operations, as the pod nears water, a proximity sensor would inflate the airbag system to cushion the landing, suppress noise, and provide the pod with extra stability. The pod could then be "sailed" for up to 50 miles (80km) by means of a small propeller driven by an electric motor. A miniature camera in the nose of the pod would transmit a picture to a multi-function display to aid navigation.

Although originally conceived for the AV-8 Harrier, it soon became apparent that the EXINT pod could also be used on helicopters fitted with weapon or utility pylons. Extensive feasibility studies have been carried out by AVPRO into using the pod on the AH-64D Apache attack helicopter as a CSAR

The AVPRO EXINT pod

Key to cutaway:
1: Hinged nose access.
2: High-intensity strobe light.
3: Radio antenna.
4: Global positioning system.
5: Instrument panel
6: Air intake.
7: Equipment bay.
8: Equipment battery.
9: Parachute retarder system.
10: Sliding door
11: Survival kit.
12: Air bags.
13: Sliding center of gravity ballast.
14: Colored warning lights.
15: Ground proximity sensor.
16: Body-contoured support.

The EXINT pod has various potential applications, including carriage of SOF couriers, extraction of rescued hostages, insertion of SOF personnel such as SEAL team members, carriage of mine and bomb disposal specialists, and delivery of special equipment.

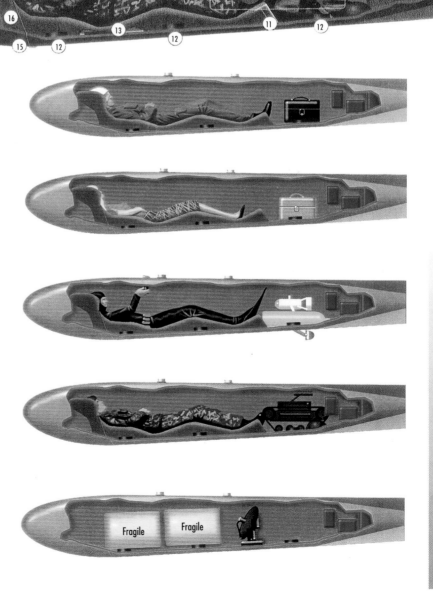

platform. The results confirmed the AH-64D/EXINT combination to be a highly versatile and flexible system capable of carrying out deep penetration CSAR missions, snap rescues, or SOF insertion/extraction. With its impressive range and sophisticated sensor/weapon packages, the Apache would require no modifications to carry EXINT pods.

In a lesser role, the pod could be used in a reversionary mode as a carrier for specialized equipment, baggage, or cargo carrier. This would extend the versatility of the AH-64D in out of area (OOA) operations. This capability could be of great value to the military planner since it would enable an Apache unit to self-deploy without the need of valuable transport helicopters in support. Each EXINT pod has been designed to carry in excess of 500lb (225kg) of equipment or, if required, an extensive medical support system for the CASEVAC role.

The pod is designed to be carried on most attack helicopters including non-Western designs, as well as advanced VSTOL attack aircraft such as JSF. The normal concept of operations (CONOPS) for EXINT is for each helicopter or VSTOL aircraft to carry two pods, but the AH-64D could carry up to four pods in the SOF role, if required.

The clandestine world of unconventional warfare in the 21st Century, with its rapidly expanding new generation assets, may hold the balance between success and failure in the growing number of out of area operations that are expected to be the pattern for future conflicts.

▶

Royal Navy Sea Harrier F/A.2 VSTOL aircraft with under-wing "people pods" being used on a special forces mission to rescue hostages who have been held by terrorists.

▶ ▼

Depiction of the EXINT pods being used in the rescue of downed aircrew by a Royal Navy VSTOL JSF operating from a nearby road while its colleague in the Sandy role fires flares for protection against enemy SAMs.

▼

Prototype of the EXINT pod, which is designed to be carried by most types of combat aircraft, including WAH-64D Apache attack helicopters (which could carry four) and strike aircraft.

THE FIFTH GENERATION, AND INTO SPACE

Recent conflicts will doubtless speed up development and deployment of unmanned combat aircraft. Meanwhile, Russia's warplane designs have shown maneuverability which surprised the West, whose designers are looking ahead to fifth-generation combat aircraft, and military planners are seeking to use the final frontier for the launching of combat operations — space.

At the beginning of the 21st Century, the development of new combat aircraft continues unabated. Following the successful NATO air campaign over Kosovo and Yugoslavia, many defense observers pointed out the fact that the air war was won by third generation attack aircraft such as the F-15, F-16, F/A-18, and F-117, aided by several even older platforms such as the B-52 and A-10. The most advanced aircraft deployed to the battle was the B-2A Spirit stealth bomber which could operate only within a package of more than a dozen escorting fighters.

The outcome of Operation *Allied Force* in 1999 put into question the need for development of costly advanced combat aircraft such as the F-22 Raptor, Eurofighter Typhoon, and JSF. However, despite NATO's overwhelming air superiority, the air war was not an unqualified success. It took almost 1,000 allied aircraft flying more than 30,000 sorties over 11 weeks to "win" the war. Despite the massive use of "smart" weapons, including the newly fielded Joint Direct Attack Munition (JDAM) dropped by the B-2A, damage done by the bombing, especially in Kosovo, was seriously over-estimated by NATO commanders. The facts are that missions were aborted because of bad weather, targets were missed due to poor intelligence, and the much-vaunted AH-64 Apache attack helicopter was not deployed before the air war had come to an

▼

The fact that the Russian aerospace industry can still surprise the West was shown by the first flight of the innovative Sukhoi S-37 Berkut (Royal Eagle) fifth generation fighter at Zhukovsky in 1997.

THE FIFTH GENERATION, AND INTO SPACE

Recent conflicts will doubtless speed up development and deployment of unmanned combat aircraft. Meanwhile, Russia's warplane designs have shown maneuverability which surprised the West, whose designers are looking ahead to fifth-generation combat aircraft, and military planners are seeking to use the final frontier for the launching of combat operations — space.

At the beginning of the 21st Century, the development of new combat aircraft continues unabated. Following the successful NATO air campaign over Kosovo and Yugoslavia, many defense observers pointed out the fact that the air war was won by third generation attack aircraft such as the F-15, F-16, F/A-18, and F-117, aided by several even older platforms such as the B-52 and A-10. The most advanced aircraft deployed to the battle was the B-2A Spirit stealth bomber which could operate only within a package of more than a dozen escorting fighters.

The outcome of Operation *Allied Force* in 1999 put into question the need for development of costly advanced combat aircraft such as the F-22 Raptor, Eurofighter Typhoon, and JSF. However, despite NATO's overwhelming air superiority, the air war was not an unqualified success. It took almost 1,000 allied aircraft flying more than 30,000 sorties over 11 weeks to "win" the war. Despite the massive use of "smart" weapons, including the newly fielded Joint Direct Attack Munition (JDAM) dropped by the B-2A, damage done by the bombing, especially in Kosovo, was seriously over-estimated by NATO commanders. The facts are that missions were aborted because of bad weather, targets were missed due to poor intelligence, and the much-vaunted AH-64 Apache attack helicopter was not deployed before the air war had come to an

▼

The fact that the Russian aerospace industry can still surprise the West was shown by the first flight of the innovative Sukhoi S-37 Berkut (Royal Eagle) fifth generation fighter at Zhukovsky in 1997.

▲

Featuring forward-swept wings (FSW), canard foreplanes, and vectoring-thrust nozzles, the Sukhoi S-37 Berkut has excellent low-speed characterisitics and close-in maneuverability.

end. The requirement for even more capable attack and reconnaissance aircraft and "smart" weapons is clearly still valid.

JSF will replace many of the US attack aircraft involved in *Allied Force* but, considering the F-15 Eagle's excellent kill rates over Iraq and Yugoslavia, deliveries of the F-22 may be delayed or even reduced. URAVs will replace many manned surveillance platforms, including the overworked U-2, while UCAV development for specialized missions such as SEAD will be accelerated in the next decade.

Much has been made of the inadequacies of the Russian combat aircraft used by both Iraq and Yugoslavia, especially the MiG-29 "Fulcrum." It must be acknowledged that the few that fought the overwhelming numbers of Allied fighters were early examples of a 20-year-old design flown by pilots trained under the flawed Soviet system and without the benefit of any airborne command and control assets such as AWACS. After the collapse of the Soviet Union, support for customer air forces virtually dried up along with spare parts and upgrade possibilities.

However, although virtually bankrupt, Russia's beleaguered aerospace industry is still capable of surprising the West with innovative designs. One of these was the maiden flight of the S-37 Berkut (Royal Eagle) on September 25 1997. Designed and constructed in secret at Zhukovsky by Russia's most successful bureau, Sukhoi, which is still producing advanced variants of its formidable Su-27 "Flanker," a type that has not yet met US fighters in air combat, the fifth-generation multi-role Berkut featured a forward-swept wing (FSW) and delta-shaped foreplanes. With FSW and vectored-thrust engines, developed for the stillborn Yak-141 "Freestyle," the S-37 will outmaneuver most of its contemporaries in low-speed, close-in air combat. Its large fuel capacity and internal weapons carriage with a warload of up to 18,000lb (8,200kg) also give the Mach 2.5 S-37 an excellent strike capability. If funds were ever available, Sukhoi's Royal Eagle could be in service with the Russian Air Force in 2010.

Sukhoi is also developing a long-range bomber to replace the dwindling fleet of aging Tu-95 "Bears," the grounded Tu-160 "Blackjack," and the still-capable Tu-22M3 "Backfire." The air-refuelable, stealthy Sukhoi T-60S will feature a variable geometry wing, and twin high-bypass ratio turbofans with two-dimensional thrust vectoring to give it high-altitude supersonic cruise without reheat at Mach 2. Although the Russian Air force currently has no funds for its Long Range Aviation force, its government's recent opposition to an expanding and offensive NATO may well change this position in the future.

Russia's once-mighty Mikoyan design bureau has also designed a fifth-generation fighter, the stealthy MiG Multifunctional Tactical Fighter (MFI) 1.44, which has yet to make its first flight. Although work began on the prototype 10 years earlier, the MFI 1.44 was not revealed to the public until January 1999. The large delta-wing aircraft, with two canted fins and canard foreplanes, is powered by twin low-bypass ratio turbofans with thrust vectoring nozzles for increased maneuverability. The squat fuselage, composite angled inlet, and fins combine to give the MFI 1.44 a low radar cross-section. To increase its stealth capability, the latest MiG is cloaked in plasma which surrounds the aircraft in electrically charged gas that renders it "invisible" to radar.

Developed by Moscow's M V Keldysh Research Center, the plasma device is yet another example of Russia's innovative approach to aerospace development, but the lack of defense funds means that the plasma-coated MFI 1.44 may never get the chance to prove its effectiveness in the air.

A Western fighter concept from AVPRO UK intended as a replacement for the F-16 bears many similarities to Sukhoi's S-37 Berkut. This aircraft should relate to the Lockheed Martin F-22 Raptor (see Chapter Two) in the same way that the F-16 relates to the F-15 Eagle. The F-22 is too costly to fill the entire US fighter inventory, a fact that was recently demonstrated by the reduction in the number to be purchased for the USAF. As research and development costs have to be paid for from a smaller number of units, this tends to lead to spiralling unit costs. For this reason, it is thought that USAF would find a relatively simple lightweight fighter a very attractive way of filling the balance of its fighter inventory.

Although this fighter concept is essentially the "low" end of a "high-low" mix with the F-22, the configuration has been laid out to match the F-22 for stealthiness and exceed its maneuverability. The aircraft has been designed to be capable of post-stall maneuver/super-maneuverability and to remain fully controllable in roll, pitch, and yaw during these types of maneuvers. The key reasons why this configuration has been selected are as follows.

▶

The stealthy low radar cross-section MFI 1.44 is designed to use a unique plasma device to render it almost invisible to enemy radars.

▼

Russia's only other fifth generation fighter is the MiG MFI 1.44 which has yet to make its first flight despite being completed in the early-1990s.

Forward-swept wing configurations are also being adopted for future interceptor concepts by the UK company AVPRO UK to improve stealth characteristics and maneuverability.

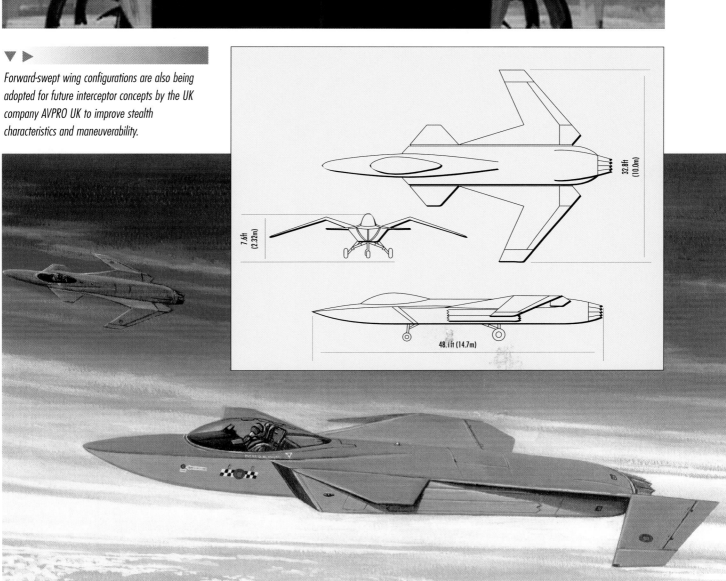

32.8ft (10.0m)

7.6ft (2.32m)

48.1ft (14.7m)

Forward-swept wing (FSW)

- The FSW offers increased maneuverability and roll control authority at high angles of attack (AoA).

- For given shock sweep, the FSW has lower leading edge sweep than an aft-swept wing (ASW). This gives it a higher lift curve slope which improves maneuverability. High lift curve slope also allows a lower AoA during approach and landing. This is particularly important for aircraft operated from aircraft carriers.

- The aft-swept inboard sections of the FSW delay flow separation and are behind the aircraft center of gravity, hence loss of lift due to flow separation is likely to result in pitch-up at the stall. The highly swept inboard section generates large amounts of vortex lift at high AoA.

- This combination of forward sweep on the outboard wing and aft sweep on the inboard section improves transonic area ruling. In turn this reduces transonic drag which results in increased acceleration and maneuverability.

- The aft-swept inboard section in combination with the canard foreplanes result in more benign stall characteristics. Tests on the Grumman X-29 FSW demonstrator in the 1980s showed that separation on the main wing began downstream of the canard tip, spreading inboard and outboard with increasing AoA. The gradual loss of lift lets the pilot know that a limiting condition is being approached.

- An additional benefit of the aft swept inboard section is that it provides a large amount of structural depth while retaining low thickness-to-chord ratio necessary for low supersonic wave drag. This also increases the wing stiffness at the root where it is most highly loaded. This results in a lighter structure.

▼

Benefitting from new technology composite materials, the FSW of future fighter designs can be stronger, lighter, and less liable to flex in high "g" maneuvering.

Close-coupled canard

- The large canard foreplanes are located as far forward on the configuration as possible, which means that the lift generated by them produces the greatest possible pitching moment about the aircraft center of gravity and hence maximises the pitch acceleration.
- The large size of the canard is necessary to provide an acceptable amount of aerodynamic pitch control during super-maneuvers when the dynamic pressure is low due to flow separation and/or low aircraft speed. Although the aircraft is equipped with pitch-yaw thrust vectoring, supplementing this with aerodynamic assistance will improve performance.
- The inboard portion of the main wing, which operates at the highest AoA on a FSW, is in the downwash field produced by the canard. This offloads the inboard section of the wing and hence delays stall.

All-moving wing tips

- Locating the roll control devices at the wingtips gives them the largest possible moment arm from the roll axis of the aircraft. This provides increased roll acceleration over trailing edge devices such as ailerons and flaperons.
- At supersonic speeds, the all-moving wingtips would provide far superior roll control to trailing edge devices and this, along with the large moment arm, was the main reason for using them.
- When the aircraft is flying at supersonic speed the wingtips influence the flow over the whole area of the wingtips. By contrast, trailing edge devices influence only the flowfield downstream of the hingeline.

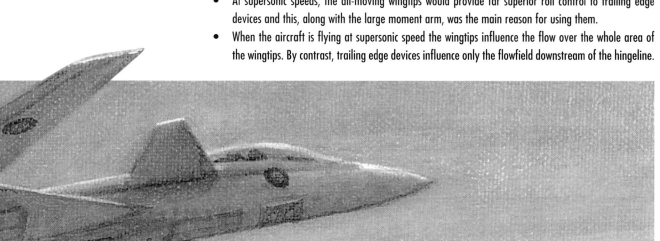

- All-moving wingtips eliminate control reversal. At high supersonic speed the ailerons cause the wing to twist in such a way that it opposes the desired rolling motion. This happens because the load on the aileron acts aft of the wind's flexural axis and hence causes it to twist. By contrast, the load on the all-moving tips acts close to the wing's flexural axis.
- With judicious flight control system programming, the tip can be made to deflect downwards as the aircraft AoA increases. This keeps the flow over the tips attached and allows the controls to remain effective even when the flow over the rest of the aircraft has separated.

Y-type inlet ducts

- These prevent radar seeing the engine face.
- They provide space for weapons bays along the fuselage sides and beneath the fuselage between the ducts.
- They also provide space for main landing gear stowage and for fuel volume.

Gull wing

- This gives the vertical depth required for directional stability.
- Although thrust vectoring gives artificial directional stability, it is necessary to have some inherent stability in the event of engine failure. This allows the vertical fin, which is a major contributor to radar cross-section, to be deleted.
- The anhedral of outboard section and dihedral of inboard section partially cancel out, giving low lateral stability. This is intentional as it reduces the stability that has to be overcome during maneuvers, and it also reduces trim drag.
- Small changes in rolling moment are induced between attached flow and post-stall, which makes the aircraft easier to control during the transition from conventional to post-stall maneuvers and vice-versa.
- The gull wing shields underwing stores, if carried, from enemy radar.

The all-composite, high-flying, long endurance Scaled Technology Proteus offers a cost effective surveillance/communications relay platform replacement for the aging U-2 "Dragon Lady."

New horizons

▲

Boeing's YAL-1A airborne Attack Laser system is a survivor of the "Star Wars" technology that was kick-started by President Reagan's Stategic Defense Initiative (SDI) in the late 1980s.

Conventional military aircraft will continue to be developed throughout the 21st Century although advanced technologies will enable new horizons to be explored for specialist missions. Examples of these include the solar-powered HALE airship featured in Chapter Six, and the innovative Scaled Composites Proteus. Burt Rutan, who was responsible for the record-breaking Voyager which flew around the world non-stop, also designed the high-altitude, multi-mission Proteus. Powered by two 2,293lb (1,040kg) st Williams-Rolls-Royce FJ44-2 turbofans, the 56ft 3in (17.16m) long all-composite aircraft has a 77ft 7in (23.65m) span rear wing and a 54ft 8in (16.67m) span canard wing. All of these dimensions can be extended by up to 12ft (4.1m) for different payloads/missions.

The unique Proteus can fly with a two-man crew or carry out unmanned High- Altitude Long-Operation (HALO) missions with an external pod for communications relay, the aircraft loitering at an altitude of over 60,000ft (18,290m) for up to eight hours on station. Other roles include that of high-altitude reconnaissance—a cost effective replacement for the U-2—and as an airborne launch platform for space rockets.

Space: "the final frontier?"

The US Air Force could push into the "final frontier"—space—if it completes its ambitious plans to form a space-based attack force. The USAF is currently engaged in several major projects to develop a range of craft that take-off from earth and fly into space on missions such as high-altitude surveillance and strike operations. On the completion of their missions, these craft would return to earth and land on conventional runways in the same manner as normal aircraft. They would be more economical to operate than the current generation of Space Shuttles which are limited to landing at highly specialized facilities such as Vandenburg AFB, California, and Cape Canaveral, Florida.

The reason for the intense interest in space-based solutions for USAF's operational requirements in the

21st Century are as follows. In the near future, USAF will have to consider either upgrading or replacing its fleet of B-52, B-1B, and B-2A strategic bombers. It will probably operate a mixed force of manned and unmanned conventional aircraft, including upgraded B-2A Spirits, along with a range of hypersonic craft capable of space flight.

The advantages of space-based attack systems are significant. A craft could take-off from fixed bases in mainland USA and be over a potential target in any part of the globe within two hours of launch. At the altitude at which the craft would fly it would be out of range of current surface-to-air missiles, giving the operating platform virtual impunity against any attack.

A system operating from space could also attack targets of opportunity at very short notice. As soon as a high-value target is detected, it could be engaged. This capability would be of great value to tactical commanders where systems such as mobile Scud missile launchers could be destroyed before they had an opportunity to fire their missiles and move to a new position.

In 1999, the US Air Force Space Command doubled its space-related research budget to $320 million to develop a series of global strike and reconnaissance space craft and the detection and destruction of theater ballistic missiles and advanced cruise missile threats. The roots of several of these projects can be traced back to programs implemented during President Reagan's Strategic Defense Initiative (SDI), known as "Star Wars," in the 1980s. SDI brought the Soviet Union to its knees as vast amounts of money were pumped into US Ballistic Missile Defense (BMD) projects, most of which never progressed beyond the concept stage.

One USAF program that did survive, albeit in a modified form, is the airborne attack laser, the YAL-1A. Based on a Boeing 747 aircraft, the airborne laser system would be able to shoot down theater ballistic missiles while they were still over the launch area. The AL-1A would operate autonomously while cruising at over 40,000ft (12,190m) hundreds of miles away from its target with wide-angle infra-red (IR) sensors providing 360 degree coverage. The US Air Force has a requirement for some seven systems which could be operational by 2005.

In 1999, a Boeing, Lockheed Martin, and TRW team was awarded a $125 million contract to develop a Space Based Laser (SBL) integrated BMD flight system with a high energy laser architecture.

With the proliferation of weapons of mass destruction and their delivery systems, several ground-based BMD systems are under development, including the Medium Extended Air Defense System (MEADS). The mobile MEADS is being offered to NATO countries using the Patriot Advanced Capability (PAC-3) air defense missile, while the US Navy is accelerating the development of its Theater Wide Missile Defense (TMD) system which is in competition with the US Army's Theater High Altitude Area Defense (THAAD) system, all of which could be deployed by 2010.

Russia is also deploying an advanced BMD system, the S-400 Triumph, developed from the very capable S-300 surface-to-air missile (SAM) system. The S-400's eight container launchers could use a variety of advanced medium and long range missiles for over-the-horizon (OTH) targets up to a range of 250 miles (400km) and a height of 115,000ft (35,000m). Meanwhile, a powerful BMD active array radar, the Multifunction Electronically Scanned Adaptive Radar (MESAR) 2, is being developed by British Aerospace for UK and US requirements as well as for a number of Gulf States.

An adjunct to the US SDI was research into manned trans-atmospheric vehicles (TAV) capable of reaching orbit, circling the earth in space and returning to land on conventional runways. Apart from conventional rocket motors, a wide variety of advanced propulsions were proposed for these TAVs, including vacuum thrust motors, cryogenic rocket motors, pulse detonation wave engines, magetohydrodynamic systems, and scramjets.

Most of the TAV funding was directed at the X-30 National Aero Space Plane (NASP) program that was eventually cancelled in 1993. To be powered by a Rocket-Based Combined Cycle (RBCC) system that was developed under a ``black" program codenamed Copper Canyon , the X-30 was superseded by the $5-8 billion X-33 VentureStar Single-Stage-to-Orbit (SSTO) Reusable Launch Vehicle (RLV) in 1996. The Lockheed Martin "Skunk Works" was selected to lead a multi-industry team to develop the Shuttle-sized X-33, which is capable of carrying a 25 ton payload. It is being built at the former B-1B facility at Palmdale, California. It will be powered by a Boeing linear aerospike rocket motor, but problems in testing

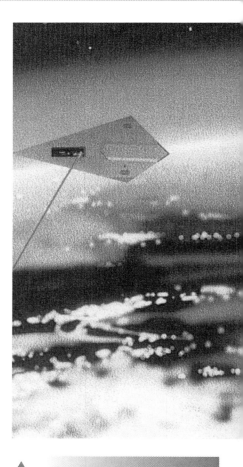

Unmanned combat aerial vehicles (UCAV) may form part of USAF's Space Based Laser (SBL) integrated Ballistic Missile Defense (BMD) flight systems.

The advanced phased array radar used by the Russian S-400 Triumph BMD system, designed to destroy over-the-horizon (OTH) targets at a range of 250 miles (400km).

this revolutionary engine, which is designed to work equally well in and out of atmosphere, have delayed the first flight of the technology demonstrator and put the program in doubt.

A smaller unmanned RLV, the Orbital Sciences (OSC) X-34, destined to carry six-man teams or small equipment payloads to space stations, made its first unpowered glide flight at the end of 1999, having been released from a high-flying OSC TriStar carrier aircraft. Powered by a 60,000lb (27,215kg) thrust Fastrec liquid-oxygen/kerosene-fueled rocket motor, the X-34 is designed to reach Mach 8. Boeing's more sophisticated X-38 Ranger Crew Rescue Vehicle (CRV) is destined to fly in 2005, while yet another product of Boeing's "Phantom Works," the X-40A technology demonstrator, was successfully flown from Holloman AFB, New Mexico, in August 1998.

The X-40A is the forerunner of the development of a new generation of small, reusable, highly maneuverable space vehicles for the USAF. The 25ft (7.5m) long, multi-mission, unmanned Space Maneuver Vehicle (SMV) will be used for satellite deployment, surveillance, and logistics missions. Designed to be deployed by 2015, the SMV will have aircraft-like operability, with a turnaround time of 72 hours or less between missions, or the capability of remaining on a flexible orbit for up to one year. It could "fly" at Mach 10 as an RLV or be used as the upper stage of Two-Stage-To-Orbit (TSTO) spacecraft.

There was a time when the Soviets led the world in RLV research. In the mid-1960s, work was begun on a "Space-Fighter," the Mikoyan Spirel, a TSTO vehicle comprising a Mach 6 jet-powered

▼

Shuttle-sized X-33 VentureStar Reusable Launch Vehicles (RLV) powered by Rocket-Based Combined Cycle (RBCC) systems are being developed at the Lockheed Martin "Skunk Works."

▼

The Orbital Sciences X-34, powered by a Fastrec liquid-oxygen/kerosene-fueled rocket motor, is a six-man space vehicle designed to operate from conventional runways.

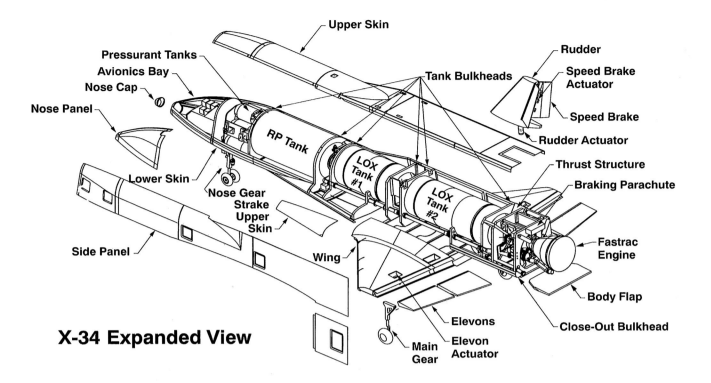

X-34 Expanded View

Upper Skin

Pressurant Tanks
Avionics Bay
Nose Cap
Nose Panel

Tank Bulkheads

Rudder
Speed Brake Actuator
Speed Brake

RP Tank

LOX Tank #1

LOX Tank #2

Rudder Actuator

Thrust Structure

Braking Parachute

Lower Skin
Nose Gear
Strake Upper Skin

Side Panel

Wing

Fastrac Engine

Body Flap

Close-Out Bulkhead

Main Gear
Elevons
Elevon Actuator

The Orbital Sciences X-34 small unmanned Reusable Launch Vehicle has already made its initial glide flight.

carrier aircraft that would carry a detachable piloted orbital craft to an altitude of 100,000ft (31,000m) and launch it into space. It would re-enter the atmosphere and land on a conventional runway. Its main role would be to destroy other space vehicles but it could also be used for reconnaissance. The project was cancelled after a technology demonstrator of the orbital craft had made a series of successful test flights following the Soviets' decision to develop its own space shuttle, the Buran.

The Mikoyan Bureau also designed a hypersonic strike and reconnaissance aircraft, the MiG-301 in the mid-1980s. Powered by two supersonic ramjet engines, known as scramjets, the Mach 4 aircraft was to be the Russian Air Force's "sixth" generation combat aircraft, while the Tupelov Bureau began work on a hypersonic strategic bomber. The giant 330ft (100m) long Tu-2000 bomber, with a payload of 330,000lb (150,000kg) and powerplant consisting of six liquid hydrogen-fueled scramjets, would cruise at Mach 6 at 100,000ft (31,000m). However, since the break-up of the Soviet Union, both of these projects have remained on the drawing boards.

The development of RBCC system powered craft using both air-breathing scramjets and pure rocket motors is continuing in the United States with the first of four 12ft (3.6m) long X-43A technology demonstrators beginning flight trials in 2000. Designed by the Boeing "Phantom Works," the X-43A is based on an engineering concept developed by the Lawrence Livermore National Laboratory in California.

A product of Boeing's "Phantom Works,", the X-38 Ranger could be used as a Crew Rescue Vehicle (CRV) for the International Space Station (ISS) or a satellite support vehicle. Here X-38 Ship No. 2 glides Earthward folliwng its release from the B-52 mothership during the program's fourth successful free flight, July 9 1999.

Known as HyperSoar, the X-43A is the first stage in the development of a hypersonic strike aircraft that would "skip" on the upper atmosphere to enable it to reach any position over the earth's surface within two hours of take-off.

The 215ft (65m) long wedge-shaped HyperSoar could carry a 99,000lb (45,000kg) payload over a range of 6,155 miles (10,000km) cruising at Mach 10. It would take off from a 10,000ft (3,100m) long conventional runway using its scramjets to accelerate to Mach 10 while climbing to to 115,000ft where its RBCC system would be shut down as it coasted out of the atmosphere. The craft would then continue to climb to some 200,000ft (62,000m) under its own momentum before beginning a gentle descent to a lower altitude, between 115,000-132,000ft (35,650-41,000m), where the engines would fire for some 20 seconds. The wedge-shaped "waverider" would literally surf through the air on its own shockwave.

The HyperSoar's military potential is significant. A small fleet of these craft could move men and equipment to any trouble-spot in the world within hours of an outbreak of hostilities, be a viable strategic surveillance platform to fill the gap left by the premature retirement of the SR-71 Blackbird, and in times of high tension perform an airborne alert mission that was last carried out by Strategic Air Command B-52s during the Cold War. It would also have a global strike capability which would enable it to carry out a precision first strike at speeds and altitudes that would be beyond any known air defenses, thus eliminating the need for large escort packages that are required for a typical B-2A mission.

Futher development of a pure rocket segment of the RBCC system would enable the HyperSoar to act as an SSTO for military satellite and space-station support missions. One of USAF's intentions is to deploy additional command, control, communications, and computers (C_4) and surveillance satellites equipped with electro-optics, space-based synthetic aperture radar, and hyperspectral imaging. These satellites may well become tempting targets for other nations and the Air Force plans to fly clusters of integrated satellites to maximize their survivability.

Looking even further into the future, a true hyper-velocity air-rider capable of speeds in access of Mach 25 combines SDI research with that of Russia's Academy of Sciences. The revolutionary US Aero-Lens

▲

Air breathing scramjets combined with pure rocket motors power the wedge-shaped X-43A HyperSoar, carrying a 99,000lb (45,500kg) payload over more than 6,000 miles (10,000km).

▲

The Mikoyan 105-11, the technology demonstrator for the detachable piloted orbital craft of the Soviet Spirel RLV, made a series of test flights launched from a Tu-95 "Bear" bomber in the late 1970s.

▼

The X-40A technology demonstrator for the Mach 10 multi-mission, unmanned Space Maneuver Vehicle (SMV), another "Phantom Works" program, made its first flight in August 1998.

vehicle, powered by silent Pulse Detonation Wave Engines (PDWE), would accelerate to supersonic speeds within the dense air of low altitude or the rarefied atmosphere of lower space. At this point magnetohydrodynamic (MHD) fan propulsion would literally explode the air around the rim of the vehicle and blast it to a velocity of Mach 25+. The system would also incorporate a plasma spike, developed by the same Russian research center that cloaks the MiG 1.44 in electrically charged gases to make it "invisible" to radar, using concentrated microwave energy projected forward of the Aero-Lens to drive the dense air from its path. The extreme speed of the Aero-Lens would enable the manned or unmanned vehicle to arrive on target anywhere on earth within minutes of launch.

The US Aerospace Force is set to become a reality within the next generation.¶

The first operational hypersonic strike aircraft could be a development of the X-43A HyperSoar that would "surf" through the upper atmosphere accelerating to Mach 10. Powered by an RBCC system, the X-43A could take-off and land on conventional runways and climb to some 200,000ft (62,000m) to reach any position over the earth's surface within two hours.

Hyper-velocity air-rider Aero-Lens three-view.

The Aero-Lens-type vehicle uses Pulse Detonation Wave Engines (PDWE) plus magnetohydrodynamic (MHD) fan propulsion around the craft's rim and a plasma spike to reach Mach 25+.

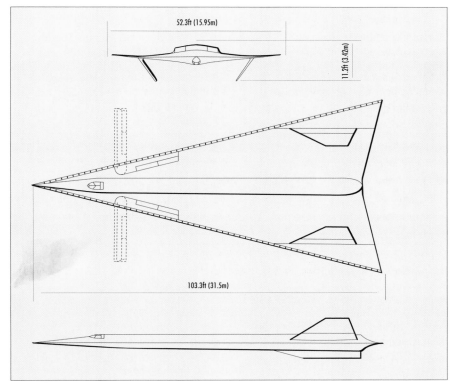

Larry Gets Lost in Portland

Illustrated by John Skewes
Written by Michael Mullin and John Skewes

SASQUATCH BOOKS
SEATTLE

Manufactured in China by C&C Offset Printing Co. Ltd. Shenzhen,
Guangdong Province, in March 2012

Published by Sasquatch Books

Book design: Mint Design
Book composition: Sarah Plein/Rebecca Shapiro

Library of Congress Cataloging-in-Publication Data is available.

ISBN-13: 978-1-57061-679-2
ISBN-10: 1-57061-679-5

www.larrygetslost.com

SASQUATCH BOOKS
1904 Third Avenue, Suite 710
Seattle, WA 98101
(206) 467-4300
www.sasquatchbooks.com
custserv@sasquatchbooks.com

This is **Larry.** This is **Pete.**

They like to ride **together** in the backseat.

PORTLAND

Marquam Bridge

Hawthorne Bridge

Morrison Bridge

Burnside Bridge

Steel Bridge

Broadway Bridge

ROSE GARDEN ARENA
Home of the Portland
Trail Blazers.

WILLAMETTE RIVER
A major tributary to the Columbia
River, the Willamette forms the
Willamette Valley, where most
people in Oregon live.

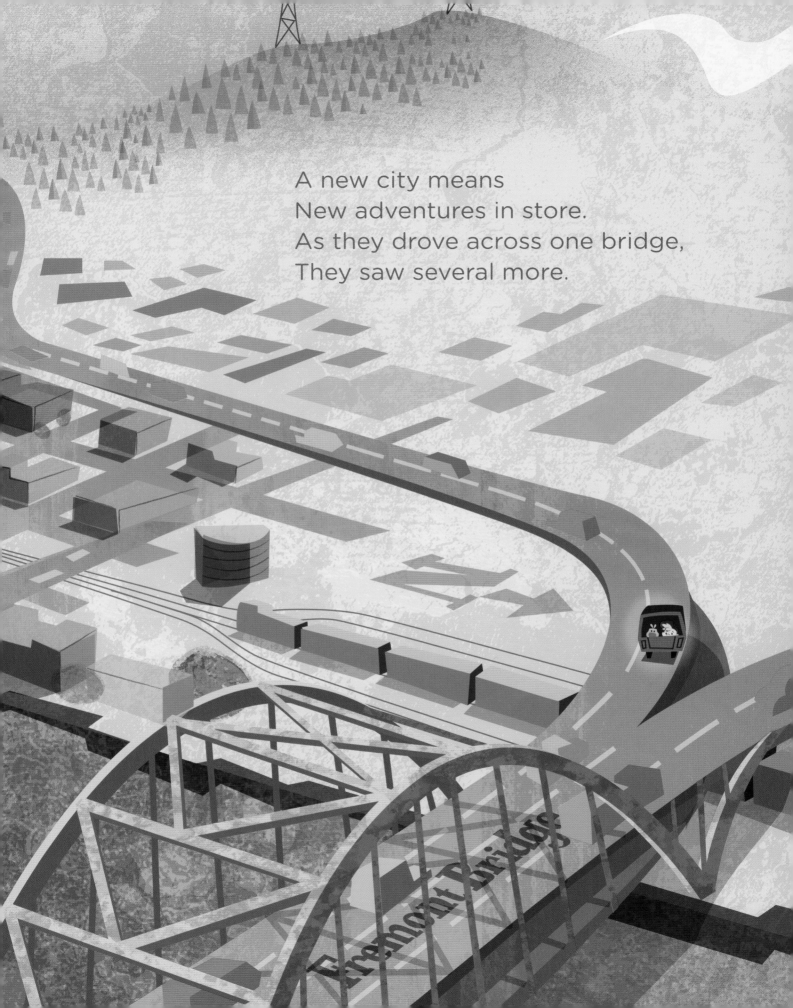

A new city means
New adventures in store.
As they drove across one bridge,
They saw several more.

Fremont Bridge

The family decided they'd first stop to eat.
They found tiny restaurants lined up on one street.

Even though Pete told Larry to **"stay,"**
Larry smelled a treat, and it lured him away.

He filled his dog tummy
Then was suddenly concerned . . .

Because Pete was **_gone_** when he returned!

It was time to get moving—to search and explore,
But each place looked stranger than the one before.

VooDoo Doughnut

24 Hour Church Of Elvis

埠華

OLD TOWN

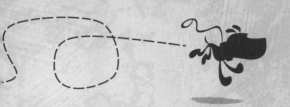

Chinatown

OLD TOWN

Burnside Bridge

Along the waterfront
Larry saw people riding bikes
And running for exercise,
Which Larry likes!

He thought he'd find Pete
In an exciting museum.
He even looked underwater . . .
But still didn't see him.

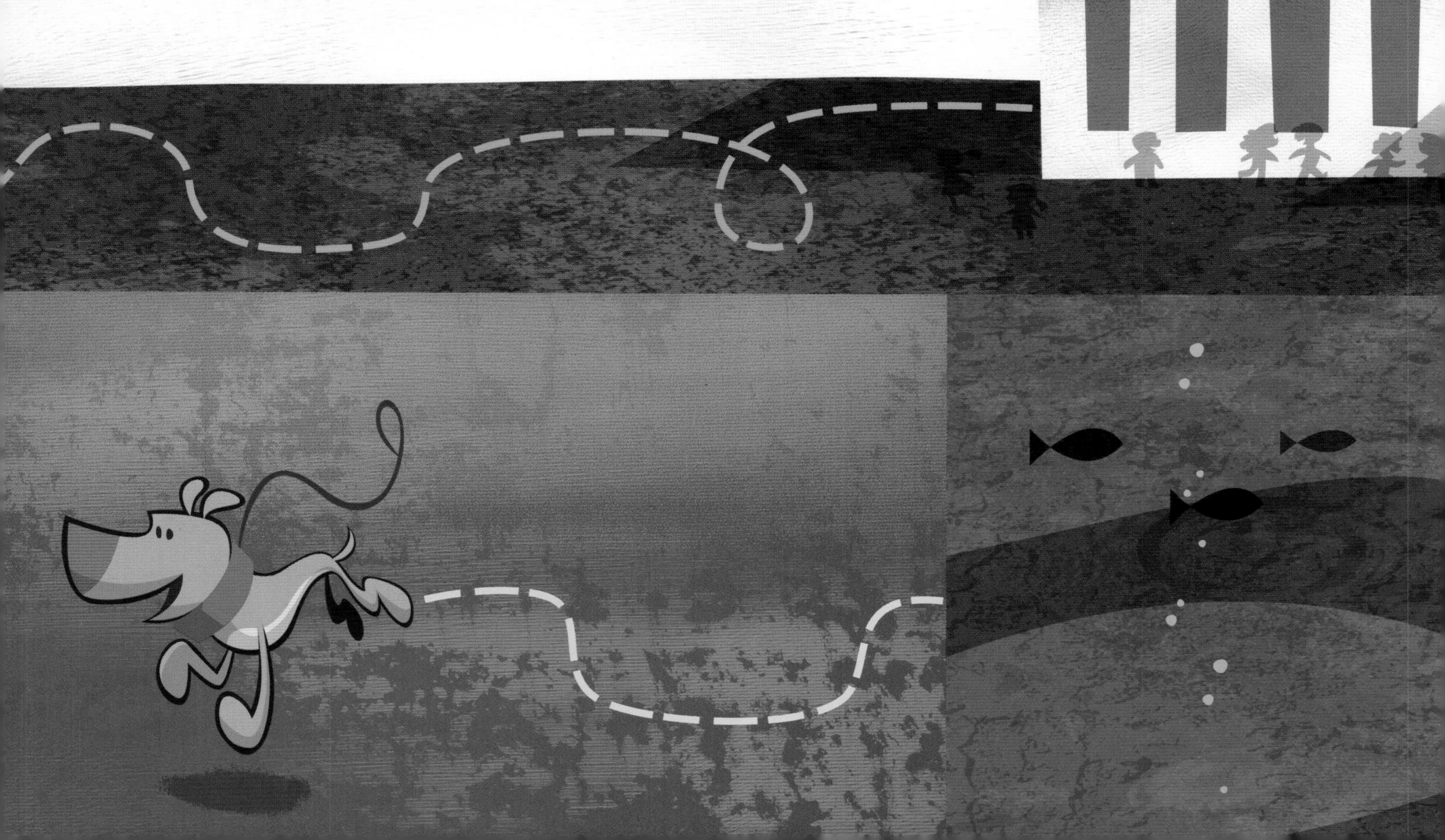

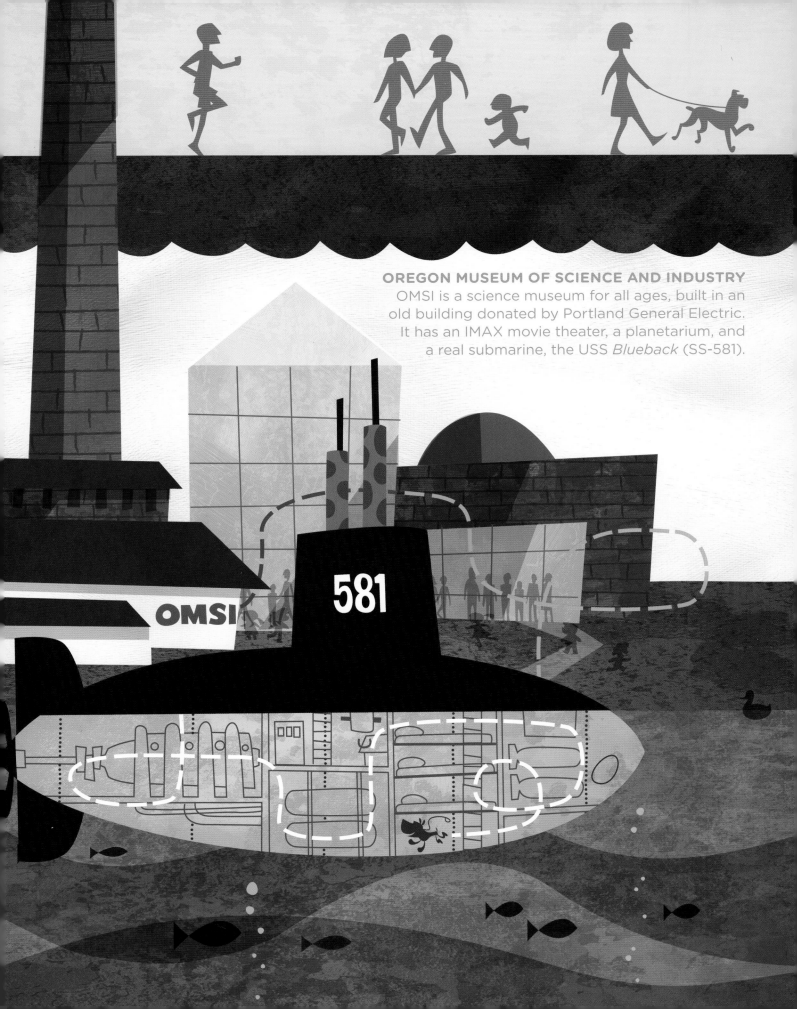

OREGON MUSEUM OF SCIENCE AND INDUSTRY
OMSI is a science museum for all ages, built in an old building donated by Portland General Electric. It has an IMAX movie theater, a planetarium, and a real submarine, the USS *Blueback* (SS-581).

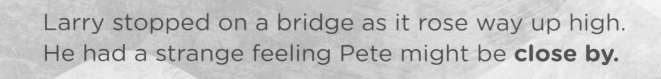

Larry stopped on a bridge as it rose way up high.
He had a strange feeling Pete might be **close by.**

HAWTHORNE BRIDGE
Because so many ships use the Willamette
River, most of Portland's bridges have to open
to let ships through. The Hawthorne Bridge
has a section that rises in the middle, known
as a "vertical lift." Built in 1910, it is the oldest
working vertical lift bridge in the United States.

PORTLANDIA

Portlandia is a nearly 35-foot-tall copper sculpture by Raymond Kaskey, built in 1985. It is the second largest hollow copper sculpture in the United States, after the Statue of Liberty.

A great giant lady
Reached down from her roof,
But she had no answer
To Larry's questioning "Woof?"

He found two streets
With a park in the middle,
But Pete's location
Remained a curious riddle.

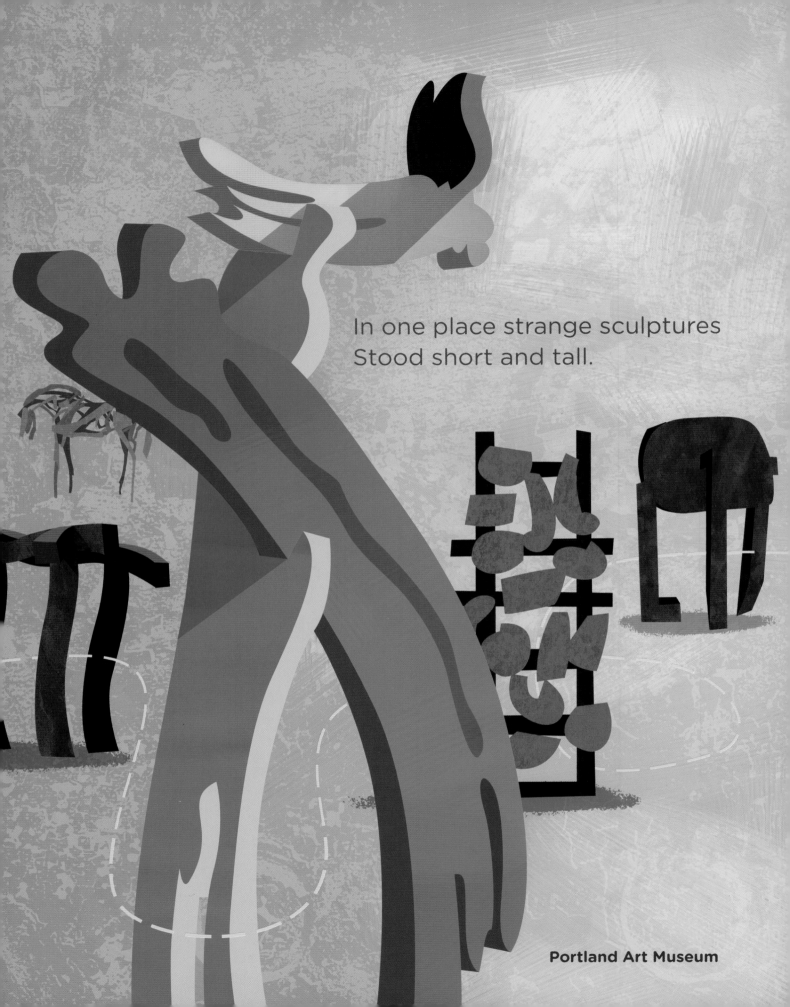

In one place strange sculptures
Stood short and tall.

Portland Art Museum

In another place a fish
Was stuck right through a wall!

SouthPark Seafood Grill

SW SALMON ST

He passed a stadium and a big smiling face.
Pete loved sports! Could he be in this place?

Portland Streetcar

JELD-WEN FIELD
An outdoor stadium, home to the Portland Timbers soccer club and the Portland State University Vikings football team.

He jumped on a train that moved without sound,
And rode into a tunnel, **deep underground.**

Light Rail

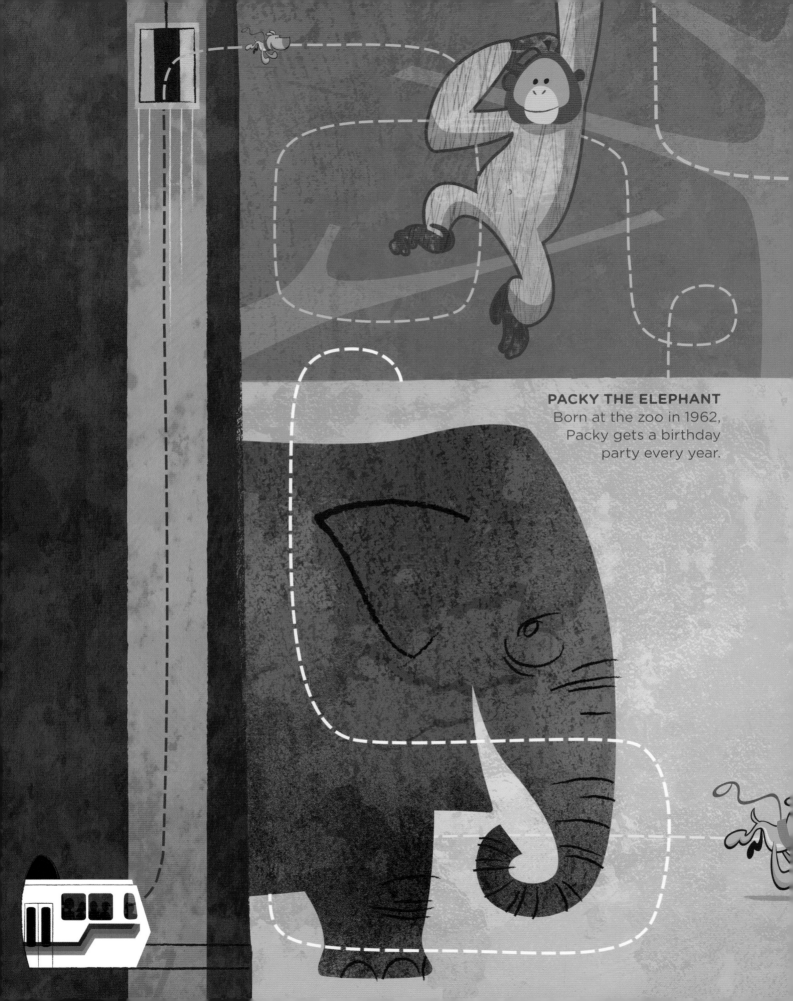

PACKY THE ELEPHANT
Born at the zoo in 1962,
Packy gets a birthday
party every year.

Larry then rode an elevator
And jumped out its doors,
He saw animals who walked
Just like him—on all fours!

He asked them for help.
He missed Pete a lot.
Most were quite friendly,
But some were *not*.

OREGON ZOO

WASHINGTON PARK & ZOO RAILWAY   WASHINGTON PARK & ZOO RAILWAY   WASHINGTON PA

He rode a small train
To a colorful place.
He'd never seen so many **flowers**
All in one place.

Even though he had much more
Searching to do,
He couldn't help stopping and
Smelling a few.

INTERNATIONAL ROSE TEST GARDEN
The rose garden has around 10,000
rose plants and more than 500 varieties.
Blooming from April through October,
the roses peak in June (depending on
the weather). This is one of the reasons
Portland is known as the City of Roses.

Back on the trail,
Down a hill Larry sped.

PORTLAND AERIAL TRAM
Part of Portland's public transportation
network, the tram rises 500 feet to take
people to and from Oregon Health &
Science University on top of Marquam Hill.

While Pete was
Traveling high overhead.

He ran into a store that
Was enormous in size.
And what they were selling
Was quite a surprise . . .

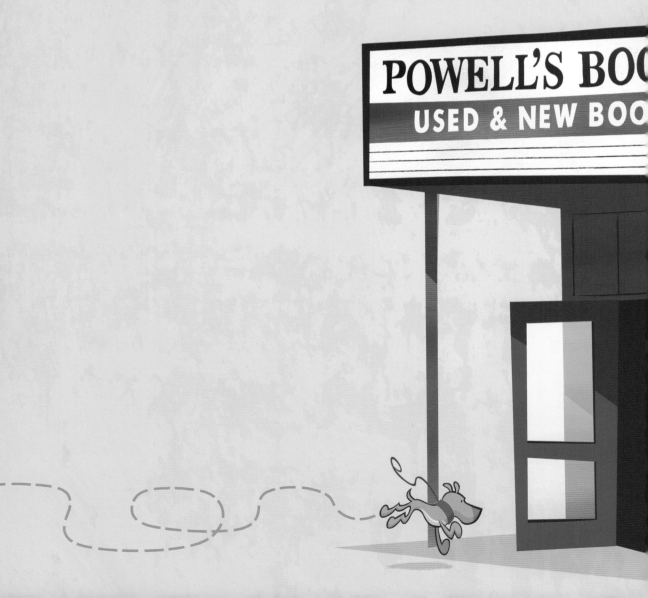

Shelf after shelf was filled
With every kind of book.
But no Pete, no matter
Where Larry chose to look.

POWELL'S CITY OF BOOKS
Believed to be the largest independent
new and used bookstore in the world,
it fills a whole city block.

Outside, something made Larry **stop.**
It was a great big mom with her kid up on top.

He tried to drink from a fountain,
But after several tries,
He soon found another
That was just his size.

BENSON BUBBLER
Donated to the city by Simon Benson in the early 1900s, these drinking fountains are all over the city of Portland.

PORTLAND DOG BOWL
Even though it looks like a dog bowl, it's actually a fountain (for dogs) by artist William Wegman.

The elephants really had nothing to say
So Larry walked on—right into a bike rider's way!

The rider stopped quickly
And nearly fell down.
Larry felt bad, but the guy
Just looked around.

Then he checked Larry's
Collar and took out his phone.
Could it be that Larry
Was done being alone?

Sure enough, at a building
Where trains come and go
He saw **Pete!** And he jumped up
And licked him hello.

UNION STATION
Built in 1896, Union Station is still a
working Amtrak station and is on the
National Register of Historic Places.

UNION
STATION

Soon Pete and Larry
Fell asleep in the car.
It was one of their most
Exhausting days by far.